LADY LOGIN'S RECOLLECTIONS

COURT LIFE AND CAMP LIFE
1820—1904

BY

E. DALHOUSIE LOGIN

WITH ILLUSTRATIONS

LONDON

SMITH, ELDER & CO., 15 WATERLOO PLACE

1916

CONTENTS

CHAP.   PAGE

 I. EARLY LIFE IN STRATHBRAAN . . . 1

 II. LEAVING HOME 31

 III. THE COURT OF OUDE 39

 IV. NATIVE SERVANTS AND CAMP LIFE. . . 49

 V. THE LAWRENCES 63

 VI. LAHORE TREASURY AND THE KOH-I-NOOR . 72

 VII. FUTTEHGHUR 85

 VIII. THE MAHARAJAH'S BAPTISM AND LORD DAL-
    HOUSIE 94

 IX. THE COURT OF ST. JAMES 113

 X. THE MUTINY — CORRESPONDENCE WITH SIR
    CHARLES PHIPPS 135

 XI. THE PRINCESS VICTORIA GOURAMMA . . 148

 XII. THE PRINCESS VICTORIA GOURAMMA—*continued* 168

 XIII. ITALY AND MR. JOHN BRIGHT . . . 195

 XIV. THE MAHARANEE JINDA KOUR . . . 206

 XV. SIR JOHN'S DEATH 225

 XVI. THE MAHARAJAH'S MARRIAGE AND CONTRO-
    VERSY WITH THE INDIAN GOVERNMENT . 237

 XVII. LATER YEARS AND DEATH OF THE MAHARAJAH
    DULEEP SINGH 256

 XVIII. FAMILY SORROWS AND ANOTHER CHARGE . 273

 XIX. OLD FELIXSTOWE DAYS 301

 XX. LATER YEARS IN KENT 323

   INDEX 341

LIST OF ILLUSTRATIONS

LADY LOGIN . . . .*Frontispiece*
From a Miniature by Fisher, 1850.

FACING PAGE

SIR HENRY MONTGOMERY LAWRENCE, K.C.B. . . 64

LORD LAWRENCE 68

H.R.H. THE PRINCE OF WALES (H.M. KING EDWARD VII.) 118
From a Photograph taken by the Maharajah Duleep Singh at Roehampton.

H.H. THE MAHARAJAH DULEEP SINGH . . . 126
From a Picture by Winterhalter.

T.R.H. PRINCE ALFRED AND PRINCE ARTHUR (GRAND-
DUKE OF SAXE-COBURG-GOTHA AND DUKE OF CON-
NAUGHT) IN INDIAN DRESS 145
Photographed by H.R.H. The Prince Consort.

THE PRINCESS VICTORIA GOURAMMA OF COORG . . 156
From a Picture by Winterhalter.

SIR JOHN SPENCER LOGIN 226

GROUP OF THE ROYAL FAMILY AT OSBORNE (WITH
EXCEPTION OF THE PRINCE OF WALES). . . 288
Taken under direction of H.R.H. the Prince Consort.

FACSIMILE OF AUTOGRAPH LETTER FROM H.M. QUEEN
VICTORIA TO LADY LOGIN 185

LADY LOGIN'S RECOLLECTIONS

CHAPTER I

EARLY LIFE IN STRATHBRAAN

ALTHOUGH few of those who saw her in her later years could fail to recognise in her a strong personality, a wonderfully clear judgment and a keen insight into character, coupled with immense force of will and vitality, I doubt if the majority of her acquaintances realised the strangely varied scenes through which my mother had passed in the course of a long life, and how closely, on occasion, she had been brought into contact with the men and women who made the history of the nineteenth century.

She was not one to speak of these things in general society, and knew, as do the wives of most Indian officials, how to keep her own counsel, and that of those who trusted her with their confidence. And often she was slow to realise that what, at the time, appeared to her just a natural condition of affairs, could possibly present itself to the mind of a younger generation as entirely incredible and marvellous !

In an ordinary way, therefore, she spoke little of the events of her earlier life, save when directly questioned by those who knew her history ; and possibly few of her neighbours in later years, who saw her immersed in her garden, poultry-yard, and live-stock, clad in the oldest and shabbiest of garments, tending her bees, superintending indoor and outdoor work in the fashion learnt from her thrifty and capable Highland mother, and with her own hands doing odd jobs of rough carpentry, ever dreamt that in other days she had been equally at home, and happy, in the atmosphere of courts, and the daily duties of official life.

But her children, and the children of the old friends and associates, with whom she still kept up intercourse during forty years of widowhood and seclusion in the country, loved nothing better than to catch her in the mood, beguile her into laying aside, for a moment, the daily paper in which she was absorbed (for her training and early association with the political service had made her an ardent student of international politics, and a careful reader of the debates in Parliament), and induce her to tell stories of the incidents she had taken part in, and of the people she had met. This she would do with a raciness and *verve* peculiarly her own, and which, alas! I can never attempt to reproduce.

We would ask her then to tell us of the old days in Strathbraan, of the grandfather and grandmother dead and buried before any of us saw the light—the former a foreigner in his ways and language, the latter, a real Highland *châtelaine* of the old school, skilled in housewifery and physic—of her voyages to and from India, during the first of which she managed to set foot on four continents, and wellnigh sighted the coast of Australia into the bargain! of adventures by field and flood in India in the old camping days, and of intercourse with native courts and zenanas, at a period when few European ladies had the chance of seeing the inside of the houses of rajahs, nawabs or zemindars.

I have tried in these pages to relate some of the stories she used to tell, sitting in the firelight in the gloaming, or in the evenings after dinner—some of the reminiscences of a condition of life no longer existent in Scotland, or in India either for that matter, and a very few of the multitudinous anecdotes, of which she had a store concerning celebrities of the time that she had met ; for the major part, unfortunately, have vanished, leaving no trace in my memory. But of the residue which remain, and which I noted at the time or shortly afterwards, I set down what I can.

So you want to know about our life at Kinloch in the old days (she would say to us), and of how the time passed so far from congenial society and from the amenities of life and society in the towns ?

I hear you even now speak of So-and-so as " living in the depths of the country," but, good people, I wonder what you would say to living seven miles from your parish kirk, as we did until the chapel-of-ease at Amulree was built ? And as for visitors of one's own class, or relatives, it was once in a blue moon they descended on us, generally without warning, and with a retinue of servants, expecting to be entertained for the whole day, when often there was no meat in the larder, and no " flesher " handier than Dunkeld or Aberfeldy !

Then the snows we had in the winter, when the roads were often blocked for weeks ! I remember my sister Lorne's marriage in 1831, and how on the eve of the wedding-day the snow came down ! By the morning the roads were impassable, and still the snow fell sullenly in huge flakes ! All thought of a marriage on that day was perforce abandoned, for not a soul ventured to the " big house " in the deep snow, even from so near as Deanshaugh and Caplea, the tiny "touns" a quarter-of-a-mile away.

Nevertheless, at midday, a procession of seven men slowly approached, literally hauling through the drifts the parish minister from Little Dunkeld, who, good man! no sooner was deposited on the doormat, than he insisted on performing the rite on the day and hour named, in the drawing-room, as was then the Presbyterian custom, and saw no reason for postponement in the enforced absence of the invited guests! Thus the bride and bridegroom remained with us, snowed up, for ten days longer, until, by dint of keeping gangs of men working in relays, a passage was cleared through the Sma' Glen, and, with infinite labour and difficulty, they were got through in a chariot-and-four to Perth, by the Glen Almond road. A wretched travesty of a wedding indeed, with no piper to greet the bride; the only music the twittering of a robin, driven in by the storm. So loud did he sing that he drowned all sound of the minister's voice!

We were a large family and I was the youngest, as you know. My grandfather, Charles Campbell, was said to have been "out in the '45;" anyhow, a brother of his was killed at Culloden—described on the roll of the slain as "Lieut. John Campbell *of Kinloch*, with Grantully's men in Roy Stewart's regiment"*—and he himself had fled to foreign parts, where he married a noble Portuguese lady, niece of the Bishop of Oporto. There was a story that she eloped with him from a convent, and that they were banished to the Brazils. At all events, it was there all his children were born and brought up, and my father—who went by the nick-

* See "Chronicles of the Families of Atholl and Tullibardine," by John, Duke of Atholl (privately printed), Vol. III., p. 297.

name of " Don Juan " in Perthshire—spoke in broken
English to the day of his death, and the style of his dress
was decidedly foreign.

When he first married he used to wear his hair in
powder, with a queue and bow of ribbons, but even my
elder sisters did not remember seeing him dressed in
that fashion. My recollection of him is with his hair
unpowdered but long, falling over the high collar of his
coat, which was of claret colour, with large gilt buttons,
and cut away into swallow-tails. At the back of the
neck a bunch of black ribbons represented where the
queue had been, just as now seen in the gentlemen's
court dress. A large soft muslin neck-kerchief, beautifully folded about his neck, took the place of the stock
then worn ; a profusion of the most delicate lace fell
as a frill down the front of his shirt, and as deep ruffles
over his wrists, while black knee-breeches and silk
stockings, with silver-buckled shoes, completed an
attire remarkable and antiquated even at that period,
and which made him singular in any assemblage of his
fellow-men. It certainly imparted to him a peculiar
air of refinement and aristocratic dignity, when viewed
alongside the other country gentlemen of his time and
neighbourhood. Out of doors he wore generally a loose
Spanish cloak with silver clasps. This added to his
foreign appearance, for it was never fastened round his
neck, but even in the bitterest wind I have seen him
stand for hours, watching the men at work, his cloak
apparently slipping off, but with one end gathered up
and flung in a peculiar fashion over his left shoulder,
so as to leave his right arm free. His inseparable
companion outside the house was a very tall walking-
stick or staff, of uncommon wood—probably Brazilian
—which he valued highly as having belonged to his

favourite brother, José. It was a yellow cane, flecked with tiny white specks, and was surmounted by a silver knob bearing the boar's head " erect," the crest of the Kinloch Campbells. He was never seen without this stick, and great was the lamentation when he lost it on a journey into Argyllshire, whither he had gone to vote on one occasion for some election ; for he regarded himself as a strong Whig and voted always for that party, though his real inclination and family traditions would have proclaimed him an out-and-out Tory !

My father was a splendid horseman, and looked a perfect picture mounted. He was an object of the fervent admiration of all the bare-legged laddies of the countryside when he rode forth on his black stallion, and to this day the tradition remains amongst the old people in Dunkeld, how on market days, when the folk stood about to watch the country gentlemen ride in on their business, the cry of " Kinloch is coming in ! " brought the townspeople to their doors, and all the children running from their games, to see the slight, dark-haired man, silent and sad-looking, clad in his strange, wide-skirted riding-coat, with the foreign cloak, and Hessian boots adorned with tassels, and the heavy Spanish spurs. I can only remember one old gentleman whose dress at all resembled my father's, and he was one of the last to wear powder.

To the end, my father spoke very broken English. He was a silent man, and seldom addressed any of us. But occasionally, when alone with us younger ones, he would break through this habit, and tell us long stories, sometimes introducing Portuguese phrases and idioms, so as to render his conversation perfectly unintelligible ! Hardly ever did he mention the events of his early life, and made only the baldest references to his brothers.

He did not appear to have cared much for any of them, save José, the eldest. Gregorio (Gregory), he would observe, was *said* to have been lost at sea, but his manner and expression betokened that he, for one, doubted the fact! Of his sisters he never spoke, and seemed to hate any mention of their names. One had married and died before he left home, the other had taken the veil. We stood in too great awe of him ever to ask any questions!

It frightened us children to see how he would sit for hours staring into the fire, and muttering to himself in a language we could not comprehend ; then, suddenly becoming aware of our presence, exclaim : " Ah, missie ! You there all the time ? What you do ? " But as often as not he would remain utterly oblivious of us all, and then unexpectedly rise, and in dead silence, put on his hat and leave the house.

Some of his ideas were peculiarly foreign, and he had certain strange prejudices—or so they appeared to us wild Highlanders—on the deportment and up-bringing of " young ladies." Accustomed to see " senhoritas " always carefully guarded, and never suffered to go abroad without the protection of a mother or duenna, he was scandalised at the liberty accorded to unmarried girls by Scottish and English custom. Never could he become reconciled to the idea of *his* daughters being seen outside the " policies " unattended ! We knew well that punishment and disgrace awaited us, if caught by " himself " outside the bounds of the garden and grounds, and when wandering, according to our wont, down by the river or over the bare hillsides at the back of Kinloch House, we caught, in the distance, a glimpse of his unmistakable figure, we would fly at breakneck speed, reckless of obstacles, for the shelter of our schoolroom. Well and good, if we got home without meeting him! But if, alas, he was near enough to recognise us individually, how have I quaked in my shoes at the sarcastic expression with which, at our next meeting, he would remark casually to our mother or the general company: "I have seen to-day some very strange creatures!—wild animals, I suppose, of some description; for it is impossible they were *young ladies!* They were rushing about through the heather 'and across the bogs, tearing up the hillsides and bounding over the rocks, exactly like a flock of goats. I wonder what they could be?"

On one occasion, I remember, he caught us red-handed, and we were summarily condemned to confinement in the old schoolroom, with a task to learn, for the remainder of the day It was a sultry summer's afternoon, and I never hear or read the story of Ananias and Sapphira—which, goodness only knows with what recondite connection with our offence, your Aunt Maria, our elder sister (named after our Portuguese grandmother "Euphrosia Maria Ferreira") had set us younger ones to learn—without its bringing back to my mind that hot, stuffy little room, and our impatient longing to be outside on the breezy braes, or in the garden with the bees, whom we could hear from our prison humming with sleepy satisfaction in and out of the roses and hollyhocks! We well knew the punishment was never inflicted with our mother's knowledge, and were quite aware that, as far as she was concerned, we had full licence to roam the woods, the moors, or the mountain-sides, to our hearts' content. Had she not herself been reared amid the wild glens and lochs of Argyllshire?

There was another point on which our father—who

otherwise seldom noticed us or interfered with our up-bringing—asserted his authority, and that, strange to say, was on the subject of *ear-rings !* " O, that's not so strange," I hear you remark at once. " Many men regard them as remnants of barbarism." He, however, was more singular in his views, according to our present ideas ; for in his opinion they were the distinction of gentle birth, and for a *senhorita* to be without them was lowering herself to the vulgar herd. " In *my* country," he would say, " all young ladies wear ear-rings. You look like little ragged children that run in the streets ! "

So convinced was he of the supreme necessity of *his* daughters being indued with these appendages as early as might be, that when my sister Maggie was only five years old, and I but three, he rode off by himself to Perth, to the jewellers, and purchased two pairs of golden " guards " set each with a single small pearl. These, on his return, were with much solemnity pro-duced, and displayed to our wondering and admiring eyes in their neat cardboard boxes. When we were told that these should be our very own, if only we would be brave and submit to have our ears pierced, the bribe conquered our fears, and we consented !

Naturally, I remember little of the incident, but Maggie used to tell —and I believe repeated the story to some of you a few years ago—how we two little ones were packed into a chaise driven by the man-servant, under escort of our father on horseback—for he took sole charge of the expedition, since our mother, though highly disapproving, offered no opposition to the pro-ject. When we arrived in Perth to undergo the ordeal, Maggie, so she herself confessed, basely took advantage of my tenderer age and inexperience, and begged that Mr. Browne, the jeweller, should devote his attention

first to me ! She said that I climbed upon the stool of
execution with great equanimity, having little idea of
what was in store for me, but that the moment the
instrument touched me, I screamed in terror, evidently
believing my last hour was come! and that my sobs
and cries so worked on her fears, that it was with the
greatest difficulty that she was persuaded to take her
turn. However, the idea that she ought to be brave
enough to undergo what one so much younger had
already endured, at length prevailed ; but even the
privilege of wearing those lovely jewels seemed scarcely
enough recompense for the agony that went before, and
it was only when we returned home and beheld the
admiration and envy in our elder sisters' eyes, and those
of our companions, that we felt rewarded for our pangs,
and gave ourselves the airs of Spartans, or Indian braves,
who had successfully passed through their rites of
initiation !

I well remember your Aunt Maria describing to me—
for, of course, I was too young to have seen it myself—the
formal state that used to be kept up at the gillies' or
tenants' dances, when my mother had not long been
married. The barn down near the mill (that gave the
Gaelic name of " Palliveolan " to the house) was
sumptuously decorated for the occasion, according to
the ideas of the day. At the upper end was raised a
sort of platform or dais, on which the " Bhantigearna "
(Lady, *par excellence*) sat enthroned, surrounded by
her daughters, to view the " revels of the retainers."
The fiddler—alone, outside that select circle, was allowed
a seat on this exalted plane.

Maria often spoke of one occasion when she, a mere
child, had been, as a great honour, allowed a place
beside her mother, in order to see the performance of a

noted dancer, who had come across the hills from Perth, to exhibit to the laird his skill and agility in a dance named the "Chantreuse" (Shantrews ?). A tall, handsome young fellow he was, dressed in nankeen breeches and waistcoat, and immensely proud of a green cloth coat, adorned with gilt buttons and a pair of swallowtails reaching nearly to his heels ! The "Chantreuse" was an old dance of foreign (probably French) extraction, and this was the only occasion on which Maria remembered to have seen it danced in public.

As soon as the performer entered the room by a door at the further end, his comical attire was sufficient to attract any child's attention. But when he proceeded forthwith to strike an attitude, with one arm thrown aloft above his head, while, in time to the music, he solemnly pointed his toes, now right now left, his coat tails touching the ground with each step, it proved too much for her sense of the ridiculous ! In vain she struggled to keep down her laughter ! in vain her mother frowned and shook her head at such unladylike behaviour ! As she watched the performer advance slowly in this fashion the whole length of the room, with a face of imperturbable gravity, and then suddenly break into a succession of leaps and bounds from one foot to the other, still advancing and then retreating, the ludicrousness of the whole performance was too much for poor Maria, who, half hysterical from fright and amusement combined, burst into peals of laughter and was ignominiously swept off by the nurses.

Whether our father had seen the "Chantreuse" danced in his early days, I know not ; or whether it merely reminded him of Brazilian dances familiar in his youth, I cannot say ; but, anyhow, from that day forward he showed the greatest eagerness for his

daughters to learn it.   His one question on their return
from a dancing-class was invariably : " Can you dance
' chantreuse,' missie ? "   He even took us younger
ones to Perth himself in order to personally interview
the dancing master, Mr. Low,* on the subject.   As far
as I can recollect, we were, in fact, taught this dance
but were too shame-faced ever to perform it for our
father's benefit, though he repeatedly asked us to do
so ; and still receiving a negative in reply to his stereo-
typed demand, he would retort angrily : " No ? You
not dance ' chantreuse ' ? You no good ! " and take no
further notice of us !

When your Uncle Colin was quite a lad (about
sixteen or seventeen years of age), and waiting for a
commission in the Honourable East India Company's
service—for, like a true Campbell, his soul was set on
soldiering and the chance of real fighting—he fell in,
while in Edinburgh, with some young men who advised
him, if he wanted to get his hand in, to volunteer for
the British Legion then being raised by the adherents of
Queen Christina of Spain, to fight Don Carlos. Recruit-
ing for this was going on actively in Scotland, and any
gentleman who could raise, or bring in, fifty men was
promised a commission in the Spanish service. Think
of that boy's dogged determination ! On his own
responsibility he went about, through our own strath,
and down to Crieff, to Glasgow, and all about the country, enlisting and enrolling men until he made up the
number ! A fine set of rapscallions some of them were ;
but many of them were our own lads from Kinloch.

We all went over to Crieff to see Uncle Colin off by
the coach. (He was my own favourite brother, and
nearest to me in age.) He picked up his men at different

* Father of the Misses Low, dancing mistresses to Queen Victoria.

stages on the route, and we heard afterwards that they
had a fearful time of it in Glasgow, where they were to
embark, and that it was with the greatest difficulty
they got their men on board !

A report had spread like wildfire through the city
that the lads were to be the victims of a Popish plot ;
that they were being decoyed from their country and
homes under false pretences, only to undergo the thumb-
screw and the rack of the Spanish Inquisition ! The
Glasgow mob was aroused, and swore that they would
prevent the embarcation by force ; and it was only by
eluding the vigilance of the bulk of the populace, and
by embarking the recruits in detachments in the early
dawn, and from a secluded wharf, that the scheme was
eventually carried out, not, however, without several
nasty skirmishes with scattered bodies of the roughs.

This, of course, we did not learn till some time afterwards ; but even had it been foreseen, our leavetaking
at Crieff could scarcely have been sadder than it was,
nor the apprehension greater with which we saw
Colin set out on an enterprise so fraught with danger
to a full-grown man, and doubly hazardous for one
so young.

Yet even the forebodings with which we saw him
depart fell short of the reality of the hardships he was to
undergo ! Fearful were the privations and severe the
fighting that was his lot with the Christinos troops ;
but the worst part of his sufferings was yet to come,
when the intelligence finally reached him from home
that he had been gazetted to the 3rd Madras Cavalry,
and he, with two companions, determined to make
his own way to the sea-coast, through a country then
entirely surrounded by the Carlists ! This they did in
the disguise of muleteers, after innumerable adventures

and hair-breadth escapes.   When at length he got
home, clad still in his sheepskin coat and quaint attire,
it was strange to watch the conflicting emotions that
crossed his father's face, on seeing him in this guise,
compounded of a melancholy gratification at beholding
once more a garb so associated with old memories, and
of shocked indignation that a *son* of *his* should so degrade
his birth, as to appear in his mother's presence in the
dress of an *arriero !*

During the first years of their married life my father
and mother had always been accustomed to spend
the winter months in Edinburgh, where their marriage
had taken place in 1804, in a house which they rented
there, as they only spent the summer months at Kinloch.
But long before my birth, the increasing number of
their children obliged them to give up making such
a wearisome and costly " flitting " twice in the twelvemonth.   They contented themselves, therefore, by
taking up their residence for half the year in the county
town of Perth, where my father possessed a house,
whether by purchase or inheritance I could not tell you.*
Thus I and my sisters were enabled to have masters,
and attend classes, during the greater part of the year,
for, as a rule, we were only at Kinloch during the summer
months.

I, myself, was born in the town house, and as my
arrival was before the expected time, it occasioned no'
little consternation and anxiety !   My poor mother was
at death's door, and there was little welcome for the
unhappy cause of all the turmoil, who was really not
expected to survive, and had been put down on a bed,
and left neglected by the nurse, while she attended to
her patient.   I was rescued from under a heap of clothes

* Two previous lairds of Kinloch are mentioned as residing at Perth.

by my mother's unmarried sister, then staying on a visit. This lady, finding the child breathed, with great promptitude hurried in search of a minister, and had it christened, in a hasty and perfunctory manner, by some stray pastor, so that it was never entered on any register, nor have I ever been able to show a certificate of birth, or know for certain by what name I was actually baptized ! It was believed that my preserver gave me her own name—spelt variously " Nellena " or " Nielina " in the family, the Campbells of Melfort in Argyllshire—but even of that there is no positive evidence, as my aunt, who was the only witness— the minister himself was lost trace of—was herself in too excited and nervous a condition, to remember with any certainty, her chief concern being that I should not leave the world *unbaptized,* and since my demise was momentarily expected, it seemed a matter of little importance under what name I made my exit !

My father was absent at the time, but he had been so frequently baulked in his desire to call one of his children after his beloved brother, that he had positively deter- mined that this eleventh one *must* be a boy and bear the name of " José." Great was his wrath and disappoint- ment on his return to be presented with an eighth daughter, and told that " it was supposed " that Aunt Nellena had had the effrontery to give the child her own name ! It was long before he could get over his vexation, and cease from constant reference to it, and to the fact that " José " or " Josephine " was equally a girl's name, and his wishes *might* have been kept in mind ! To the end of his life he refused to call me by my (supposed) baptismal name, and I think it was the unquestioning manner in which I accepted the name of " Josephine " as my proper one, that made him adopt me as his special favourite. When he heard the others calling me " Lena " he invariably turned round on me with the indignant remonstrance : " You Miss Josephine ! You Miss José ! " and it made him quite happy to find that when asked my name, I promptly replied, without a shade of hesitation : " Josephine Campbell."

My father and his brothers and sisters were all brought up as strict Roman Catholics. Indeed, our Uncle Gregorio, and, after his death or disappearance, my father himself, had been sent to the granduncle, the Bishop of Oporto, to be educated for the Roman priesthood. This was done much against my father's will, and in the end he prevailed on our grandfather (who had meantime returned from exile, and made his submission to King George's Government), to allow him to join the army instead. For some reason or other a commission was applied for in a Highland regiment, and though not a syllable could be extracted from him with reference to the two or three years he served in it—years of purgatory they must have proved to the shy, foreign lad, thrust into companionship strange and unsympathetic, even if not absolutely hostile—there was one single point connected with this period, on which he could always be " drawn " by malicious acquaintances and mischievous juniors, a point on which he quickly waxed vehement, if not eloquent— and that was his undisguised aversion to the Highland dress ! Think of the horror of the youth who had never seen or heard of the kilt, on being informed that it was henceforth to form an article of his attire ! How every sentiment of modesty was up in arms at the outrage ! And picture his joy when, on receiving his father's permission to throw up his commission, he felt that he was quit for ever of this source of humiliation! The expression of scandalised horror with which he always alluded to the garment in question, and the reluctance with which he acknowledged that he had ever been brought to don it, never failed to convulse his hearers with merriment.

The only other subject on which he sometimes launched into speech, was on the iniquities of the priests, to whom he seemed to have developed a very violent aversion during his time of training in the seminary. After his father's death he and his elder brother had turned Protestant, and he was regular in his attendance at the parish kirk, though probably totally unable to follow the minister's discourse, given in the broadest Perthshire.

One festival of the Church, however, then much neglected by the Presbyterians, he to the end observed as a day of rejoicing; and much to the amazement of his dependents, who thought such doings a reprehensible relic of Popish up-bringing, always had a gathering at the "big hoose" on Christmas Day. He would go round himself to issue the invitations on these occasions, and make them all promise to be present, repeating impressively: "Christmas! Christmas! Remember—do not forget! The twenty-fifth of December! Remember!"

To him, with his old associations, the royal family of Portugal stood on a far higher plane than that of Great Britain. When he wished to compliment any one of his daughters on their appearance or attire, he would exclaim: "Here comes the Queen of England!" But should another appear to merit still higher approbation, the acmé of approval was denoted by the epithet: "Here comes the *Queen of Portugal!!*"

My mother having been unable to nurse me herself, I alone, of all my brothers and sisters, was brought up by a foster-mother, one of the Kinloch women. In consequence, I in the family was the sole proud possessor of a foster-sister, my devoted slave and adherent as I grew up. How I triumphed over my sisters on this account, and revelled in the exhibition of my authority before their envious gaze! Thinking over it now, I realise what cruel little tyrants children often are in their dealings with one another.

I can remember how, on summer evenings, Maggie and I would go down by the burn, where we could watch the children going home from school along the Aberfeldy road on the further side, and I would signal Kirstie Crichton to come across the stepping-stones and report herself. Whereupon, if not satisfied with her progress at her tasks that day, or should she otherwise fall under my displeasure, I would forthwith proceed to administer severe chastisement on the spot, or admonish her to be more careful for the future!

So great was the veneration in which the " young leddies " were held, that I positively believe that Kirstie *enjoyed* the importance of her close connection with " Miss Lena," even though it was made to entail such painful consequences! And I know that the sight of me, her junior in age, enacting the part of " dominie " to another child, so roused the jealousy of my sister Maggie, that she *bribed*, with sweeties and bawbees, a much bigger girl, known as Bessie " Homish " (her father being *Thomas* Crichton), to allow her the same privilege in watching over her morals. Thus it came about that the edifying spectacle might be frequently beholden, of the two youngest daughters of Kinloch engaged in belabouring their liege subjects!

The catering for the immense household needed to be on a large scale, for the farm-servants, both men and women, lived on the premises, the men having their sleeping-quarters over the stables. Farm and indoor servants took their meals together in the outer hall, near the kitchen, and there were always a few hangers-on or outsiders to swell the total. The providing for this company formed an important part of the cook's daily duty, and the careful mistress superintended every detail to see that there was no waste. The old style of Scottish cookery was founded on the French, and had many points of resemblance. Huge joints of meat were never seen on the hall-table save on high days and holi-days, but every morning the enormous *pot-au-feu* called the " kail-pot " was placed on the kitchen fire, and into it were thrown meat, vegetables, pease, a handful of oatmeal, and any scraps of bread remaining from the family table. If a sheep or bullock were slaughtered, the head, heart and liver, etc., would be added ; not a scrap would be lost, though great care was always taken that any intestinal portions were left unbroken and hanging over the edge of the pot, so as to be easily lifted out when their goodness was absorbed. We mischievous children, who were perpetually in and out of the kitchen, led the cook an awful life, by playing continual pranks with the kail-pot whenever her back was turned. We would lift the lid surreptitiously and drop in all sorts of unusual culinary additions, to the no small perturbation of that much-harassed functionary!

This broth was the standing dish of the servants' dinner. The meat was either served in it or removed and given separately. In the centre of the table stood a large flat basket, piled high with barley bannocks, for

white bread was never seen in those days in the servants'
hall. These bannocks, ten inches in diameter, were the
test of a woman's value. If she was known to bake
good bannocks there was little fear of her ever wanting
a husband! And the men were connoisseurs on the
subject, and not easily satisfied.

Sometimes, for a change, potato or pease-meal flour
would be mixed with the barley meal; and, for a treat,
oat-cakes were given now and again. Oatmeal porridge
formed the staple breakfast and supper, the women-
servants alone being allowed tea instead.

The laying-in of winter stores for the household
exercised the forethought and powers of organisation
of the lady of the house, as much as those of an officer
in the commissariat preparing a garrison for a siege!
The factor had to be advised of the exact number of fat
beasts to be purchased at the Dunkeld Martinmas fair,
when the cattle arrived in droves from Argyllshire. Two
or three were the usual number, and these were salted
down and pickled, along with the mutton-hams for
winter use.

The annual slaughter of these beasts was quite a
marked day in the calendar of the year to the inmates
of Kinloch. Then began the regular manufacture of
tallow candles, or " dips," for the winter, a long and
tedious operation. Each woman had two tubs in front
of her, one empty, the other partly filled with hot water,
on which floated a thick layer of liquid tallow. Strands
of hemp or flax, the length of the candle required, were
hung over a stick, forming a loop at the top of each,
through which the stick passed. About ten strings
were on each stick. The woman dipped the strands into
the tub of grease, and set the stick across the empty
tub, to dry the strings and drain off the extra grease.

She repeated the process with another stick. By the
time she had dipped the strings on about eight sticks, the
first were sufficiently hardened to receive a fresh coating.
Thus the operation was continued till the dips were
thick enough. This was the usual Highland practice
in the early part of the nineteenth century.

The relations between landlord and tenant still par-
took of the old feudal character. Only part of the rent
was paid in money, for it was far easier to the farmer
to pay in kind. Money payments therefore were very
small indeed, and the rents were made up to their value
by certain seigneurial rights. For instance, each tenant
was bound, according to the size of his holding, to give
so many days' labour on the laird's land in " hairst "
or " hayseln " (hay or corn harvest), providing a sub-
stitute if unable to come himself. His wife or daughter
besides was expected to do so many days' spinning or
carding for the " leddy." Moreover, each crofter and
cottar paid as their due annually, in lieu of a portion of
the rent, a certain number of fowls, termed " Kane-
chickens," which were the perquisite of the laird's
wife. It may well be imagined that much depended
on the latter's disposition, and her consideration for
the tenants, whether this tax was irksome or otherwise,
as it was left entirely to herself *when* to exact it ! Some
ladies, who had little thought and kindliness for their
poorer neighbours, demanded their rights when fowls
were scarce, and commanded a higher price in the
market, but those who, like my mother, acted fairly by
all, and whose sympathy sprang from knowledge of their
difficulties, asked only for the tale of " Kane-chickens "
when they could best be spared. The duty of warning
the tenants when the tribute was to be exacted, was the
office of a special functionary—in our case, old Peter

Anderson ; and occasionally when, on an emergency, he was bidden to collect and bring them in himself, I can remember seeing him returning in triumph, like an Indian brave decorated with the scalps of his enemies, hung round the middle with the bodies of the dead ducks and fowls, their heads passed through his waist-belt ! The great point was that these seigneurial rights were regarded as no hardship by the tenants, to whom it was infinitely easier to pay their rents in this manner than in the form of hard cash, which would have entailed the cartage of their produce over execrable roads, to Dunkeld, Creiff or Aberfeldy.

One important duty of the " Bhantigearna " * (lady) was the supervision of the " spinning-women," who came in their turn to render their tale of work, and assembled each morning at the " bothy," a building attached to every large Scottish manor or homestead, where the farm-servants were lodged and usually fed. At Kinloch this consisted chiefly of a large room, barely furnished, with the spinning-wheels standing in rows the whole length of it, the " lady's " chair and wheel in the post of honour at its head.

How the picture comes back to me of that long, low room, filled with the musical hum of fifteen or sixteen wheels all going at once, and the cheerful sound of voices lowered to a discreet murmur ; for was not the lady there herself, spinning busily, and setting an example of industry to all, while ever keeping a watchful eye upon the work and behaviour of the others ? Ever and anon she would leave her place, and pass down the line of spinning wheels, stopping at each to examine the thread, to test its fineness and evenness, and to see that there were no knots or faults. She herself was a noted

* Pronounced " Vynegerna."

spinster; none other could produce from the " spool " a
thread as fine as gossamer, yet smooth and even as
a silkworm's web.

The fleeces of the Highland sheep that pastured on the
Kinloch moors and hills, were spun into wool yarn,
and sent to the Trochrie weaver, and to Aberfeldy, to
be woven into plaids and homespuns; but the staple
yarn was the flax, grown in large fields, a lovely crop in
flower, covering the hillside above the house with its
rich, bright blue, like a wide patch of summer sky held
captive between the shoulders of Meall Mhor.   This
flax crop was an important item in the revenues of the
Kinloch estate.   When ready, it was cut in bundles,
and after the seed had been shaken out, it was taken
down to the Cochill burn below the house, and left to
steep in the shallow pools by the mill, that seigneurial
water-mill which gives the name of Pall-i-veoollan,
or " Milltown," to the house itself, " Bhantigearna
Pall-i-veoollan " being the full Gaelic title of the laird's
lady.

When sufficiently rotted by the action of the water,
the flax was removed, and beaten with heavy clubs,
to separate the fibre.   Then the carding and the winding
on the spools began, ready for the winter spinning.

As the shades of evening fell, and the work of the farm
perforce ceased, the spinning-room at the bothy had an
irresistible attraction for the "lads," whether "hinds"
or "herds"; and they would gather bashfully in groups
about the door, watching the women industriously ply
their wheels in the gloaming.   The long, low room was
lighted only by the firelight, whose ruddy glow as it
flickered and fell on the spinsters' figures, and was
caught and reflected by the whirling wheels and
rockers, formed a scene marvellously picturesque and

harmonious. A favoured few of the lads, as a very special privilege, were permitted by the "lady" to enter, and take a seat at the further end of the room, where a lad might have a quiet "crack" with the lassie of his choice, screened by the shadows cast on floor, walls and ceiling, by the movement of the spinsters' hands and feet working in concert—the one on the treadle, the other with a constant back-and-forward motion that twisted the thread betwixt finger and thumb. But all must be conducted with bated breath and the utmost decorum, for was not the eye of the "leddy" herself ever upon them, or that of her confidential maid, a very rigid exactor of the strictest propriety?

Strangely enough a day came—was it to foster the new linen trade of Ulster?—when the home manufacture of linen web was strictly prohibited by law! Then the fields of flowering flax, which had been a feature of the hillside of Meall Mhor, behind Kinloch Lodge, were grown in sheltered spots screened from the view of passing excisemen. And when the "leddy" spread her woven clothes to bleach in the full sun, the bairns of the countryside would be set on watch and guard, and whenever a signal, waved from Cablea, the hill facing the house across the Cochill burn, warned the household that scouts had sighted the "gaugers" on the Aberfeldy road, instantly the bleaching greens were black with human ants, every man, woman and child from the four "touns" (or hamlets) of Cablea, Innercochill, Milltown and Deanshaugh, turned out to lend a hand, for fear the minions of the law should catch their beloved "Bhantigearna" in the act of defying them! Though well they knew she still span and wove her linen sheets and napery, oft though they came by stealth, having word of the bleaching, never a pocket-handkerchief did they sight in the policies, though the greens and braes but a half-hour syne had been white as if covered with a snowdrift!

From going in and out so much amongst our own people, we were closely associated with their daily lives, and the feudal feeling was strong between "the family" and those of the tenants who had held their lands for generations. Whenever any one among them died, word was at once sent to the "hoose," and some member of the family was expected to come as soon as possible, as a token of respect. If any of us children were seen passing, we would be sure to be called to come in and "view the body," and terrified as we might be at the notion, we knew it would be the occasion of dire offence if we ever omitted this duty. Apart from the idea that it showed respect to the dead, and sympathy with the relatives, it was judged a sure precursor of ill-luck to ourselves if we failed to do so, and many a time have I, a wee bit bairnie, been dragged into the chamber of death by an officious servant-maid or cottar's wife, and, terrified out of my wits by the sight of the still, stiff form, been compelled by actual force to touch it with my trembling finger, to ensure that it should not "walk," and haunt me all my life after!

The sister next above me was credited with second sight, as seventh daughter of a seventh daughter; but I myself, having been born with a "caul" (or "happy how"), was held in special veneration, as endowed by Heaven with the power of passing on to others the gift of good luck imparted to me at my birth! They believed that my touch had healing powers, and that any prayer or charm uttered by my mouth was more effectual, and received with greater favour on high, than that of an ordinary, ungifted mortal. Specially

was this the case with any " beast " bewitched by
malice, or " overlooked " by the evil eye ; for our
Strathbraan folk were true Celts in their superstitions,
and firm believers in kelpies, brownies, and the " guid-
people."

So, whenever any of their cattle were stricken with
a disease they could not account for, I would be sent
for. Many a time, when the summons was urgent,
have I been roused out of my sleep in the middle of
the night (unknown, needless to say, to my mother and
the governess !), dressed hurriedly by the servants, and
carried, rolled in a plaid, on a man's shoulder, over the
hill to some farm or other, where, in the byre, still
dazed with sleep, and bewildered by the lanterns
flickering against the darkness, I would be made to
stand in the stall by the side of a sick cow or calf, and
holding the creature by the ear, repeat a Gaelic charm,
of whose meaning I had not the faintest conception !
Again, I would be in request by those starting on a
journey, or projecting some new venture in business,
in order that I might pronounce over them some magic
formula or incantation, prompted by one of the bystanders, which, uttered by me, would assuredly bring
success to the undertaking !

My father's shyness and taciturnity made him go
very little into society, and as my mother was much
engaged looking after the household, and managing
the estate, we girls would have seen little outside our
own strath, were it not that the old Marquess and
Marchioness of Breadalbane were fond of having
young people in the house, and as the Kinloch and
Breadalbane properties " marched," and the families
were connected, the " Kinloch girls " would be sent
for when there was a large house-party to entertain.

Thus we met many noted strangers from the south and elsewhere, as well as the Tayside gentry. The ways of Scottish society were still much as described by Sir Walter Scott, and as it was not yet considered a disgrace for a gentleman to be seen intoxicated, the sole distinction observable between certain old topers was that, while some of them were *frequently* tipsy after dinner, one or two were never seen quite sober ! There were many honourable exceptions to this low code of manners in Highland society, but, as a rule, the English guests were pleasanter associates for girls in their teens, though often ridiculed for their simplicity and refined habits by their Highland acquaintances.

The old Duchess of St. Albans, who had been the widow of Mr. Coutts the banker, when the Duke, much her junior in age, married her, was one of the habitual visitors at Taymouth. My first view of her, however, was at the Crieff Hotel, on her way through to Kenmore. It was on the occasion when we saw my brother Colin off on his adventurous campaign with the Christinos. After the coach in which he travelled had left for Glasgow, and while we were waiting to return home, the Duchess and her retinue arrived in eight carriages ; for though by birth of no family, she had a most exalted idea of her own importance, and when paying a series of short visits to country houses, was so convinced of the savage condition of the Highlands, that she travelled always with her own *chef* and *patissier*, who alone were permitted to cook her meals at the inns she stopped at on the road.

I shall not easily forget the sight of the disgorging of the Duchess's own chariot when it pulled up at the inn door. First emerged her Grace herself, an enormously fat woman ; then followed her three nieces, daughters of Sir Francis Burdett, whereof the youngest and best-looking, became inheritress of her wealth, and Baroness Burdett-Coutts. These young ladies, evidently in mortal terror of their awful relative—not without reason !—followed the Duchess in single file, dutifully carrying each some article necessary to her Grace's comfort, reticule, cushion, wraps, books, foot-stool, and bag of toilet requisites, the Duchess's favourite lapdog, and her pet parrot in its cage ! After them came her Grace's private physician, who travelled always in the same carriage as herself so as to be on the spot ; while the Duke preferred the coachbox to the company inside—and no wonder !

All the time, the Duchess's tongue was heard going, scolding, complaining, abusing everybody, from her husband downwards, in unmeasured terms. The unfor-tunate nieces came in for no small share of her harangue, and earned painfully any share of her fortune she may have left them in her will, for she swore at them unceas-ingly, like a trooper, or a Billingsgate fishwife !

What a bustle and confusion the whole place was thrown into !   Nothing in the inn was good enough for the Duchess ; she must have her own footman lay the table, with her own glass, silver and napery ; her own cooks produce a dinner ; her own confectioner make the pies and pastry. Her appetite for dainties was enormous, and after her departure—for she halted only for the midday meal—the innkeeper's daughters brought us children in the remains of the pies, that we might taste the richness of the crust made by the Duchess's baker.

The Duke appeared a very mild, quiet little man, completely lorded over and swamped by the personality of his overwhelming spouse.

The old Marchioness of Breadalbane dearly loved to

tell a good story, and was not averse to doing so occasionally at the expense of her English guests.

She and the Marquess had a large party of sportsmen once staying at Taymouth Castle for the opening
of the stag season, mostly gentlemen from the south,
desperately anxious to acquit themselves creditably
in what was then a more unusual form of sport, and
extremely desirous that nothing in their attire or
appearance, should betray the fact that they were tyros
in deer-stalking.

The Scotsmen of the party, naturally, wore the Highland dress, both for the hills and (in full paraphernalia)
in the evening, and the effect of its enhancement of a fine
masculine figure had the usual consequence, in exciting
the jealous admiration of their English associates, who
were not to be deterred from attempts to follow their
example. The results, in spite of the Highland dictates
of courtesy, were the cause of considerable amusement
and sarcastic comment, amongst themselves, to the
native-born mountaineers, especially the gillies. In
the smoking-room, too, a tender solicitude had been
manifested for the pain and injury caused to their delicate white skins by the rude abrasion of granite rocks,
and the scorching rays of the sun in the corries! The
taunts and raillery, it would seem, had hit the victims
on the raw. For in the very early morning, when the
first glimmer of the " false " dawn was scarcely showing
in the east, Lady Breadalbane was roused by strange,
stealthy sounds on the sweep of the drive at the entrance-
door of the Castle, which, as is the case in all Highland
residences, was laid with a surface of about four to
six inches of large, round, loose shingle, the object of
which is to remove all traces of mud off the boots of the
sportsmen ere they enter the premises.

Thinking that the hour must be later than she imagined, and the darkness boded a wet day for the hills, the Marchioness drew back the curtain, and peered forth. An inky blackness met her eyes, with a faint white light breaking on the horizon where perhaps in an hour's time the sun might show his face. And still those mysterious, creepy sounds went on in the gloom below ! Alarmed, she listened for a few moments ; then, as her eyes grew accustomed to the darkness, she made out strange shadows crawling to and fro on the white surface of the stones. Gradually they took form as the light strengthened, and just as she felt quite positive that the prize herd of black cattle must have got loose from its paddock, were now engaged in routing the gravel and the turf with muzzle and hooves, and would presently attack her cherished shrubs and gardens, and had laid her hand on the bell to give the alarm, one of the " beasts " reared itself on its hind legs, stood erect, and marched in at the front door ! In the second " quadruped ?" that followed suit she recognised a human form ; the third revealed himself as the Duke of L —— in an extraordinary garment, and one by one she identified her English guests as they raised themselves from their hands and knees, on which they had been grovelling for the last half-hour amongst the stones, and filed slowly back into the house before her amazed vision, in every variety of *deshabillé*, but with the air of men who had·shown their contempt of personal agony and discomfort, and could now exhibit with triumph their scars in the field of slaughter ! Who can deny to such a race the virtue of stoicism and the proof of pure breeding ?

CHAPTER II

LEAVING HOME

I HAVE little doubt that it was to the possession of that "happy how" that our Strathbraan folk attributed the fact that I was preserved from a watery grave on my first voyage to India! Even for those days of sea-risks it was an exceptionally long and dangerous one.

My father and mother were both dead, and my eldest brother, the laird, afterwards General Charles Campbell, invited me, and my next sister Maggie, to come out to him, in the North-West Provinces, where he was stationed. We were under the escort of a married sister, going out to rejoin her husband, who was herself young, very handsome and amiable, and not much accustomed to making all the arrangements for a sea-voyage. She was therefore easily persuaded to engage cabins in a freshly painted and decorated ship, sailing for Calcutta—of course round the Cape of Good Hope—commanded by a most delightful and courteous captain, quite a gentleman, and with most charming manners, and a bachelor to boot! His officers appeared equally affable, and anxious to oblige. The vessel was large and spacious, and so little crowded with passengers that the accommodation was palatial for those days. In fact so resolved was the skipper to be agreeable to his lady-passengers, that he even placed himself at our disposal, to assist us in making the necessary purchases of outfit for the voyage!

We left the Thames, therefore, with the happiest anticipations, hoping that the time at sea might prove as free from discomfort as it was reasonable to expect, considering the stormy oceans to be traversed. But, alas ! scarcely had the Start Light faded from our view, when a curious clanking noise began, which we, in our ignorance, did not recognise, but which sounded ominous in the ears of the few passengers on board more experienced in the ways of ships. From that moment forward the dread sound was hardly ever stilled, but as we entered the Bay of Biscay the full force of an Atlantic gale met us, and I and my sisters knew and cared little for what was happening !

Our voyage was a series of disasters. No sooner had we weathered one gale than another overwhelmed us, and for many days we were driven before a hurricane out of our course, caught by the great Equatorial current, and many times within an ace of foundering, till suddenly, after days and weeks under close hatches, we found the ship erect, sailing through calm waters, and woke one morning to be told that the fair scene we saw before us was the harbour and city of Rio de Janeiro, the storm having carried us to the opposite coast of the Atlantic ! Thus, for the first and only time of my life, I saw the continent of America !

We remained only a day or two at Rio, and lay in the outer harbour with little communication with the shore, while repairs of the damage done by the gale, including an immense amount of carpentry and caulking, were carried on in the hold of the ship, in a sort of feverish haste.

We left as unexpectedly and hurriedly as we came, and it was only after the coast of America had faded into the blue distance, that Captain ——, first swearing

us to secrecy (with an oath so solemn and terrible, that
we two girls, aged respectively twenty-two and twenty-
four, shook with terror as we repeated it after him!),
confided to Maggie and me a fact known only to himself, the first officer and the carpenter, viz., that the ship
had been leaking ever since we left the Channel, and
that in the hurricane she had received such injury that
there was now a great hole in her bottom! This had
been patched after a fashion as we lay at Rio, and it
was *hoped* that, with fair weather, and the pumps
going, we might reach Cape Town in safety, where it
would be possible to effect more thorough repairs!
Not a word of this dire state of things were we to dare
to breathe to a living soul, least of all to our elder
sister! under pain of eternal perdition!

As it came out later, he was sole owner of the vessel,
a notoriously unseaworthy craft, which he had purchased
as a speculation, for a low sum, and had repainted,
done up, and advertised for this one voyage, risking
his own life and that of all who sailed in her, like the
gambler he was, for the chance of making his fortune
at one bold stroke!

You can imagine the feelings of relief with which
Maggie and I, and, indeed, all on board, hailed the sight
of Table Mountain; but again, to our disappointment,
the ship did not enter the port, but lay outside in the
offing!

Actually, she lay in the Bay for nearly a fortnight,
during which time she was in the hands of shipwrights,
tinkering her up as best they could without putting her
in dock, for the continuance of the voyage. Meanwhile,
confiding in our sympathy, and exacting fresh pledges
of secrecy from us two younger ones, the Captain
positively engaged rooms at his expense, for us three

sisters, at the best hotel, where we were entertained royally, much to the gratified surprise of our chaperone; and we spent the time visiting the places of interest, and the country round, in a coach-and-four, which the gallant mariner hired for our delectation, and drove himself! Not many birds of passage to India by the Cape route in those days saw so much of Cape Colony, and in such agreeable fashion!

Our sojourn came hurriedly to an end, however; for, as it turned out, the authorities' suspicions were aroused by certain rumours flying about, as to the unseaworthiness of the ship lying without the jurisdiction of the port, and the Captain found it necessary to sail unexpectedly, leaving behind some of the cargo and passengers he had anticipated, and cutting short the work of repair to the ship. Of course Maggie and I believed implicitly his assertion that all was now right, and the vessel as sound as when she first took the water. But we soon had a rude awakening, and it was not very long before all on board became aware of the actual state of affairs.

No sooner had we weathered the Cape than the trouble began. Doubtless the Antarctic rollers began the mischief, and then gale after gale caught us, the leak started afresh, and the water gained so fast that all hands were at the pumps in relays, day and night. Off Mauritius we were caught in a hurricane and all but foundered, and as we slowly made our way northward we were struck by the monsoon. The Lascar crew, overworked, overdriven, miserable and terror-stricken, were several times in open mutiny, and with all his criminal recklessness, one could not but admire the magnificent nerve and seamanship of our skipper. That alone, under a merciful Providence, brought us at

length through that terrible voyage of over five months'
constant peril, when, to the amazement and joy of our
friends, who had long given us up for lost, and the
relief of the underwriters at Lloyd's, where the ship
had been "posted" for weeks, we were signalled off
the Sunderbunds, and came at length up the Hooghli!
There the vessel was seized and condemned by the
authorities—as she would have been at once had she
entered the port at Cape Town—the Captain and
officers were arrested, and for a long time she was an
object of curiosity in the dock where she lay, crowds
visiting her to inspect the great hole in her bottom,
and marvel that she had ever been brought so far!

Mingled with all the terror and tragedy of that
voyage, one ludicrous episode comes back to me sometimes. Oddly enough, it is in church that it recurs to
me, for it is associated with a once very popular hymn-
tune, to which, to this day, I have a violent antipathy.

It was somewhere in the Indian Ocean, between the
Cape and the Bay of Bengal—I have forgotten the date
and the exact latitude—when the weather had slightly
moderated, that the Captain, whose temper and nerves
were in a highly-strung condition, accused the second-
officer of leaning over the poop-rail, to peep in at the
ladies' cabins! The latter protested his innocence,
and we all declared our disbelief in his ever having done
such a thing. We liked the young man, who was very
quiet and civil; and really much preferred his society
to that of the Captain. But, curiously enough, the more
we took his part, and assured the Captain that we felt
positive the accused had never dreamt of behaviour of
the kind, the more furious grew his superior against
him! To our horror, and that of the other passengers,
though every man was needed to work the ship, the

Captain ordered the unfortunate young man into close confinement, *in irons*, below in the hold! There in the darkness, the foul air and the stench, he was kept, in the heat of the tropics, and with a head-sea on! Our entreaties on his behalf only made the Captain more obdurate. Through the cook, and the steward who gave him his food, we sent him messages. "We were not to worry about him," he said. "He was all right; only he craved for music to beguile the weary hours. Would we get permission for him to have his instrument, and he would be perfectly happy?" The boon was granted, and we rejoiced to think that we had obtained this slight solace for the prisoner. We pictured him as a marine Orpheus, charming the rats and cockroaches with his violin. Suddenly from the depths of the hold there arose the most appalling groans and wheezes! It was the second-officer's efforts to produce harmony on a *concertina*, and the one and only tune he apparently knew, or attempted to play, from that time forward, in fair weather or foul, by night and day unceasingly, through the clanking of the pumps, and the bellowing of the wind, was "Jerusalem, my happy home!" Never do I hear that refrain without it bringing back to me the smell of that awful ship and her wallowing in the trough of the sea, day after day, week after week, punctured by those heartrending howls unceasingly emitted from her very vitals!

We were met at Calcutta by another married sister and her husband, with whom Maggie remained until her marriage shortly after. I, meantime, went on up-country, with my sister, Mrs. Hope Dick.

Those were curious days in India. Ladies were scarce, and unmarried girls few and far between. Men used to write home for their wives, proposing to women they had only heard of, and never *seen* in their lives. I had a sister, Patricia, engaged to a brother-officer of my brother's, who was afterwards a General on the Staff of the Viceroy. She died, poor thing, after only a week's illness, on the very day that had been fixed for her marriage. Would you believe it ? General B. saw a portrait of me on my brother's table, and though my poor sister had been dead only a month or two, he wrote straight off to me, a girl in the schoolroom, and asked me to be his wife ! And I—oh ! I was terrified lest I should be made to marry a man I had never set eyes on !

I knew a girl, passing through a station on her way up-country, who went to a dance, and had seven proposals in one night ; and one of her suitors, a very fat Major, waylaid her palankeen as she was continuing her journey, and poured his offer of marriage through the closed chits ! *Palki-dâk* journeys were made by night generally, and it was hardly dawn. The young woman, scarcely awake, did not realise at first that he was serious, as he enumerated the carriages, horses and jewels he would be able to afford her, culminating in a statement of the amount of pension she would draw as his widow ! Becoming alive to the fact of what he was aiming at, she begged him to say no more, and bade the *ayah* with her in the palankeen tell the bearers to hasten, as they had dropped into a crawl when the officer appeared. But the woman, who had been heavily bribed, gave contrary directions, and the Major, in Hindustani, did the same. Angry and alarmed at such persistence, and at the distance that she had now dropped behind her chaperone's *palki*, she thrust her head out of the opposite side from her persistent admirer, shouting to the bearers her one phrase of the language, the first that comes naturally to every European : " *Jaldi, jaldi jao !* " The bearers, grasping the situation, set off at a run, while the Major ran panting alongside, continuing his arguments to the lady, interspersed with roars of bad language at the bearers, who, hearing the girl's peals of laughter at the figure he cut, chattered and giggled as they tore faster and faster, till the last she heard of the gentleman was an expiring shriek as he dropped behind : " Five thousand rupees, dead or alive ! " Oh, yes, it's quite true, I assure you ! How do I know all the details, you say ? *Of course it was from the ayah !* She was dismissed, naturally.

You ask if, among the seven offers mentioned, one proved to be from " Mr. Right " ? No, I may tell you; for the very good reason that they came too late. She had met *him* for the first time, four-and-twenty hours before, at the previous station—and there never was any question on the matter !

Well, I never got as far as Cawnpore, or joined my brother ; for I stopped at Lucknow with my sister, Mrs. Dick, and there I was married, on July 28th 1842, and spent my honeymoon in the Beebeepore Palace at Lucknow, put at our disposal by the King of Oude, Mahommed Ali Shah.

CHAPTER III

My husband twice held the post of Residency-Surgeon at Lucknow, and had in addition many other appointments under two successive Kings of Oude, including that of Physician to the Court.

The Princesses and Begums of the Royal Family showed me the greatest friendliness, from the Queen-Mother downwards. Indeed, Malika Geytee, the King's favourite wife, treated me always as an intimate friend, and all the Princesses made a point of presenting me, on the birth of each of my children, as a sign of personal regard, with a complete outfit of native dresses for myself and the newcomer, of their own handiwork, gorgeously embroidered in gold and silver bullion. These I still possess, as evidence that these native ladies do not all pass their lives in complete idleness, as is commonly supposed.

Malika Geytee kept up a correspondence with my husband for many years after we left Lucknow, and even when we had returned to England letters in the most beautiful Persian script continued to reach us from her. Many of these Princesses were women of great intelligence as well as high lineage, and we used to discuss all sorts of subjects, though not often religious matters, unless they specially questioned me, for my husband had a great dislike to any attempt to teach Christianity except with the husband's permission; but their curiosity was great concerning European clothes and customs.

Being thus thrown into the society of native ladies of rank for over seven years, I naturally got to speak the Court language, and as I was about the only English-woman at home in England during the Mutiny time who did so, when the old Queen came to plead the cause of her son (the wretched Wajid Ali), with our Queen Victoria, she begged that I might be the inter-preter on that occasion. I much feared I should have to undertake the office, as Her Majesty approved of the idea, for having had such constant kindness from the poor old lady, it would have been terrible to have been the instrument of making plain to her that her mission was in vain—the treatment meted out to that worthless caitiff was far more lenient than he had any right to expect. He was finally awarded a pension of £70,000 per annum, which he was allowed to squander as he pleased in the most profligate debauchery. However, the difficulty was got over by placing an Indian official as interpreter, behind a screen, in the room at Windsor where the two Queens had their interview.

Talking of screens reminds me of the scenes I fre-quently assisted at in Oude, when my husband was sent for to prescribe for a *purdah* patient. Of course he was never permitted to have a full view of her face! In-stead, he had the fleeting vision of a *hand*, or of a *tongue* " without visible means of support," waggling through a hole cut in the curtain, by which to judge of her general condition!

But I was privileged to view, at close quarters, the comedy that was being enacted behind the *purdah*— the solemnity of the eunuchs supporting their mistress, while they assisted her to open her mouth and thrust her tongue through the orifice! the shouts of laughter from the entire zenana, present *en masse* at the proceedings, the hysterical giggles and fidgeting of the patient, not at all averse (if good-looking) to making use of an opportunity to view eye-to-eye, and unveiled, such a popular Englishman. Undoubtedly, most of the Begums, and especially my friend Malika Geytee, thoroughly entered into the humour of the situation, once their minds were relieved of the dread lest my jealousy might be aroused by the undoubted attractiveness of many of these patients !

His many personal friends amongst the Nawabs also welcomed me to their zenanas, and I had a chance of seeing the native ladies, and their children, in a social intercourse very unusual in those days between the two races. These purdah-women exercise an influence and a power that is only slowly being realised by Europeans, and as the zenana is the actual source of all the intrigues that constitute Oriental diplomacy, I learnt to be of real use to my husband in his political work.

He never would take any fee for medical attendance on the natives, and the expedients that some of these Nawabs adopted to show their gratitude were often absurd in the extreme. He had saved the life of the Wuzeer (Prime Minister) Nawab Ameenoodowlah, by his promptitude and skill, when the latter was waylaid and cut down by dacoits, and he also cured the Wuzeer's only child, the little Begum Wuzeeroolniza, when far gone in consumption. She had been given over by the native *hakim*, and wise women, when, at the Wuzeer's earnest request, Login closely examined her, and discovered that the unfortunate child was slowly pining away, owing to the fact that her skin was encrusted with a hard shell, formed by the succession of ointments she had been plastered with, since to wash a patient in illness is regarded as fatal in native medical science! His prescription of a warm bath was received with indignant horror by the Begum, who only consented to try it, after much persuasion *through the purdah*, if the " Mem-Sahib " would come and see it carried out herself!

So I and my ayah arrived at the zenana, armed with a supply of soft towels, scented soap and sponges, and it was the interest and excitement aroused by the first sight of the latter that finally overbore all the opposition.   Never in their lives had the Begums and their attendants beheld a sponge, or the European scented soap, for that matter!   At first their alarm was great when the unknown marine monster swelled in the water, and they shrieked when we held it towards the child, for fear it should bite her!   But, once reassured on that score, they regarded it as a piece of magic, and were enraptured at being presented with it on my departure. They amused themselves with it for hours, filling and squeezing it, and throwing it at each other, accompanied by peals of laughter!

It was a long and delicate process softening and removing the poor little mite's coat of armour, and when accomplished, her emaciation and weakness were pitiful to behold, so that even then there seemed little hope for her life, unless placed directly under our eye in the cantonments, with a few trusty servants to carry out the doctor's orders.   The child herself begged to be allowed to go, and a bungalow was taken for her next our own, where she became an object of great curiosity and interest to the English children, as she took her daily morning and evening drives in a gorgeous chariot, shaped to represent a peacock, the outspread tail forming a sort of canopy, beneath which she sat, attended by her zenana guards. When, after some months, she recovered, her grateful parents actually presented this fairy coach to my children, who were greatly envied in its possession by all the other juveniles.

The Chota Begum came every day to me to learn to read and write English, and always afterwards addressed me as "Mother." For many years she kept up an affectionate intercourse with us, and Login was constantly teased by his friends about his "Indian daughter." There is a letter of hers sixteen years later, dated "Lucknow, February 25th, 1859," when she had been for some time the wife of a Nawab, and the Mutiny a twelvemonth over, and addressed to him at Church House, Kew, which commences, "Worthy Pappa," and winds up, "your most affectionate daughter, Wuzeeroolniza Begum."

Many of these native friends wrote to him throughout the Mutiny, when we were in England, thus keeping him informed of much unknown to most Europeans. The poor Wuzeer made the most extravagant presents to show his gratitude, and the King his master, to make things worse, used to *suggest* (otherwise command !) his unfortunate Minister to bestow on the Doctor Sahib this or that object dear to his heart.

Thus, when your father was absent once in the district (for he was Surveyor of Roads, Postmaster of Oude, and in charge of the *daks* or posting-houses), a *chobedar* in the royal livery requested an interview, and addressing me in grandiloquent language, pointed with his *chobe* (mace) to the portico, where stood a magnificent equipage, well known to me in all the royal processions of which it was a much-admired feature ! This, he said, had, by the King's special direction, been sent for my acceptance by the Wuzeer !

In consternation, I gazed at its glories—London-built, it was lined in satin and gold! the horses, enormous milk-white creatures with pink noses, had tails of brilliant scarlet, which literally swept the ground! their pace the native amble, great action, but little progress, pawing the air on their hind legs, in the attitude affected by the steeds on the old classic friezes! It needed an immense exercise of tact and politeness to convince the poor Wuzeer that we really could not deprive him of the object of his chief pride and delight.

Other presents sent in the same fashion, by different Nawabs, included a brace of baby elephants, gaily painted and adorned,with two negro boy-slaves, chastely attired in a necklace a-piece of bright beads, and a very inadequate loin-cloth! two huge Persian cats, more like leopards, chained to *charpoys* and accustomed to kill and eat their food! These were sent as playmates for the children! Indeed, so generous were our native friends that at one time I remember *fourteen pairs* of carriage horses, with their equipages, in our lines, not counting our own riding horses, and the elephants kept up for our private use by the King of Oude, and I found it quite an undertaking to make my daily round of the stables, with our old *derogah;* Ali Bux, in attendance, bearing a basket of sugar-cane.

Mahommed Ali was the King of Oude when I first went there. He was succeeded by his son, the notorious Wajid Ali, of Mutiny renown. The latter had been rather popular, as a young man, with the European community, as he was a sportsman, active and athletic. But no sooner did he come to the throne than he allowed himself to be hoisted about as if he had lost the use of his limbs. Only once did I see him, when paying his first visit of ceremony to the Resident, conscious of the ridiculous figure he cut—his attendants who tried to lift him bodily, chair and all, to the howdah of his elephant, having failed *twice* to do so—seize the ropes in his hands and run rapidly up the ladder, in his old "form."

Yet in no other way did he abate a jot of his correct ceremonial attitude. At the public tiffins which he occasionally gave to the European officials, his chair was surrounded, as had been his father's, with a crowd of attendants, each with their special office to the royal person, rigorously defined—the chowri-waver, the wielder of the regal fan of peacock-feathers ; the hookah-bearer ; the bearer of the golden ewer and basin (*chil-lumchi* and *lota*) ; the holder of the royal napkin, to wipe his mouth between each morsel ; the cup-bearer, and a seventh who stood in readiness with the royal pocket-handkerchief, and deftly—to quote an old doggerel—" blew his royal nose," as if his master were a babe-in-arms !

While his guests ate at other tables, special dishes were served to the King, who, as a mark of distinction—just as in Biblical times we read that Joseph as " lord of the land " showed favour to his brethren—sent helpings from it to specially honoured guests. I remember one occasion, when Wajid Ali had bestowed on my husband a *khillut*, or dress of honour, and a seal bearing his title of " Bahadur," that His Majesty took it into his head to take from the *plat* in front of him a handful of kabobs-and-rice, which was brought to me with great ceremony, with " The King's salaam to Mem Sahib Login," he, and all the assembly, watching with intentness, while I struggled to consume some morsels of the dainty thus honoured by the royal hand !

Colonel Low was Resident when my husband first

went to Lucknow; after him, Sir William Nott, Sir
George Pollock, heroes of the First Afghan War, Colonel
Davidson, and Colonel Richmond. Most of these had
been known to Login before in Afghanistan. He was
always hoping that his great friend, Sir Henry Lawrence,
was to receive the appointment, but that did not come
till after we had left ourselves.

Of my husband's friends of the First Afghan War
and the Mission to Heràt, I only knew these Residents,
the Lawrence brothers and their wives, Major D'Arcy
Todd and his wife, who were god-parents to one of our
children,* Sir Henry Rawlinson and Sir Frederick
Abbott. The travellers Mitford, General Ferrier, and
Professsor Vambéry, I was only to meet in later years.
But many of the men who made their names in the Punjab War were with us at Lucknow besides the Lawrences. There was especially Patrick Vans Agnew, one
of the Resident's Assistants, and a great friend of my
husband's, whose assassination at Mooltan was the
cause of the Second Sikh War. Later on, at Lahore, my
husband had charge of Moolraj, and the other chiefs
implicated in his murder. Vans Agnew was always most
grateful to Login for his good offices on his behalf with
Mr. Thomason, the Lieutenant-Governor of the North-
West Provinces, and Mr. Hamilton, his chief at Lahore.
He was a very warm-hearted fellow, devoted to his
people at home—his letters were full of them—and making
most particular inquiries after all his friends at Lucknow.
His description of Eldred Pottinger (whom your father
was associated with, and very fond of, both at Heràt
and in Kohistân) always amused us. He spoke of him
as the " little man with immense mustaches " whom he
never imagined could be " The Hero of Heràt ! " He was

---

* Louise Marion D'Arcy Login, died at Aylesford in 1909.

very reckless in his remarks about authorities, and once referred to Lord Ellenborough as " a great brute in his behaviour to Pottinger and Outram."

Some of the chaplains we had there were not shining lights, and their lack of the sense of humour provided merriment to the rest of the station. There is an institution common in India called a " mutton club." As a rule, mutton is not obtainable from the ordinary bazaar-butcher, who substituted for it generally the flesh of a venerable he-goat of age and authority. In most stations, therefore, the Europeans join together to purchase a few sheep of tenderer age than those usually obtainable, put a man in charge, and have them fed on " gram " till fit for table. Then the secretary of the club, an office frequently filled by the chaplain, as more stationary in the place than the other officials, sends round a notice that a fat beast is ready for the butcher, and members are requested to select the portion of the animal they would prefer for their own use, putting their names against the joint chosen. In the case I am thinking of, the chaplain was the secretary of the mutton club, and apparently was so bound to the usual formula he employed in addressing his congregation, that when desirous of altering one of the club rules, he sent round a paper asking each member, if they agreed to the new arrangement, to signify the same by an affirmative in their own hand, the document being headed : " My dear Flock." The paper came first to my husband. Anxious to respond as fully as possible to the pastoral suggestion conveyed, he promptly wrote " Ba-a (!) " in token of assent, and sent it on to the next man. Naturally on its return to the sender, from its peregrinations round the station, the rest of the " flock " had followed suit, and the document bore nothing but " baa-baa " all down the page, which brought the chaplain upon us in a towering rage, demanding apologies for the insult offered to his sacred calling !

One other rather unusual incident connected with a church service it occurs to me to relate here.

My eldest brother, afterwards General Charles Campbell (usually known as " the Bukshi " because in the Paymaster - General's Department), was married at Cawnpore to a Miss Wemyss. It was commonly reported that he showed but little eagerness as a suitor, and certainly as a bridegroom took a very languid interest in the ceremony, being very slack and hesitating in answering the first responses. The Eurasian clerk thereupon took upon him to prompt him in his part ; but when it came to the question—" Wilt thou take this woman to be thy wedded wife ? " and the zealous official replied for him in a loud nasal chant, " I-i weell," your uncle electrified the congregation by turning round in a towering passion, and shouting at him : " I'll be d——d if you do, sir ! "   Anyhow, it put more life into his participation in the rest of the service

CHAPTER IV

NATIVE SERVANTS AND CAMP LIFE

I SUPPOSE my husband had a special faculty for gaining the devoted attachment of those who served him, but anyhow, I hold in grateful and affectionate remembrance many of the servants we had in those days. How could one fail to do so in the case of old Ali Bux, the Kalipha, our major-domo, and afterwards Derogah of the King's Gharib-Khana (Hospital)? He had followed my husband to Afghanistan, and remained with him throughout the whole three years of the Political Mission at Heràt, refusing to return to India with the other Hindu servants. Although prepared, as he said, "to die in his master's service in those uncivilized regions," as it might be years before he ever rejoined the wife he had left in Lucknow, he announced his intention of solacing himself, under the circumstances, by taking to him as second wife a Heràti, whom he informed his master he was sure he would approve of, since she was "fair as a *Belati Bibi*" (European lady)! She proved as courageous as she was fair, and a first-rate rider, accompanying the party through all the dangers of the forced marches on their retreat, her child tied to her back in Turcoman fashion. When the camp was looted by marauders, she helped her husband to defend the most valuable of his master's papers and property, by assuring the wild tribesmen that they contained the *dawai* (magic) of the famed "Hakim of Heràt," Login having established a hos-

pital and dispensary there, producing the Wizard's staff
—Login's walking-stick, carved with a coiled snake and
the hieroglyphics of Major D'Arcy Todd's nickname,
"Bhuggut Ram," in Persian characters—as proof of
their assertion !

The Kalipha's real troubles began when he presented
the fair Fatimah to his first wife. The quarrels between
the two were incessant and vociferous, and Ali Bux
often compared himself to Jacob, betwixt Leah and
Rachel, for Fatimah was the apple of his eye ! His only
method of quieting them was to threaten them with the
wrath of the Doctor Sahib.

At once, when we married, I found myself the special
charge of Ali Bux, who considered himself responsible
for my well-being whenever my husband was absent,
and wrote him daily reports. Often was I thus sent
alone in his care to the hills, for change, whenever
Login was kept in the city. He it was who chased and
re-captured my recreant palki-bearers, a big stick in
one hand, and a formidable knife in the other, because
they had dropped, and abandoned, their burden incontinently in a jungle-path at a sudden alarm of a man-
eating tiger ! And when the melting of the snows in
the mountains turned a brook in our road into a wide,
swift-flowing river, and my palki was floated over, tied
to *mussucks* (inflated skins) in a pitch-black night, the
water washing over the floor, so that the ayah had to
put the baby on the shelf amongst the eatables, for
safety, it was Ali Bux himself who swam alongside,
turbanless and stripped to his waist-cloth, to assure
me all was safe !

His zeal occasionally led him into odd expedients,
and he was much mortified to find that I did not
invariably appreciate his methods.

I was under his care in a lonely bungalow in the hills when the baby's ayah fell sick, the child itself being ailing. In the middle of the night I also was taken very ill, and there was no woman to attend to the baby! Moreover, the supply of milk ran out.

Ali Bux was in despair! He could never face his master if aught happened to me or the child! Assuring me he would return with a nurse, he vanished down the *khudd* with half a dozen servants, and returned in triumph two hours later, dragging an unfortunate young woman with a baby-in-arms, who seemed in mortal terror, and spoke no known language! She was fair and blue-eyed, and it turned out, had been absolutely *kidnapped* by him out of a camp of Cabuli traders, whose fires he had marked in the valley below! Her complexion and colouring convinced him that here was the very thing to please his Mem-Sahib, and he bitterly upbraided the poor creature for her ingratitude when, at the first chance, she fled with her baby, and it all came out! She was discovered at daybreak on a circular drive running round the top of the hill, made for me to take the air and enjoy the views, having spent the whole night seeking in vain for a path leading downwards! Ali Bux never could understand my sympathy for the poor thing, and my horror at his cruel conduct.

And then there was Hinghan Khan, the orphan boy of good family, who had followed my husband from Heràt. His parents had been carried off in a Turcoman raid; but he himself was rescued by Eldred Pottinger, and attached himself to Login on his arrival, following him about like his shadow, and sleeping at his door at night until, won by his silent adoration, the Doctor Sahib took him into his service.

And well did Hinghan repay this act on his part!
He proved invaluable, adapting himself to all circumstances and places. Like all his countrymen, a splendid
rider, he was of great service on the march whenever
there were difficulties with the tribesmen. He accompanied his master to Candahar and Cabul, went with
him to Charikar, in Kohistan, when he joined Eldred
Pottinger there, and returned with him to India when
he resumed his work at Lucknow. He was a light
weight, and used to exercise my Arabs for me, accompany me on my rides, and ride postillion in a very
pretty phaeton, drawn by a pair of Cabuli ponies, or
rather Heràtis, for they had been brought by Login
from that place.

They were brothers, and as long as they had been
in Afghanistan had been most affectionate together,
always occupying the same stall. But the strange thing
was that after they reached India they developed the
most extraordinarily quarrelsome disposition, and had
regular stand-up fights, even when in double harness!
To cure them of this habit, we had them harnessed with
an extra rein to the " off " pony, to keep his head away
from his fellow. But this did not prevent the " near "
one, if his rider was off his guard, from making a snatch at
his companion across the pole ; and then they both went
at it "tooth and hoof" to the terror of the bystanders,
whether at the bandstand of an evening, or on the road!

I got so used to it, that I thought nothing of sitting
for twenty minutes or so till the combatants were
separated or tired out. All I could do to help
Hinghan was to hang on to the rein, to keep the " off "
pony from crushing his leg against the pole. But when
driving them myself, I had to have two reins fastened
either side to the bar, to keep their heads apart.

Poor Hinghan was devotedly attached to his master's children, and his gallantry and presence of mind helped on one occasion to save them from an awful peril.

The kings of Oude used to delight in elephant fights at their entertainments, and for this purpose a certain number of male elephants were kept in a place apart from others, where they were trained and made *must* (mad, or ferocious), to prepare them for these fights.

One morning, very early, the boy Hinghan Khan was out exercising his master's horse, Kamran.* On passing this place he found a terrific battle going on between the *mahout* and a large elephant which was to fight next day at the Palace entertainment.

Hinghan only remained long enough to see the unfortunate *mahout* thrown down and trampled to death, while the elephant rushed out quite mad, straight through the city. Suddenly it flashed on him, that the two babies of the Doctor Sahib had started for their early morning airing with the *ayah* on their elephant, and would be now on their way home, right in the track of this infuriated beast, whose trumpeting was rousing the whole city ! Instead of turning home, therefore, the boy gave rein to the Turcoman he was riding, and flew like the wind to give the alarm to the children's attendants. He met them returning about a mile and a half away, their elephant already excited by the distant roaring of the mad one, and refusing to proceed. Instead of obeying the *mahout's* goad, it stood still, quivering with rage, and trumpeting loudly, eager for the fray, for it was a large and powerful animal, noted in the *shikar* after tigers for its courage and speed,† and could

* So named because presented to him by Shah Kamran, at Heràt.
† It was afterwards nearly blinded by a tiger in the Terai, when out on *shikar*.

hardly be induced to turn its back on the prospect of
a fight. When, therefore, Hinghan appeared shouting :
" *Hathee! hathee! must! must!* " (Elephant ! mad
elephant !), and waved to the *mahout* to leave the road
and strike into a byway, it was with the greatest difficulty that the man endeavoured to follow his directions.
When at length he succeeded, the *must* elephant was
almost upon them, and then ensued a terrible race for
life !

It requires practice to accommodate oneself to the
pace of an elephant, even when the animal is only walking, and what the motion is like when at a gallop or in a
race, is past description ! Suffice it to say, that the
mahout managed to outstrip the mad brute, whose
terrific roaring seemed to strike terror into all other
animals. Hinghan Khan created a diversion in every
way he could, to distract the *must* elephant's attention,
and would have succeeded better had not his poor
Turcoman been wild with terror and unmanageable.

Handsome Hinghan Khan, always spick and span,
and dressed to perfection in the blue and silver livery
he was so proud of, was an object of admiration to the
Europeans of the station, and quite a distinctive
feature of our establishment. He accompanied us on
most occasions when riding or driving, for even when
not doing postillion he acted as outrider, and to his
great delight his master had him fitted out with English
top-boots, which rendered him the envy of all native
beholders !

From time to time, poor Hinghan had periods of
depression, when he seemed as if he could not exist for
a moment out of the sight of the Sahib, the Mem-
Sahib, or the " Baba-log," and these coincided generally with the season of the great fairs, when many

Afghan horse-dealers were about. My husband always suspected that communications were made from Hinghan's cousins and other relatives, who were a haughty race, and probably felt it derogatory that one of their lineage should serve in any capacity, however confidential, in the household of a " feringhi."

But these interludes passed, and Hinghan always became his bright self again. Then it.came about that I was ordered to, Europe for my health, and the children went with me, and your father was away in the Punjab. The household was left in charge of Bhugwan Doss, then our major-domo, who wrote in great distress to tell his master that Hinghan Khan had suddenly and totally disappeared, and, in spite of search and inquiries in all directions, not a trace could be found of him ! It was said that previously some Afghans had been seen hovering about the place, and fellow-servants told that Hinghan had been noticed for some days in floods of tears, brushing and folding his livery, and *fondling* his boots, which were found, after he left, carefully put away, and not a *pice*-worth (coin less than a farthing) of his master's property had he taken with him ! Hinghan's disappearance remains to this day a mystery, but I don't think we ever ceased to miss him, nor do I believe it would have ever taken place had either of us or the children been near him at the time.

The number of followers with even a small camp is astonishing, as each hanger-on is accompanied by his whole family. But as ours consisted of over two hundred servants, without counting the escort, the encampment presented a lively, bustling aspect in the evenings, when all were assembled round the various camp-fires, chattering and cooking the last meal, before rolling themselves up for the night.

One evening, after dark, a tremendous uproar was heard in camp, and every one rushed out to see what was the matter. The word was passed from mouth to mouth that a grass-cutter's child had just been carried off by a wolf out of its mother's arms! Parties were sent in all directions, and a strict search made all night, with no result ; but at day-dawn, in a neighbour-ing gully, the skull of the child was found—picked clean! The mother had been sitting at the fire, baking *chupatties*, with her infant in her lap, when the wolf, taking advantage of the darkness, came up behind her, put his head over her shoulder and seized the infant. It was only the shriek of her opposite neighbour, who caught the gleam of the beast's eye in the firelight, that told her what had happened!

Next day it was pitiful to see the poor mother trudg-ing along, as before, among her companions, with all her household goods on her head, but *without* the child, whom she had been wont to carry also, seated astride on her hip!

For some time after this incident there were perpetual wolf scares in the encampment, and my English nurse, Herdman, who was quite new to the country, was the cause of a terrific panic one clear, starlight night. The whole camp was roused by an outburst of shrieks, and from all directions men came running, the sentries firing wildly, under the impression that there must be a general attack by dacoits. The uproar came from the direction of the nursery tent, and those who hurried to the spot discovered Herdman in her sleeping attire, throttling an enormous hound tethered to a post of the *semiana*, which she firmly believed was a wolf come after her babies! It was with difficulty that she was persuaded to loose the unfortunate animal (which luckily had been so surprised by her sudden onset from behind, that he had been unable to bite her), for she swore positively that she *knew* for a fact, that the two Indian princes, then in my husband's charge, were already devoured, as she had seen a *whole pack* of the same animals looking out of their tent-door (which was next to hers), licking their lips ! and who could doubt that the children would be their next victims !

It was some little time before the wolves in question were identified as a pack of greyhounds belonging to the Maharajah Duleep Singh, which he, in his eagerness to go out coursing early the next morning, had privately ordered to be brought, before dawn, into the outer division of his tent. Seen in the faint light, the woman's mistake might be excused ! Anyhow, one could not but admire her reckless courage, in defence, as she thought, of her charges.

Wolves, you see, were prevalent, and much dreaded in the jungles over large districts of Oude, and there have been several authenticated cases of children carried off by these treacherous beasts, yet spared and suckled by them with their own cubs. The story of Romulus and Remus therefore has its foundation in fact. I myself only saw one of these " wolf-children," as they were called, during my husband's time as Superintendent of the Gharib-Khana.

It had been found in or near the Terai, a district of jungle and swamp on the confines of Oude and Nepal, appeared about four or five years old, and had fine, soft, downy hair covering the whole body. Though undoubtedly human, it was very animal in its instincts and ways. It walked and ran on all-fours, and could utter only a weird cry, like the yelping of a hound. Though guarded most carefully, it several times escaped into the woods,

In spite of all efforts to coax it, it refused food, and gradually pined away and died, for they are always very difficult to rear after being taken from their foster-mothers.

We were always careful when travelling through the robber-districts to have special guards supplied by the headmen of the villages, and the dacoity-chiefs, to whom we paid a sort of black-mail not to let other people rob us ! For of course you know thieves and robbers in India are a special profession, caste, or clan, by themselves. They are marvellously expert, and often have I been entertained by the stories told me by prisoners in the gaols, of how, sometimes for a wager, they would steal clothes (and even the sheets they were lying on) from sleeping travellers, by tickling them to make them turn over, while these light-fingered gentry pulled away the desired garment !

On one occasion the Maharajah Duleep Singh, having made large purchases from the jewellers at Delhi, and not caring to part with his treasures to the Toshkhana (treasury chest under guard) that evening, asked me to keep them for him till the morning. Very unwillingly I consented, as I dreaded the responsibility, and placed the articles in my dressing-case, which always remained in camp under my *charpoy* (bed), where also slept my small black-and-tan terrier. Just before I lay down, I hardly know with what intention, I unfastened the dog's chain from the leg of the bed where it was usually attached, and passed it through the handle of the tin case. Being somewhat nervous, I lay awake tossing and listening to every sound, and dropped only into fitful dozes. All of a sudden I was startled awake by a most awful commotion in the tent—barks, shouts, a musket shot, and yells—and was just in time to catch a fleeting glimpse of a slight, dark form, stark naked, disappearing through a slit in the tent wall, while my poor little " Fan " lay choking, snarling, and howling, all at once, full length on her back ! My first thought was for the dressing-case—it was gone ! but there stood the dog, frantic with rage, tugging furiously at one end of her chain, the other being in some mysterious manner passed out under the tent, outside which the box lay safe on the ground ! The thief had been foiled, and had made his escape, after dropping his prize, on discovering its unexpected pendant ! He had effected his noiseless entrance by crawling under the tightly-pegged tent ; the faint light burning showed him the dressing-case, but *not* the small dog coiled at a distance from it. He had a very narrow escape, for on rising to his feet he fell over a servant sleeping there, who made a grab at him, but the miscreant had so plentifully anointed his naked body with oil, that he slipped through the hands of the other like a fish. He did not, however, escape un-scathed, for drops of blood for some distance on the ground showed that the sentry's shot had told !

The favourite occupation in the afternoon in camp was to inspect the horses, and see them groomed and fed, to walk down the lines where they all stood in per-fect order, picketed with head-and-heel ropes, and to feed them with pieces of sugar-cane provided for the purpose, which they looked for with the greatest eagerness.

The elephants, too, had to receive a visit, and be offered biscuits and lumps of sugar. One of these animals was particularly docile, and constantly to be found acting nurse to its *mahout's* baby, which lay asleep between its huge fore-feet. It was curious to watch the great beast gently fanning the child and brushing away the flies from its face with a branch off the nearest tree, held in its trunk; while, with its funny little eyes, it meantime kept a sharp look-out on the fast accumulating pile of enormous *chupatties* which the child's parents were engaged in making, and which, it knew well, were destined for its own supper. Sometimes, if wakeful and lively, the baby would crawl away a little distance from its guardian, but the latter—aware that its allowance of *chupatties* depended on its attention to its duties as nursery-maid—would never allow the little one to get beyond reach, but lifted it back to its former position with its trunk, in the gentlest manner possible.

My Arabs got so accustomed to following me about all over the place, that when we were once more settled in our bungalow, one of them—" Black Satin " by name, usually mis-called " Black Satan ! "—when I was not looking, followed me up the steps, across the verandah, and into the drawing-room, in search of more sugar ! I, all unconscious of my visitor, only became aware of his presence when he stretched his neck over my shoulder, seized an antimacassar off the sofa, and swallowed it whole before my eyes !

My husband had one nasty adventure with a riding horse of his, whom we were feeding with sugar in his loose-box. Suddenly the brute, a rather vicious country-bred, seized his master's thumb in his teeth, regularly crunching the bone. Nothing would make him let go, and he kept throwing up his head out of reach, so that his victim could not free himself, and the syce was not at hand at the moment. I only was with your father, and in desperation, rather to his terror, managed to pass my hand into the horse's mouth, behind his teeth, seize his tongue and twist it, at the same time startling the beast with a blow on the nose. It was, of course, a risky manœuvre, but successful. The injury was already severe and *tetanus* dreaded, the wound being in such a dangerous position.

In view of this possibility, Login himself made all the preparations for amputation of the thumb, and, as it was that on his right hand, and he therefore could not himself perform the operation, he sent for his apothecary, and gave him most minute instructions how to proceed, undertaking to do all that he could personally, short of using the actual knife !

On the other hand, my Arab " Sultan," I verily believe, saved my life on one occasion when I was riding alone at Mussoorie, accompanied only by my syce. I happened to be away from my husband in the Hills. He had bought a small property at Mussoorie, on which were two or three bungalows, so I was often sent up there with the children in the hot weather.

I had been out for my early morning ride, and was coming homewards, following a track on which there was room for only one quadruped, the cliff overhanging the pathway on the one hand, while the other fell sheer away in precipices of many hundreds of feet. Turning the corner of a projecting rock, I saw a horseman advancing towards me on the same path, and to my horror and that of my syce, recognised him as an officer I knew, mounted on a notoriously vicious, country-bred animal, the aversion and absolute terror of the other riders in the station !

As he came nearer, I perceived that he was pale with terror, and quite incapable of exerting any control over his beast, which, the instant it caught sight of us, came tearing on in a mad fury, seized my horse's neck with his teeth, absolutely trying to shake him as a terrier does a rat! In the moment that the two horses closed, the Englishman—I regret to have to say it!—slid off over his horse's cruppers, leaving me to my fate! I could not, if I would, have followed his example, for my feet in the side-saddle were already overhanging the precipice, and it was all I could do to keep my seat, as the horses went at it " tooth and hoof "! They fought, standing erect on their hind feet, biting and striking each other with their fore-feet. The syce behind me was powerless to do anything. I helped " Sultan," who fought really in my defence, all I could, by hitting the other horse vigorously with the butt-end of my whip, but with very little effect.

Mercifully, in the end, " Sultan," with an heroic effort, threw his opponent over the *khudd* (precipice), while retaining his own balance, and I was spared to return to my children in safety!

I had to leave " Sultan " behind in India when I went home with the children. My husband took him through the Sikh War, and had him in Lahore for some time, but finding him too light for his weight, had to sell him. John Lawrence, who kindly managed the sale of his stud for him, sold him to Brigadier Wheeler for his daughter's use, and it may be that he perished with his mistress in the awful tragedy at Cawnpore.

CHAPTER V

THE LAWRENCES

DURING our time at Lucknow it was that we made the acquaintance of the Henry Lawrences, and, as you know, they were from that time forward till their deaths our very dear and intimate friends. He and your father were inseparables, when they could be together, and—what is more uncommon—I think that I and Honoria Lawrence were quite as devoted to one another, and perhaps even better correspondents ! I have never met a woman quite like Honoria, never a wife who more entirely shared in, and helped, her husband in his work, yet without in any way bringing that fact to the knowledge of the world at large.

Both of them were god-parents to our children ; and I have Henry Lawrence's letter from Nepal, dated February 11th, 1845, in which he mentions that fact. This is what he writes :

" MY DEAR LOGIN,
    " My wife has been very ill, so ill that for a week I feared for her life. . . . I am sorry to hear that your dear wife has been so ill too. I regret much that you did not make up your minds earlier to spend the hot season with us here. . . . Let your brother Tom come to us . . . . my invitation is for the whole year for certain. After that I will launch him, and if he is *your* brother he'll find his own legs ! . . . My dear wife will gladly undertake the office of god-mother to the

last arrival * (remember our compact, that the next boy is to be *my* godson†).

· " Yours,
"H. M. L."

Lawrence and his wife stayed with us at Lucknow on his way to Khatmandoo. He was then writing articles for the *Calcutta Review*, of which Sir John Kaye was the editor, and urged Login to do the same. We were living in the very house in the Residency into which Lawrence was carried wounded to die ; and in that same verandah where the two friends sat over their *chota hazri*, in the delicious cold weather mornings, after their early ride, discussing all things in heaven and earth, and especially in India, Henry Lawrence was to breathe out his last sigh, and compose that pathetic epitaph graven on his tomb : " Here lies Henry Lawrence, who tried to do his duty ! "

His letters from Khatmandoo were full of humorous and quaint remarks. "Our Prince here has put down his papa," he wrote on one occasion, " and is giving me a lot of trouble. Last week they murdered (' killed ' *they* call it !) sixteen of the opposition party, so now all hands can call the boy to the throne ! " " I have no wish to get Lucknow unless I am allowed full swing to carry out my schemes for the amelioration of the people," he says in another letter, " . . . but if I were employed in Oude I should certainly stipulate to have the benefit of your services. Don't you think we could make something of that fine country between us ? . . . I wish I had your brother James here for companionship, for my rides are very lonely. F—— and his wife are

---

* Lena Margaret Campbell Login, died at Pau, February 20th, 1866, aged 21 years.

† Rear-Admiral Spencer Henry Metcalfe Login, C.V.O., died January 22nd, 1909.

SIR HENRY MONTGOMERY LAWRENCE, K.C.B.

respectable people according to the fashion of the world's
respectability, but their hearts are *gizzards!* He has
only three ideas in his head : (*a*) There is no such thing
as poverty in England. (*b*) The English Church is purity
and propriety personified. (*c*) Antigua. We have never
any disagreement ; simply we don't *milao* (assimilate)."
His letter acknowledging ours on his wife's death is
very touching in its simple reference : "My trial is a
sore one, and hard to bear—God's will be done ! Yes,
I will try to go to Roorkee. Napier will probably be
there, and I wish to meet him, also to see Cautley, and
Mr. Colvin, and your party." In one from Mount
Aboo, dated June 18th, when we were already back in
England, he thanked Login for helping his son Alec,
and asked him to spur the boy on to use his powers, "as
he is amiable but unenergetic, I fear. You have been
accustomed to youths, and might influence him much.
. . . I will be obliged by any help you can give."

Honoria Lawrence's letters stretch over a period of
nine years ; some are from Nepal, and one, a farewell
one, from Serampore, on her way home, 21st February,
1846, speaks of her "little Prince Waldemar" (he was
godchild of Prince Waldemar of Prussia, then travelling
in the Himalayas, who also stayed with us at Futtehghur,
accompanied by M. de Tocqueville, the French explorer)
as "the Prince of babies, such a little bundle of fun and
sweetness ! Kiss both of your babies for me, and a
double share for my god-child. Love to Dr. Login,"
she concludes, "from your very affectionate, H. LAW-
RENCE." In the last one written from Lahore, December
20th, 1852, she again inquires after my eldest boy, and
her little god-daughter, and says : "Just nine years
ago I was receiving your kindness at Lucknow, and
enjoying my visit very much. Since then I am become

a very old woman, feeble and tottering, but with great happiness in my lot. . . . In spite of all appearances to the contrary " (she was a most irregular correspondent), " affectionately yours, HONORIA LAWRENCE."

My husband, of course, knew George Lawrence and his wife at Cabul, and it was during his Afghanistan service he first met Troup and Colin Mackenzie, Henry Havelock, Outram, Sir George Pollock, Pottinger, D'Arcy Todd and many others. He acted at Cabul as Private Secretary to Sir William Macnaghton, the murdered envoy, while Lieutenant Conolly was away on a mission to Kandahar. Indeed, he only came down the Cabul River, by raft, from Jellalabad to Attock, in August, 1841, two months before the insurrection broke out at Cabul. He had been attached to the political mission at Heràt since 1838, taking over from Eldred Pottinger the charitable works he had started there, and adding to them, amongst other things, the revival of the carpet-weaving, for which Heràt in earlier times had been famous.

Afterwards he became closely associated in his work with both Henry and John Lawrence, when he served under them in the Punjab Government, and it was with breathless interest and heart-sick anxiety he followed every detail of the glorious tragedy of Lucknow, and from his situation at home, was able very materially to assist in obtaining for the Lawrence brothers and their children public recognition of their services to their country.

Although the question of a baronetcy for Henry Lawrence's son, and a peerage for John Lawrence, was mooted 'and discussed, and openly debated, so that friends wrote to congratulate the latter on the honour awarded him, the Government procrastinated and haggled, in the most galling manner, and up to April or May, 1858, John Lawrence had not a line from anyone in authority regarding a peerage, or indeed of any intention of doing anything for him ! And Alec Lawrence, Henry's son, though the fact that he was to have a pension was mentioned in the newspapers, had received no account of it. Sir John Lawrence, of course, would not move in the matter, and, as he said himself, though he should like to have a peerage if it were given freely and gracefully, with a pension for two generations, " on the other hand I shall not be unhappy if I get nothing. It is highly satisfactory to me to feel that I have to any extent done my duty ; that I have not lived in vain ; that I have been useful in my generation ; and that my services have been acknowledged by my country. I was very much pleased at receiving the thanks of Parliament." In this same letter, written to his brother-in-law, he adds : " Thank Sir John Login for so kindly thinking of my interests."

In another letter written about the same date from Rawul Pindi, he speaks thus of the position of affairs in India :

" Affairs out here are slowly coming round. The great masses of the Mutineers and Insurgents have broken up. We hold Lucknow now in strength, and have reconquered Rohilkund. But we have little footing in Oude beyond the range of our guns. It will take another cold weather, at least, before we can put down all opposition. The guerillas are now trying their hands at guerilla tactics, and if they only persevere, must do us infinite damage. In the best seasons they can walk round our troops, encumbered as they are with baggage and other impedimenta. But in this weather, exposure is certain death to many of our men, sunstroke, apoplexy, fever, and dysentery, will terribly thin our ranks before

next October. I myself am a strong advocate for some
kind of amnesty. But few are of my way of thinking.
The general cry is for a war of extermination ! No one
seems to count the cost. Had we done this, when we
last advanced on Lucknow, affairs would have been in
a better state than they are now. We should then have
only had the desperadoes to deal with. Now we have
all united in one common bond against us. We cannot
run down and kill 40,000 or 50,000 of such fellows
without suffering ourselves.

"Policy, therefore, to say nothing of humanity,
dictates a compromise. People in England seem to
think that we can hold India without a Native Army !
However essential Europeans are to us, Native Troops
are still perhaps more so. We can do nothing without
the latter. Much misfortune here has doubtless arisen
from keeping up too small a body of European troops,
but we must take care not to fall into the opposite
error.

". . . The danger now is, that a feeling of hatred
will continue between the two races, which must
assuredly sooner or later bear bitter fruit. The Punjab
continues peaceful and prosperous. Under God's
mercy, the secret of administrative arrangements is to
care for small things—to prevent mischief recurring.
Matters have come to that pass down below, that years
will probably elapse before order and security are
restored. . . . At the present mode of going on, we
shall require a steady influx of European Troops, to
the extent, probably, of 20,000 per annum, to enable us
to overcome all opposition."

I give these quotations, only because it is always of
interest to know the opinion of the great men of the
moment on the course advisable in stupendous crises
of our history ; also one likes one's children to know how
closely associated was their father with the central
facts of Indian statesmanship. Sir Charles Trevelyan,

LORD LAWRENCE.

then at the Treasury, wrote that John Lawrence had appealed to him to see that the Lawrence Asylum Fund got proper endowment, and begged Login to help him with his counsel, but not to show John Lawrence's letters, or take any steps, till they could confer together on the subject. He asks him at the same time to introduce him to Lady Lawrence, who was then in England.

Mrs. Bernard, sister of the Lawrences, interested my husband to get a cadetship for the son of her brother Richard, which he was very pleased to do, and she also suggested that the same distinctions and help conferred on Sir Henry Havelock's family might very properly be given to the three orphans of the defender of Lucknow. " Could you, dear Sir John, without pain to yourself," she remarks, " bring this subject before any of the high personages in the realm ? . . . You will excuse my writing to you, as I do not know Lord Stanley personally, or anybody who has so much communication with the Court as yourself. . . . But I would much rather leave it in your hands, knowing well how his memory is revered by you, and how much he thought of you when he was alive." Three days later, she writes to express " the gratitude that we all feel to you for your most kind and successful exertions. The recognition of our dear Henry's merits will be most grateful to his family. . . . Richard has five sons, and in regimental rank is only a captain, so you can easily imagine the service you have done him ! "

Sir John W. Kaye wrote some months later :

" MY DEAR LOGIN,

" A move is to be made in the Court of Proprietors against the grant to Sir John Lawrence, partly on religious, or rather anti-religious, grounds ; his offence

being that he made a public manifestation of his respect
for Christianity, and his desire to do justice to native
Christians. I am not sure that the *party* is strong enough
to make much fight, but we ought to muster, not only
the friends of the Lawrences, but the friends of Christianity. . . . Let me hear from, or see, you, as soon as
possible. . . ." *

Dr. Bernard, guardian of John's children, also
thanked him for expediting Alec's baronetcy, saying it
would be " an additional pleasure to dear Alec to hear
how, at the last, as at the first, you have been concerned
in this matter. . . . I am thinking of writing myself
to Lord Derby, and enclose draft, as I should not dream
of using the arguments I do without your sanction.
Except to John himself, and to Harriet (Lady Lawrence),
what transpired as to the peerage went not beyond
our own house, which included Mrs. Hayes. . . . What
he has himself said about it is very little. I believe,
in fact, that you have seen it all. . . . I cannot but
feel disappointed at the shabby way in which the present
Government are dealing with him in the matter of the
peerage " (after the offer of one had actually been transmitted to him unofficially but with the highest authority,
many months before !). This was the way in which the
Cabinet at home translated the wishes of the nation who
hailed him as the " saviour of India," merely because,
having spent his life in the service of the Empire beyond
the seas, he was unknown personally to Government
officials, or to political parties at Westminster ! Dr.
Bernard adds :

" *Quem Deus vult perdere dementat prius.* . . . These
sad Indian experiences seem likely to be thrown away.
How much of increase, or return, of European influence,

* See " India under Victoria," Captain Trotter, Vol. II., p. 105.

would accrue to our country from having India put into vigorous and able hands ! I fear that most things there are drifting back into the old channels, except the native mind, which will *never* fall into the old channel ! *That* will have gained power by the experience of the last year, at any rate. Under the mask of these despicable routinisms, one cannot but see a want of manly courage in our home administration, quite as much as in that of India. John would be an unpopular G.G., for under him men would have to do their work honestly or vacate their offices ! . . . Our lads * give an amusing account of how he stopped three days at Rawul Pindee, where Herbert Edwardes and Becher came to him by appointment, and the three talked over public affairs from 10 a.m. to 6 p.m. each day, sometimes one, and sometimes another, taking a short nap and waking up to join in the conversation. The third evening the two departed and John went on. They don't work like this at home ?

" Yours very sincerely,
" JAMES F. BERNARD."

* Alec Lawrence, Sir Henry's son, and Charles Bernard (afterwards Sir Charles Bernard, K.C.S.I.), son of the writer.

CHAPTER VI

My husband left Lucknow in October, 1848, at the breaking out of the Second Sikh War, in order to resume field service, and was present at several of the principal engagements. It was a current joke against him often during the early part of his career, amongst his brother-officers, that he was as keen to distinguish himself in *laying the guns* at the beginning, as he was in carrying off the wounded under fire afterwards!

It was at Gujerat, I believe, that a bullet was discovered to have passed through the chair he was seated on, while amputating a man's arm. All standing round rushed from the spot, but Login never even looked up until the operation was safely finished.

Meanwhile, I, in November, started for England with my three eldest children, and after spending some time in London and Edinburgh, and paying a flying visit to Kinloch, settled first at St. Roque and then at Clifton, and leaving my children in charge of a lady living in Edinburgh, rejoined my husband at Futtehghur.

My husband's letters from Lahore, where he was hard at work under Henry Lawrence, kept me informed of all the wonderful events of that time. At first he was unofficially employed making an estimate of military expenditure and the cost of raising several Irregular Cavalry Corps. He was also sent out into the district to receive the submission of the Khâlsa regiments—one European with a small native escort, by moral influence, inducing hundreds to lay down their arms! He was recommended to Lord Dalhousie for the appointment of Guardian of the young Maharajah Duleep Singh by Henry Lawrence, Head of the Punjab Commission, and John and George Lawrence. He consulted John Lawrence first, he told me, as to whether he would be wise to continue in the political department, rather than return to professional work, as his prospects were so high in the surgical line, because he thought his opinion would be less biassed than Henry's, less influenced by personal friendship and intimacy, since he had known Henry for so long.

On the 6th April he was installed by Henry Lawrence, with the Governor-General's sanction, as Governor of the Citadel and its contents, including all the political prisoners and harems of the late Maharajahs, the Toshkhana, or Treasury, with its jewels and valuables, amongst which was the Koh-i-noor, kept always under a special guard, and also as Governor to the young dethroned king, Duleep Singh, a very lovable, intelligent and handsome boy, of twelve years of age, who very speedily developed a great affection for his guardian, and came to Login four days later with a portrait of himself to be despatched to me with his salaam! He begged me to be informed that he had written his name below that I might be sure it was genuine, and was very proud of being able to do so himself in Persian and in English! This was only a first sample of the genuine simplicity and cordiality of his relations with us, all throughout our intercourse, and the very real interest and sympathy he showed to us and our children. By his directions, a sketch of the Palace and its surroundings was made for me at the same time. His great amusement then (as it was later on) was hawking or falconry,

of which he was passionately fond, and he was busy
getting up a book on the subject in Persian, with drawings and paintings of all the various species of hawks,
which took up his whole time and attention.   He employed several native artists at this work, and tried his
hand occasionally at drawing and painting himself.
He was unusually well educated for an Indian prince
of those days, reading and writing Persian very well,
and having already made some progress in English.

My husband at first lived in the Residency at Lahore,
with Lawrence, where George Lawrence and his wife
after their release from captivity joined the party,
and Herbert Edwardes was also there for a time, on
leave from Mooltan.   But after he was made Governor
of the Maharajah, he was apportioned a part of the
Palace, enclosed in a very beautiful garden, with five
marble *baradurries* (hall, reception-room), fountains,
etc., somewhat in the style of the Shah Munzil at
Lucknow, only more magnificent, being in marble.
He soon had a door of communication opened between
his rooms and the Maharajah's apartments, as he found
his charge was happier when he knew he had him always
within call.   He gravely informed his new Governor
that he would not trust himself again amongst the
Sikhs, and declined to go out for a ride or drive unless
he was with him.   As soon as the Maharajah heard that
the opening had been cut, he wanted to go with him to
see it !   There was a small hole, only just large enough
to pass through in a crouching position, and a drop of
several feet into the doctor's room.   Login having leapt
down, the Maharajah called to him to catch him, and
sprang into his arms ! and his whole retinue, some of
them stout, elderly courtiers, punctiliously followed
suit, as in duty bound, looking as solemn as if assisting

at a Court ceremonial! Guardian and ward appreciated the humour of the scene, and mutually recognising the efforts it cost to preserve a semblance of gravity, cemented on the spot a lasting friendship.

As "Killah-ki-Malik" (*i.e.*, Lord, or Master) of Lahore Citadel, Login had complete authority there, had charge of all guards, stores, magazines and treasures, as well as the State prisoners. He had some European assistants, and some sergeants of Horse Artillery, four European writers, and several *moonshees* and *mutsuddies*, to assist him in making out lists of the arms of all kinds, and of the vast camp-equipage of all the late rulers of the Punjab. Such a collection it was of splendid Cashmere tents, carpets and purdahs, with horse and elephant trappings! My husband himself took the listing of the jewel department, with Misr Makraj (the late Maharajah's Treasurer, whose family had been custodians of the Koh-i-noor for two or three generations) as Assistant-Keeper of the Toshkhana. The way in which jewels of the highest value were stowed away was extraordinary. On one occasion Login found some valuable rings, including one with a beautiful portrait of Queen Victoria, huddled together in a bag, and suggested that it would be well to tie a label to each with an account of their history and value, attaching it by a string, until the velvet rolls that he had ordered for them were ready. The next time he saw them they had all been strung on strings, dozen by dozen, like so · many buttons! His first rough estimate of the jewels in the Toshkhana, *exclusive* of the Koh-i-noor, was little short of a million pounds.

The Koh-i-noor was always kept under a strong guard and in a safe in the Toshkhana. Lord Dalhousie, in his

letters, relates * how Login used to show it, on a table
covered with black velvet, the diamond alone appearing through a hole cut in the cloth, thrown up by
the blackness around it. Before this arrangement was
made, your father always followed the advice of the old
native Treasurer when showing it to visitors, and continued the practice observed by Runjeet's Toshkhana
officials, viz., never to let it out of his own hands, but
twist the strings securing it as an armlet firmly around
his own fingers.

The original stone, as most people know, was found
in the mines of Golconda, and remained for generations
in the possession of the Rajahs of Malwa, from whom
the Emperor Alad-ed-deen obtained it by conquest.
In 1526 it came into the hands of the Moguls, till Nadir
Shah, the Persian, who conquered Mohammed Shah in
1739, got it from his vanquished foe, by the clever
ruse of exchanging turbans in sign of friendship! But
Nadir's son, Shah Rokh, lost it to the Durani Ahmed
Shah, and so it remained with the Afghan Dynasty,
till Shah Soojah, when driven from Cabul by Dost
Mahommed, brought it, in his flight, to the dominions
of Runjeet Singh, who stipulated that the famous jewel
should be the price of his hospitality and support to the
fugitive. Shah Soojah exhausted every expedient to
avoid giving it up; and as everything connected with the
history of the jewel interests most people, you may like
to hear the account which your father got from Misr
Makraj, who remained on as his assistant in charge at
the Toshkhana, eloquent in his expressions of relief at
being set free from the sole responsibility; for, as he
said, " the Koh-i-noor had been fatal to so many of his

* " Private Letters of the Marquess of Dalhousie," by J. G. A. Baird, pp. 124,
172.

family that he had hardly hoped ever to survive the charge of it !"

According to Misr Makraj, Shah Soojah-Ool-Moolk, at the time the Koh-i-noor was taken from him by Runjeet Singh, was in confinement, with his family, in the house of the Dewan Lukput Rai.

When the Maharajah's officers, amongst whom was Fakeer Azizoodeen, came to him to demand the jewel, " he sent by their hands," says Misr Makraj, " a large *pookraj* (topaz) of a yellow colour, which the Shah stated to be the Koh-i-noor." But the Maharajah's jewellers, who were sent for to test it, soon told him the trick that had been played. " He kept the topaz," writes the worthy Treasurer ; " but sent immediate orders to place the Shah under restraint (*tungai*) and to prevent him from eating or drinking until the Koh-i-noor demanded was given up, as he had attempted to impose upon the Maharajah ! After this restraint had been continued about eight hours, the Shah gave up the Koh-i-noor to the Vakeels above named, who immediately brought it to the Maharajah in the Summun, where it was shown to the jewellers, who had remained with the Maharajah at the palace until the return of the Vakeels. The Maharajah had dressed for the evening Durbar, and was seated in his chair, when the jewel was brought to him. It was brought in a box lined with crimson velvet, into which it had been fitted, and was presented to the Maharajah, who expressed great satisfaction.

" It was at that time set alone (singly) in an enamelled setting, with strings to be worn as an armlet. He placed it on his arm, and admired it, then, after a time, replaced it in its box, which, with the topaz, he made over to Beelee Ram, to be placed in the Toshkhana under the charge of Misr Bustee Ram Toshkhaneea." Afterwards, under charge of Beelee Ram, it was carried along with the Maharajah, wherever he went, under a strong guard.

" It was always carried in a large camel trunk placed on the leading camel (but this was known only to the people of the Toshkhana), the whole string of camels, which generally consisted of about one hundred, being well guarded by troops. In camp, this box was placed between two others alike, close to the pole of the tent, Misr Beelee Ram's bed very close to it, none but his relatives and confidential servants having access to the place.

" For four or five years it was worn as an armlet, then fitted up as a *sirpêsh* for the turban, with a diamond drop of a *tolah* weight (now in the Toshkhana) attached to it. It was worn in this manner for about a year, on three or four occasions, when it was again made up as an armlet, with a diamond on each side, *as at present.* It has now been used as an armlet for upwards of twenty years."

Shortly before the death of Runjeet Singh, Rajah Dhyan Singh, Wuzeer, sent for Beelee Ram, and stated that the Maharajah had expressed by signs, for he was by then speechless, that he wished the Koh-i-noor to be given away in charity. But to this Misr Beelee Ram objected, saying that it ought to remain with the Maharajah's descendants, and that already twenty-one lakhs of rupees, and jewels and gold, etc., had been given away to the Brahmins. When, therefore, Rajah Dhyan Singh obtained uncontrolled power, he threw Misr Beelee Ram into prison, where he was kept for four months, the keys of the Toshkhana being handed over to Tej Chund.

But on the accession of Maharajah Shere Singh, Misr Beelee Ram was at once again called into office, and continued during his reign.

Again, the day after Shere Singh's death, Beelee Ram was seized by Heera Singh's people and sent to the house of Nawab Sheik Imamoodem, by whom he was *disposed of* in the *Tykhana* (underground room) of his house, along with his brother and another official!

Beelee Ram's nephew, Gunesh Doss, who was with him at the time, was also put in confinement, along with six others of Beelee Ram's family, including Misr Makraj. They still had to perform their duties in the Toshkhana, though the keys were taken from them.

Misr Makraj's statement, which my husband countersigned and preserved, concludes by saying that, " At Heera Singh's death, Misr Makraj and his six relatives were released, and after the removal of Lal Singh from power, the charge of the Toshkhana and Koh-i-noor again came into the hands of Misr Makraj, *with whom it continued without intermission until made over to Dr. J. S. Login* on 3rd May, 1849, when taken possession of by the British Government."

As to the notion that the Koh-i-noor brought ill-luck to its possessors, we know what Lord Dalhousie thought of such an idea.* He enumerates the long line of conquerors who held it, from Akhbar to Runjeet Singh, and scoffs at the bare supposition ; and then tells how when the last-named desired his plundered guest, Shah Soojah, to tell him the real value of the diamond, the latter replied : " Its value is ' good fortune,' for whoever holds it is victorious over his enemies." This anecdote was told the " great Proconsul " by Fakeer Noorooddeen, who had himself been one of the messengers from Runjeet Singh.

I, myself, of course, never saw all the magnificence

* " Private Letters," etc., pp. 139, 395.

of the treasures in the Lahore Toshkhana ; but this is
how they were described to me by my cousin, Colonel
Robert Adams, afterwards second-in-command of the
Guides, and Deputy-Commissioner at Peshawur, where
he was assassinated by a Ghilzai in 1864.

" CITADEL, LAHORE,
" November 2nd, 1849.

" . . . I wish you could walk through that same
Toshkhana and *see its wonders ;* the vast quantities of
gold and silver ; the jewels not to be valued, so many,
and so rich ; the Koh-i-noor, far beyond what I had
imagined ; Runjeet's golden chair of State ; silver
pavilion ; Shah Soojah's ditto ; Relics of the Prophet ;
Kulgee plume of the last Sikh Gúrú ; sword of the Persian hero Rustum (taken from Shah Soojah) ; sword
of Holkar, etc.; and, perhaps above all, the immense
collection of magnificent Cashmere shawls, rooms full
of them, laid out on shelves and heaped up in bales—it is
not to be described !   And all this made over to Login
without any list or public document of any sort ; all
put in his hands to set in order, value, sell, etc.   That
speaks volumes, does it not, for the character he bears
with those whose good opinions are worth having ?   Few
men, I fancy, would have been so implicitly trusted."

By Login's special request, the Governor-General
raised Misr Makraj to the rank of noble, as a mark of
appreciation of his integrity.

In his letters to me from Lahore, Login mentioned
to me on two occasions that Lord Dalhousie had paid
private visits of inspection to the Toshkhana, but their
real object was not revealed to me till two months had
elapsed.   On January 2nd, 1850, he wrote :

" . . . It was a great relief to me to get away from
Lahore . . . . Macgregor took over charge from me. . . .
I got Moolraj, Chutter Singh, Shere Singh & Co. (the

political prisoners), to sign a *Razeenama* in Persian, which they did with great readiness. . . . I shall deposit it along with the receipt for the Koh-i-noor, which was written by Lord Dalhousie himself, in the presence of Sir H. Elliot, Sir H. Lawrence, Mansel and John Lawrence, and countersigned by them all. They also affixed their seals, as well as my own, to the State Jewels, when I delivered them over. This document will be worth keeping, I think, and something for my children to look at when I am gone."

Six months later, he says :

"Futtehghur,
"*July 16th*, 1850.

" I see by the papers that the Koh-i-noor arrived in England. . . . I was one of the *very few* entrusted with the secret of its disposal. Indeed, they could not have got access to it without my knowledge, seeing that it never left my possession from the day I received it in charge ! I may tell you now that it is safe that Lord Dalhousie came to my quarters before he left Lahore, bringing with him a small bag, made by Lady Dalhousie, to hold it ; and after I had formally made it over to him, he went into my room, and fastened it round his waist under his clothes, in my presence. Lord Dalhousie himself wrote out the formal receipt for the jewel ; and there my responsibility ended, and I felt it a great load taken off me ! All the members of the Board of Administration were present, and countersigned the document. The other jewels were also sealed up and made over.

"Thus Runjeet Singh's famous Toshkhana of Jewels is a thing of the past ! "

The receipt itself is in this form :

" I have received this day from Doctor Login into my personal possession, for transmission to England, the Koh-i-noor diamond, in the presence of the members

of the Board of Administration, and of Sir Henry Elliot,
K.C.B., Secretary to the Government of India.

"(Signed) DALHOUSIE.*

" LAHORE,
    " *December 7th*, 1849.
(Signed) " H. M. LAWRENCE.
          C. G. MANSEL.
          JOHN LAWRENCE.
          H. M. ELLIOT."

I think this account of the Koh-i-noor may be considered sufficient to dispose of a legend that has obtained
very wide credence, and which it has even been attempted
to father on Lord Lawrence, the very last man to have
originated it, knowing as he did all the facts of the case.

To imagine for a moment that the Koh-i-noor, set
as an armlet, as described by Misr Makraj, and enclosed
in a box, could ever have found a resting place in any
person's waistcoat pocket, however capacious, is taxing
too much the credulity of the average individual, and
has caused infinite amusement to the large number of
officials aware of the ceremonial always observed in its
transit, and the strong guard placed over it both in and
out of the Toshkhana.†

---

* In the lately published "Private Letters of the Marquess of Dalhousie,"
edited by J. G. A. Baird, pp. 124, 172, occur the following reference to this
incident :—

"The Koh-i-noor sailed from Bombay in H.M.S. *Medea* on 6th April. I
could not tell you at the time, for strict secrecy was observed, but I brought it
from Lahore myself ! I undertook the charge of it in a funk, and never was so
happy in all my life as when I got it into the Treasury at Bombay. It was sewn
and double-sewn into a belt secured round my waist, one end through the
belt fastened to a chain round my neck. It never left me day or night, except
when I went to Dera Ghazee Khan, when I left it with Captain Ramsay (who
has now joint charge of it), locked in a treasure-chest, and with strict orders
that he was to sit upon the chest till I came back ! My stars, what a relief it
was to get rid of it ! "

Sir John Login in after years remarked that his skill with the needle then
stood him in good stead, as it was he who acted *dirsi*, and sewed the jewel
securely into its chamois-leather wallet.

† As time has gone on, the story has received fresh additions, and we even

My own connection with the famous jewel was non-existent at this period ; but later on I will relate how I had a very close view of it, under circumstances historical and dramatic, of which I am now the sole surviving witness.

My husband often told me that the medley of articles in Runjeet's Toshkhana was indescribable. He found a fine portrait of Queen Victoria in a " go-down " (shed) among a heap of other valuables, all covered with dust ; amongst them several good drawings and fine old engravings, and a little wax-cloth bag containing a copy of Henry Martyn's Persian Testament, the fly-leaf inscribed " From Lady William Bentinck to Joseph Wolff ! " One of the largest emeralds ever seen was accidentally discovered set in the pommel of a saddle ! The saddle had been already condemned to be broken up or disposed of, when the piece of *green glass* (as it was supposed) was observed, set in the position in which the Sikh noblemen often carry a mirror when riding in full dress, to make sure that turban and paraphernalia are all *en régle*.

Besides the jewels that he was allowed to pick out for the little Maharajah—you may be sure that he was careful they should be some of the finest ones—your father wrote to me from Lahore that he had taken care to select some of the best tents for his use, before any were made over for sale, and had ordered that those to be used for his servants and establishment be at once pitched on the parade ground in front, at the same time

find the late Duke of Argyll retailing it in an article in the *Windsor Magazine* of June, 1911, which gives the impression that John Lawrence actually pocketed the diamond before the astonished eyes of the native Treasurer and his master, while still the Maharajah of Lahore was an independent sovereign, on the plea that he would be a safer custodian than its legitimate possessor ; and proceeded to make good this assertion, by rolling it *in an old stocking*, placing it on a shelf and forgetting all about it ! !

giving his people a plan of encampment to which they were always to adhere.*

"Now, when I tell you," he wrote, "that the tents for the little man himself are all lined, some with rich Cashmere shawls, and some with satin and velvet embroidered with gold, *semianas*, carpets, *purdahs* and floor-cloths to match, and that the tent-poles are encased in gold and silver (like a *chobedar's* mace), you may fancy that we shall look rather smart! I should say that for camp-equipage old Runjeet's camp was the very finest and most sumptuous among all the Princes of India!"

* A water-colour sketch of the Maharajah's camp was afterwards made by one of Lord Dalhousie's staff, and hangs in my house at Aylesford.

CHAPTER VII

DULEEP SINGH was proclaimed Maharajah at the age of five years. He and his eldest brother, Khurruck Singh, were the only two sons of Runjeet Singh, who were born of his wives and " acknowledged " by their father. Shere Singh, Duleep's immediate predecessor, was only an " adopted " son. Of *his* children, only an infant of four months, Sheo Deo Singh, survived him. To him your father was also made guardian.

Duleep Singh's mother was the beautiful and notorious Maharanee Jinda (or. " Chunda "), sometimes known as the " Messalina of the Punjab." She, with her brother, Jowahir Singh, and her favourite, Lal Singh, governed the country, until the Board of Control, consisting of the two Lawrence brothers, Mr. C. G. Mansel, and (at one period) Sir Frederick Currie, took over charge, in conjunction with the native Council of Regency, of whom six out of the eight members remained loyal to the agreement with the British Government during the rebellion of 1848, though the Maharanee was proved to have been in communication and accord with the rebel Sirdars.

As a matter of fact, throughout the Second Sikh War, Lahore remained perfectly quiet and unaffected by the disturbances in the northern and western provinces. The Resident continued to exercise supreme authority, assisted by the Durbar (except one member who had gone into open rebellion), and the little Maharajah remained in profound ignorance that any unusual events, which could affect him or his sovereignty, were passing in the country without.

He knew only that Golâb Singh, the son of Chutter Singh, and his own personal companion, was suddenly removed from his attendance, and placed in confinement, and that, later on, the palace itself was guarded by a British regiment.

The insurgents were proclaimed as rebels " against the Government of the Maharajah Duleep Singh ; " and the Resident, on the 18th November, issued a proclamation (approved by the Governor-General), telling " all loyal subjects to the Maharajah " that the British Army " has entered the Lahore territories, not as an enemy to the constituted Government, but to restore order and obedience. All who have remained faithful in their obedience to the Government of the Maharajah Duleep Singh . . . have nothing to fear from the coming of the British Army." *

For having instigated her little son to offer an open insult to the Resident, Sir Henry Lawrence, and the native Durbar, the Maharanee Jinda had been separated from the Maharajah Duleep Singh, and on August 19th, 1847, removed to Sheikopoora, twenty-five miles from Lahore.

On the 8th May, 1848, she was discovered to be implicated in a plot to poison, and otherwise dispose of, the Resident and other prominent British officials, so she was removed from Sheikopoora to Ferozepore, and ultimately to the fortress of Chunar. From here, however, on the 18th April, 1849, she managed to escape, in the disguise of a fakirnee,† and took refuge in Nepal, where my husband's younger brother, Dr. James

* " Punjab Papers," pp. 260, 438, 449, 562.
† Female mendicant.

Dryburgh Login, was then Acting-Assistant-Resident at Khatmandoo.

Dryburgh Login was in great favour with Jung Bahadour, the famous Nepalese Prime Minister, and had been selected to accompany him to England on the visit which he paid just before the Mutiny broke out, a visit which turned the balance in our favour, and made him into a zealous ally of the British " raj " during the troublous times of 1857—1858. But alas! poor Dryburgh did not live to take up the appointment ; indeed, I am not sure that he was ever aware that he had been chosen for it, for my husband thus wrote to tell me of the sudden death of this dear brother, at Dinapore, on the 13th November, from cholera, after twelve hours' illness.

" He had come down from Khatmandoo in high health, to pass his examination in Calcutta, and was suddenly struck down on his way back. . . . I was to-day introduced by John Lawrence to Lord Dalhousie, with much warmth of commendation. His lordship said that he had heard on all sides how much satisfaction I had given in discharging my duties, which were of no ordinary delicacy, and that I had acquitted myself *well*. He appointed to-day, noon, for a long conversation with him, from which I have just returned, in which he gave me full instructions regarding the future disposal of the young Maharajah, and said it was a great relief to the Government to have me in charge of him, and that the way in which I had acquitted myself, both towards him and the Government, was in every way satisfactory to both. He was really very kind and cordial indeed, and did not wish me to restrict myself to Futtehghur as a residence, but allows me to take him to visit other parts whenever I like, and eventually to England. I then had an opportunity of giving him my ideas regarding the advantage of sending some of the young Sikh noblemen to England, and so forth. And what came next ? Why, poor Dryburgh was to have been appointed this day to the charge of the Nepalese Mission to England ! I told Lord Dalhousie what had occurred, and he was much shocked, and sympathised with me most cordially."

Everyone was struck with the young Sikh Sovereign's charm of manner ; his geniality and love of truth, and his straightforwardness was very unusual in an Oriental. One could not but have great sympathy for the boy, brought up from babyhood to exact the most obsequious servility ; and it was greatly to his credit that he submitted at all to any direction or discipline, or to the idea that his education was to be enforced by any system of authority. My husband was really fond of him, and the two got on famously together ; yet there were occasional contests of will between them, and the first real exercise of discipline on the part of his guardian arose out of a matter so trivial as to give it an exceedingly absurd aspect. Duleep Singh had run out into the garden during heavy rain, and got thoroughly drenched. Finding him in this condition, Login wished him to change his clothes, but, half in play, the boy said he would do so at the usual time, and when urged to change at once, he turned obstinate. Then, in the quality of his governor, my husband gave him half-an-hour to do it, of his own accord, and when he still held out, told him how he grieved to coerce him in any way, but that he advised him, as a friend, not to make it necessary to have to use compulsion. Poor little fellow ! In a few minutes he came sobbing to his guardian's room, and " pleaded the Treaty of Lahore, which stipulated that he was to be allowed to do as he liked ! ! "

When I came to join the little community within the
confines of "Futtehghur Park," as it was called, I
found myself in a strange comminglement of European
and Oriental arrangements. There were several bungalows dotted over the estate, each surrounded by its
own compound. The largest one was occupied by the
Maharajah, another by ourselves, the third by the
Ranee Duknoo, mother of the little Shahzadah Sheo Deo
Singh, who had refused to be separated from him. With
her, besides her boy, lived her brother and uncle, both
men of great charm and cultivation, for whom I had a
sincere respect and liking. The other houses were
allotted to the native gentlemen in attendance.

The daily evening reception in the drawing-room was
unusual in an ordinary European household, and was
one of the few semblances of royal ceremony retained
by the young deposed monarch. During the day he
was supposed to be occupied in his studies, or taking
his out-door exercise, and the gentlemen of his suite
were free to follow their own devices ; but in the evening Dewan Ajoodeah Pershad, Fakeer Zehoorudin,
Sirdar Boor Singh Butaliwallah, and the other nobles
and ministers who had followed their sovereign into
exile, made their appearance in full dress to pay their
respects, and hold themselves at his disposal for a few
hours.

, Duleep Singh then was to be seen seated in State on
a couch or chair, with his attendants grouped about him.
Each of the suite on entering made low obeisance, then
stood erect, his folded hands to his forehead, and gave
vent to the one word "Maharaj!" with the sudden-
ness of a pistol-shot! This salutation was made on
entering and on leaving the presence, the Maharajah
receiving it—according to native ideas of kingly dignity

—without visible sign of acknowledgment. Intercourse with Europeans, however, soon made him a little more gracious in manner.

Naturally, my arrival upon the scene was an event of immense interest to these worthy gentlemen, who vied with each other in showing me the greatest courtesy and deference. Many were the interesting conversations I had with them, comparing and discussing the differences between Eastern and Western manners and ideas. How endless were their questions about all I had seen, and done, while at home in England! And I, on my part, had much to learn from them on various matters.

Then the incessant dissertations and arguments on the meaning, and wording, of the Treaties between the British Government and the Sikh Maharajah, especially the Treaty of Bhyrowal, and the last Treaty of Lahore, by which the Maharajah Duleep Singh was deprived of his kingdom! All these things formed the subject of conversation in the evening, diversified by the round games, hide-and-seek, blind man's buff, etc., in which the Maharajah and his young companions delighted, and into which the Sikh chiefs were dragged, whether they would or no! If they felt them inconsistent with their dignity, they were far too good-humoured to show it, and entered into all the Maharajah's fun and teasing as if they were children themselves.

One of the prettiest sights at Futtehghur of an early morning, or in the cool of the evening, was the perfectly appointed *sowarree* * of the young Sikh Maharajah out for his daily ride, accompanied by the Shahzadah and his English friends, with his retinue of warlike Sikh attendants, handsomely-dressed and well-mounted, fol-

* Cavalcade.

lowed by a detachment of the Governor-General's
Body Guard * in their scarlet, and Skinner's Irregulars
in their saffron uniforms, the whole effect was both
picturesque and brilliant. If, instead, the Maharajah
went out on his elephant, with its splendid trappings
and silver *howdah*, or in his carriage, with its four grey
Arabs, driven by his English coachman, the same
finish in every detail was observable.

I always regarded the Ranee Duknoo as one of the
most beautiful—if not *the* most absolutely beautiful—
woman I ever met! Tall, slender, graceful, and very
fair she was, with a peculiarly gentle and winning
expression of countenance. Clothed, as befitted a
widow, in sad colours, without ornament or jewel, the
soft white muslin *doputta* draped about her shapely
head, its transparent folds shrouding the lower part of
her face, her large mournful eyes bearing a look of
appeal and innocence, she was a living presentation of
the Madonna, as depicted by the old Italian masters.

She was of ancient Rajpoot lineage from the Kangra
Hills, and had been specially selected for her beauty
for the harem of Shere Singh—Runjeet's adopted son—
on his coming to the throne. Thus the little Sheo Deo
Singh was only a few months old when his father
was murdered, and Duleep Singh was elected by the
Khâlsa (Sikh Commonwealth).

Her son therefore she looked upon as in very deed
a " prince," born in the purple, and was never so happy
as when encouraged to talk about him. Like most
Eastern mothers, she was intensely jealous of any other
influence over him, and would have kept him in the

* By an order of the Governor-General in Council, a detachment of the Body
Guard, consisting of " twenty-five good men and two trusty native officers,"
remained with his Highness at Futtehghur, " so as to lessen the duty of the
Irregular Corps."

Zenana, close by her side, without troubling about other teaching. It was my part to try and convince her in a friendly way, of her real duty as a mother, to take full advantage of the education offered him by the Governor-General, in association with the Maharajah. She was fully sensible of the sacrifice I myself had made in like manner, by separating myself from my own children, and sending them to England to be educated, and was filled with astonishment at it.

I made a practice of visiting her constantly, as she led a very retired life, and rarely went outside her house, and we used to compare notes about our respective children. She, on her part, remonstrated with me on the way in which my youngest boy,* born since my return from England, as he grew beyond the age of a toddler, was encouraged to walk out, and ride a pony (albeit only in a ring-saddle), all day long, amongst a crowd of men-servants and the troopers of the escort, instead of being kept in the Zenana with the women-folk! Harry was a spoilt young monkey, it is true, and was never seen without a tail of followers, hanging on to him and the pony, wherever he went, all kept occupied by some special work enjoined by the "chota Sahib!" This peculiarity he retained all his life, and I used to tease him about his faculty for never undertaking the smallest job himself without "making up a party," as he called it, to "assist" by looking on!

And, later on, when, to counteract the coddling of the womenfolk, and the little airs of arrogance he occasionally assumed, the Shahzadah was allowed to attend, at Mussoorie, as day-pupil, a private school for the sons of English officers and civilians, much to the horror of his mother and uncles—the first foreshadowing

* The late Rear-Admiral S. H. M. Login, born 1851.

of the Kunwar College, to be established a generation later!—how often have I been a witness of the boy's tempestuous return from his lessons, leaping from his pony, on which he went to and fro ceremoniously escorted by his *sowarree*, and bursting into the room where we were seated, to tell, in high delight and excitement, of all the tussles and games he had joined in, his relatives vainly striving to suppress, in my presence, their scandalised consternation at such undignified pastimes!

The little Shahzadah was a charming little fellow, with very pretty manners and great personal beauty, inheriting the delicate, refined features, and aristocratic bearing of the Rajpoots, rather than the coarser beauty of the Sikhs.

It was a quaint sight to observe him making his daily short progress from his mother's house to the Maharajah's; to note, on the one hand, the dignified bearing of the little Prince, stepping daintily along in his beautiful and picturesque national costume, his snowy turban fringed with gold (a becoming spot of colour being given by the crimson under-turban which confines the knot of long hair peculiar to the Sikhs); and on the other, the reverential demeanour of the uncle and granduncle in attendance, walking respectfully one step in the rear, answering dutifully the remarks which the child vouchsafed to them over his shoulder, and always careful to address him as " Shahzadah-jee," while the little man accepted as his due the admiration he excited.

CHAPTER VIII

It was while my husband was absent on leave, having come down to Calcutta to meet me, that the Maharajah suddenly announced to his temporary Governor, Captain J. Campbell, 7th Madras Cavalry, his intention of embracing the Christian religion ! Such a resolve was an entire surprise to all in authority over him, who were totally unaware of all such idea on his part ; and Login returned in haste, with instructions from the Governor-General to ascertain whether he, or any European, had introduced the subject of religion to his notice, talked upon it, or engaged him in any question regarding it. His two English playfellows were also to be examined on the subject.

After careful inquiry, Login wrote a report to the Governor-General that he had got the evidence in writing of the Maharajah's Sikh retinue, the Dewan Ajoodhea Pershad, Fakeer Zehooroodeen, the Porohut Golâb Rai, family priest of the Maharajahs of Lahore, and Sirdar Boor Singh, that no improper influence had been, in their estimation, made use of to make him change his belief in the religion of his people.

As a matter of fact, very little effort was made by his own people to instruct him in the Sikh religion. Though every inducement was made them, very few of his Sikh attendants, none of his Sikh priests, or *Grunt'hees*, and only one Brahmin *porohut* (family priest) consented to come with him from Lahore. The last-named had been

prevailed on by Login with difficulty, making many
conditions. When his favourite Mahommedan attendant,
Meeah Khema, who had been with him from childhood, asked to be allowed to return to Lahore, Login
procured in his place a young Brahmin of good family
of Furruckabad, named Bhajun Lal, educated in the
American Mission Schools, but not known to have any
leanings towards Christianity. His father was a wealthy
bunniah of that city, and he himself afterwards set up
a large tent-factory at Futtehghur.

This young man, nevertheless, was the only creature
in his entourage who had any inkling that Duleep Singh
was turning his inquiries in the direction of the Christian faith, and that he was sceptical with regard to many
of the " pious stories " in the Shastras, *e.g.*, that of the
virtuous Rajah who distributed daily in alms *ten thousand
cows* before he broke his fast, and yet came short of
eternal salvation, because his servants, unknown to him,
had placed amongst the daily tale of cows one that had
already been numbered in the charitable dole !

But although he used to make Bhajun Lal read the
Bible to him, and discuss it together, it was, as the young
Brahmin quaintly put it, " sometimes Bible—sometimes a few conjuring tricks (of which he was very fond)—
sometimes games in ' Boy's Own Book '—and all he
did, he did of his own wilful will," it was plain that
neither Bhajun Lal—who himself never had the courage
to sacrifice his worldly prospects by embracing Christianity, though evidently convinced of its truths—nor
any European, had exerted their influence over the
Maharajah in order to turn his mind in that direction.

After hearing all, Lord Dalhousie expressed himself
as " entirely satisfied . . . that no improper influence
had, either directly or indirectly, been used by you

(Login), or by any other English gentleman connected
with his Highness's establishment."

Such an unheard of thing, however, as that a native
Prince, under the Governor-General's immediate guardianship, should desire to become a Christian, had to be
referred to the authorities at home, and for four months
he was not allowed to make any public declaration of his
intentions, or any change in his religious observances ;
and it was not until March 8th, 1853, or two years
and three months after he had intimated his earnest
wish, that he was permitted to receive Holy Baptism.
He had meantime been very solemnly warned of the
serious step he had taken, and was thoroughly grounded
in the doctrines of the faith he wished to embrace,
to the satisfaction of the Bishop of Calcutta (Dr. Wilson).

By Lord Dalhousie's special injunction, repeated
in several private letters to my husband, the rite was
administered by the chaplain of the station, the Rev.
W. J. Jay,* with a total absence of fuss and ceremony,
" In order," as Lord Dalhousie put it, " that I may feel
satisfied in my conscience that the boy has not been,
unintentionally by us, or unconsciously to himself,
led into the act by any other motives than that of
conviction of the truth. To that end," he added,
" your management of the matter has been most
judicious and highly satisfactory to me."

As the church of the station was at the time under
repair, the baptism took place in his own house, in the
presence of about twenty of the European residents
of Futtehghur, and about an equal number of the Maharajah's principal native servants, who had been invited
to attend. As witnesses to the entry in the register
(since god-parents are not obligatory, though customary,

* Father of the Rev. Osborne Jay, Vicar of Shoreditch.

in the baptism of those of riper years) the signatures of three persons, my husband, myself, and Colonel* Alexander were affixed, also that of Mr. Walter Guise, who had been the Maharajah's tutor. The names of some of the Maharajah's native attendants were also added, amongst them that of Jewindah, a favourite Sikh servant. At the last moment, by a happy inspiration, I made the suggestion that there would be a special appropriateness in the use of Ganges water for the sacred rite, seeing the veneration in which the river Ganges (*Ganga-jee*) is held by all Hindoos, since thereby it would be henceforth sanctified to Duleep Singh with a new and holier association. Even so do Jew and Mohammedan alike hold in reverence the waters of Jordan, but to the Christian alone it typifies the "water of baptism," wherein Christ Himself was baptised. Jewindah hailed with joy what he regarded as a special concession to Hindoo prejudice, and begged to be allowed himself to fetch the water in his brass lotah.†

The ceremony was felt, by those permitted to be present, as very touching and impressive. I well remember the earnest expression on the young boy's face, and the look, half-sad, half-curious, on those of his people present by their own wish.

Nothing could have been more admirable than the fatherly interest and constant supervision exercised at this time by Lord Dalhousie over his ward. Had he been his own son he could not have manifested more tender solicitude for his well-being, both bodily and spiritual. He was above all things desirous that the young prince should be solely influenced by the highest

* Afterwards Lieut.-General Sir James Alexander, K.C.B.
† Strangely enough, a form of baptism forms part of the *pahul* or initiatory rite of the Sikhs.

motives in the step he took, for the Viceroy expressed himself as intensely disgusted at the display and "tamasha," as he called it, that had a little time previous to this been made over the baptism of the daughter of the Rajah of Coorg, of which I shall have more to say presently.

Lord Dalhousie's letters to my husband, and to the Maharajah on this occasion, were marked by the same spirit of cordial friendliness in the one case, and of almost parental affection in the other, that characterised his intercourse towards them both at this period.

To Login he wrote :

"GOVERNMENT HOUSE,
"*March* 16*th*, 1853.

"MY DEAR LOGIN,

"I have the pleasure to receive yours of 8th, enclosing one from the Maharajah. I rejoice deeply and sincerely in this good issue to the great change the boy has passed through, with so much satisfactory evidence of the reality and genuineness of his convictions. I regard it as a very remarkable event in history, and in every way gratifying.

"Let me add that, under circumstances of peculiarly great delicacy, and of great difficulty, I have been most highly satisfied with the judgment and discretion, the prudence and kindly tact, which have been exhibited by yourself through them all.

"Believe me to be, my dear Login,
"Yours very truly,
"DALHOUSIE."

And again, later :

"*January* 31*st*, 1854.

"MY DEAR LOGIN,

"I have just received the Court's leave for the Maharajah to go to England, and I beg you to deliver the enclosed to him.

" I hope he will do me credit, for they have had a sickener of native grandees* at home lately.

"Yours most sincerely,
"DALHOUSIE."

To the Maharajah himself Lord Dalhousie had written when first informed of his resolve :

" SIMLA,
"August 2nd, 1851.

" . . . . Your Highness will readily understand that my wish to refer the subject to the Court of Directors did not proceed from any reluctance on my part to meet your views, still less from any doubt of the wisdom of the step you wished to take. I was desirous only that it should be clearly seen that the act was your own, springing from your own heart, and that you had not been led into it hastily, and while you were yet too young to have deeply considered the importance of your act. I rejoice to learn that your Highness remains firm in your desire to be instructed in the doctrines of the Bible, and that you have resolved to embrace a faith, whose teaching, if duly practised by the help of God, will tend to increase your happiness in this life, and will secure it in another that is to come."

He now expressed himself as " thanking God and the Saviour of us all, that He had put into his heart a knowledge of, and belief in, the truth of our holy religion." " I earnestly hope," he continues, " that your future life may be in conformity with the precepts of that religion, and that you may show to your countrymen in India an example of a pure and blameless life, such as is befitting a Christian prince.

" I beg your Highness to believe in the strength and sincerity of the regard which I shall ever feel towards

---

* Referring to Jung Bahadour and the Rajah of Coorg.

you, and to remain, now and always, your Highness's sincere and affectionate friend,

"DALHOUSIE."

On Christmas Day, 1851, Lord and Lady Dalhousie came to Futtehghur, and dined with my husband and myself in the evening, Duleep Singh being present. Lord Stanley was there at the same time, also M. Rochussen, the late Governor-General of Java, to whom Lord Dalhousie had privately asked Login to render any attention that was in his power.

It was really very charming to observe the Governor-General's thoughtful care for the comfort and happiness of the Maharajah, and how very thoroughly he inspected all the arrangements of the establishment, and the laying-out of the place and grounds. So kind-hearted and genial did he show himself, in his intercourse with his ward and with ourselves, that it was hard to believe that this was the man his detractors accused of being so uncompromisingly frigid, and autocratic in bearing, to his subordinates. He was much pleased with the improvement that a year's constant intercourse with European ladies and gentlemen had effected in the young prince's ease of manner, and proficiency in English. His shyness about speaking it had been the reason for a system of fines on anybody who spoke a word of Hindustani in his presence, the proceeds to go to certain charities he was interested in. To revenge himself for the constant fines at first levied on himself, he used to profess deafness, and ignorance of English words, in order to trap the unwary, till with a shout of laughter he called on his victim to " fork out " the required amount for breaking rules !

And as to his chivalrous courtesy to ladies—the result of his adoption of English ideas of what was due

to them—I may mention an occurrence that took place
at this time, and is strongly stamped on my memory,
though it is only one instance among many others.

There was a subdued excitement among the Ranee
Duknoo's people, when it became noised about that
Duleep Singh was forsaking the Sikh religion, and seeking to learn the new faith ; of course, if it were so, then
the Shahzadah would naturally become of more importance, and would be looked upon by all Sikhs as the true
representative of the Khâlsa Raj. It was reported that
the Ranee encouraged these ideas, and it was observed
that the little boy had begun to take upon himself
consequential airs, and to make remarks derogatory
to his uncle. There was also an affectation of avoidance
of his society which was very unusual and impertinent,
as the Sikhs attach little importance to the strict pre-
servation of caste, though the Rajpoots are very
punctilious.*

No doubt the Ranee wished to ascertain for certain
if the rumours she heard were true, for she asked
me several times why the Maharajah had discontinued
his visits to her ?

One day, when on my way to visit the Ranee, I met
the Maharajah and his party hawking in the park. On
learning whither I was bent, he asked, with some eagerness, if he might go with me, as he did not care to go
alone ? Of course I agreed, but was careful to send a
chobedar beforehand, to warn the Ranee of the coming
visit.

We were received, and announced by the little Shahzadah and the Ranee's handsome young brother, Meah

---

* The Ranee herself had lost caste by marrying a Sikh, and her people did
not eat with her in consequence ; nor did they eat with the Shahzadah, the son
of a Sikh.

Ootum. There was unusual constraint observable
during the visit; even the little Shahzadah seemed not
at ease, and as if expectant of something about to
happen. The Ranee offered refreshments, and called
for fruit-sherbert, for which she was famous. The tray
appeared with only *one* glass upon it. This the Ranee
filled, and offered with deep reverence to her Sovereign;
but the Maharajah courteously handed the glass first to
me. Drinking part of the contents, I replaced it on the
tray. To my horror, it was immediately refilled, and
once more presented by the Ranee to the Maharajah,
while significant glances passed between the brother
and sister! Perceiving that a premeditated insult
was intended, I exclaimed in a low voice, in English:
"Don't touch it, Maharajah!" But, rising and turning towards me with a courteous salute, he took the glass
in his hand, drank off its contents, and abruptly t rn-
ing on his heel, left the house, giving the slightest possible gesture of farewell to his sister-in-law, who gazed
after him in consternation, now alarmed at the result
of her experiment!

I took my leave, you may be sure, directly after this
insult to my husband's ward, and was much touched to
find the Maharajah had waited outside, in order that I
might not return without his escort. Asking him *why*
he took the glass, and thus permitted himself to be thus
affronted—"What?" he replied, his eyes flashing;
"you would have me let them *insult you too?* They shall
see that I honour you! And I am not ashamed thus to
show that I have broken caste!"

It was about this time that he brought to me a very
curious, common, little brass idol, asking me to take it
out of his sight, as he did not wish to be reminded that
he had ever done "poojah" to a thing like that! He

added, with a twinkle in his eye : " It is the last one left to me now! Had it been silver or gold, like the others, it would have disappeared long ere this, as they have done, one by one, once my fellows saw I had no further use for them! Well, they are welcome to them for all I care ! " *

He had been long anxious to show that he was no longer a follower of Nanuk, the Sikh Prophet, by cutting off the long tress of hair which he, in common with all Sikhs, wore twisted up into a knob above the forehead, and covered with the bright-coloured under-turban. When, at length, after a year's probation, he was suffered to cut it off, he brought the coil, long and abundant as a woman's, and presented it to me as a token that he had now done with all it represented. By his request, he, with several of his native attendants, was present at my little son's christening, and much disappointed that he was not permitted to act proxy for Sir Henry Lawrence, who was god-father, though absent in the hills.

The Shahzadah continued to share Duleep Singh's studies at Futtehghur and at Mussoorie, and was very anxious to accompany his uncle when it was decided that the latter was to visit England. But now came in the power of the Zenana. The Ranee Duknoo opposed the Governor-General's project of education for her son, threatening to commit suicide if ever he were sent over the " black water." And her determination, of course, won the day. In spite of Sheo Deo Singh's own earnest desire, he had to be left in India ; and although from time to time he continued, up to the year 1861, to write to his former guardian, it was evident that his English education had stopped short, and his

* This idol is now in my possession.

writing and power of expressing himself deteriorated,
though he never failed to send affectionate messages to
me, of whom I think he was really fond, and also to my
little boy Harry. In a letter from Calcutta in 1861,
when he was the guest of his uncle Duleep Singh, he
begs that both of us would write to him often.

He was, of course, quite a small child when he came to
us, and such an attractive, lovable little fellow that it
was a great wrench to part with him in the end, so much
had he twined himself round both our hearts. There
is a very touching little note of his to my husband, that
I have always cherished among my treasures, dated
the 9th June, 1853, in which he implores his " dearest,
kind and beloved *Uncle* " (as he always insisted on dub-
bing Dr. Login), who had punished him pretty severely
for some childish fault, that he was " very sorry for his
faults, and hope by grace of Almighty God I will not do
so any more, and beg that you will pardon your most
beloved nephew, SHEO DEO SINGH."

On the 16th April, 1859, the Ranee Duknoo wrote
to your father from Benares : " I am very glad to see
Harry's letter to Shahzadah and to find that he has made
so good a progress in his education, and is become a
strong and active boy. If you make a sailor of him*
undoubtedly he will become a famous navigator to
keep up the honour and power of England." On the
29th June, 1860, she wrote to us, and to the Maharajah,
to announce the completion of the marriage ceremonies
of her son the Shahzadah (he was then about seventeen),
and sent to *me*, as well as to the Maharajah, the customary presents, of splendid native dresses, given by
the bridegroom's parents to their near relatives. It

---

* He had apparently already selected his profession at the age of seven-
and-a-half years !

was really exceedingly nice of her, and intended as the highest and most friendly compliment.

When, in February, 1861, the Maharajah went out to India for a short time, and Sheo Deo Singh met him in Calcutta, I am afraid the uncle was a bit disappointed to find how much the nephew had lost, in the meantime, of his European habits and education. Duleep Singh wrote :

" The Shahzadah is staying with me, but is a thorough native in his manners, I regret to say. He is a very quick, intelligent lad, and wishes to marry another wife ! You will be surprised to hear that he has no objection to read the Bible now, and often reads a chapter to me ! . . . I have no doubt that he will one day become a Christian, and before that come to England ; as he does not care if he touches a *mitra* (sweeper), provided none of his people see him ! He tells me he does not believe in his religion, and wishes to accompany me wherever I may go, even to England, if he could do it without his mother knowing it ! "

When it was decided that the Maharajah was to be allowed to go to England, we proceeded by slow stages towards Calcutta, or rather Barrackpore, where Lord Dalhousie offered him the use of his country-house. We stopped a few nights at Lucknow, where we were invited to the Palace, and a special *khillut* given to my husband, the King insisting on my accepting a pair of diamond bracelets and a ring, as a souvenir. Colonel— afterwards Sir William—Sleeman was then Resident, and was exceedingly interested in Duleep Singh, and very anxious that he should understand that he was of the same race as the men of Kent ! Sir William was an ardent ethnologist, and had satisfied himself that the Jâts of the Punjab and the Juts of Jutland (the race

of Hengist and Horsa) were originally the same, and came
from about Kashgar and the Caspian.

He was celebrated, too, as the man who put down
"Thuggee," the devotees of Kali, who murdered to do
her honour ; and many a time have I been left in the
verandah with a number of venerable and mild-looking
convicts from the gaol (the guard, of course, within
call) who entertained me with tales of how they enticed
their victims, and obligingly illustrated, with a hand-
kerchief, how they strangled them in their sleep ! while
my husband and Colonel Sleeman took measures of
their crania, to make casts for the medical and ethno-
logical museums. There is a story to the effect that, as
these skulls were only *numbered*, and my husband
included a cast of their guardian's head as well, the
savants at home pitched on this last as the one that
showed the most *undoubtedly* ferocious criminal pro-
pensities !

At Benares there joined our party a very remarkable
and interesting personality, the Pundit Nehemiah (or
Nilakanth) Goreh, a young and learned Brahmin, one
of the earliest converts to Christianity of that caste,
distinguished alike by his saintliness, his talents, and
his ability. He had been working as a missionary
amongst his own people, and desired to accompany
the Maharajah to England for three years, as his tutor
in Oriental languages, and Christian *Gooroo*. He was
then a candidate for Holy Orders, and had an earnest
wish to visit England. As to remuneration, he said
that he "wanted to be a *Byragi*,* but his body won't
let him, so all he asks for is food and raiment ! " We
found in him indeed a saint and a gentleman, and he
made a most favourable impression on all with whom he

* Hindoo ascetic.

came in contact, even amongst the highest in the land,
Her Majesty the Queen, and the Prince Consort, by
their own special desire, on two occasions receiving
him in private audience. When at length the time came
for his return to India, it was with the greatest sorrow
that we all saw depart from the household one who
seemed to radiate an atmosphere of holiness and purity
about him. Before departing, he begged to see our
little baby-girl, in order to bestow his blessing upon her
in true Oriental fashion. Bending over her, as she lay
asleep in her cradle, he uttered a very fervent prayer for
her future life, and then after solemnly contemplating
her in silence, he remarked in his quaint idiom—later
on, he spoke perfect English—" Ah, yes ! When I look
at her, lying like that, I think of my own little daughter !
When I left India, she was just such another—such
another—little beast ! "

Letters continued to come from him from time to
time, but he was always a bad correspondent. As he
himself wrote to Sir John in December, 1859 : " My
mind has been made, and is being made daily more and
more, to disrelish everything that does not belong
directly to the line of work which I have chosen for
myself. I employ my time in going out to preach at
set times, and in reading and writing, and holding
conversation on religious subjects with people that come
to visit me, and going to visit people for the same purpose. Whatever does not directly belong to this line I
have neither time nor curiosity, nor a relish for. With
regard to such things I am as if I did not live in the
world ! " Living thus the life of a Christian *Yogi*, he
wielded an immense influence amongst the natives of
the district in which he worked, who flocked to hear
him preach from immense distances, all, of every creed,

regarding him as a holy man, learned in the Shastras, as well as in the Scriptures. Even to this day testimony is borne to the immense love and veneration in which he was held. He had of course held priest's orders in the Church of England for some time, and afterwards joined the branch of the Community of the Cowley Fathers in Calcutta, who, finding that his books and lectures were doing such great work among the educated Hindoos, withdrew him from outdoor mission-work, and he was kept principally employed in writing theological works, and learned treatises, and in philosophical debates with Hindoo pundits. His daughter was educated partly in England, and was herself the author of several poems. After he became a Cowley Father he was often in England, and he died not many years ago, much respected in the Community. It was through him, while he was still at Benares, that we used occasionally to hear of the Shahzadah Sheo Deo Singh, the sons of the Coorg Rajah, and the Maharanee Jinda.

While at Barrackpore, before sailing for England, a certain native gentleman, who had been sent to Europe to present a claim or petition, on behalf of the Nana Sahib at Cawnpore, to the Court of Directors, came to pay his respects to the Maharajah Duleep Singh. He was a man of no rank, in fact, of low caste, who had been selected as his envoy by the Nana, partly because he was a favourite and a boon-companion of the latter, and partly as a sort of studied insult to the "feringhi-log," in order to sneer at their incapacity to distinguish between one native and another. How he and his master must have chuckled over the reception accorded to this creature in London, for he was received and fêted as a native "prince" by many who ought to have known better! The Governor-General had this man in mind, amongst others, when in a private letter to Login he wrote : " The visit of Jung Bahadour whom they spoiled, and still more, the present visit of the ex-Rajah of Coorg, whom, in spite of all my precautions and warnings, they have lifted out of his place, making a fool both of him and of themselves thereby, has disgusted the Court and Board of Control, with native, and especially with princely, visitors." This man, then, his head completely turned by the adulation offered him at home, and the licence allowed him in etiquette, came swaggering up the stairs to the Maharajah's apartments, of, course in full dress as to his turban, etc., but clad, as to his feet, in a smart pair of European boots. At the top of the flight he confronted my husband, who, pointing to his footgear, remarked : " Excuse me, you have forgotten ! " The other, at first, blustered and refused, arrogantly declaring that he had never removed his shoes for any grandee in England, and he was not to be bound by such antiquated and childish customs ! " How you have behaved in England is not my affair," said Login, who well knew the whole incident was planned as an attempt to insult Duleep Singh in the eyes of his servants, because he was now a Christian, " but I may tell you that, either you remove your *turban* (the greatest affront possible to a native) *or your shoes* before entering his Highness's presence, or—I and the *chobedar* here kick you down these stairs, like the scum you are ! "

Confronted by the wrath in your father's eyes, and the menacing looks of the servants around, the now trembling wretch fumbled to undo the laces of his shoes (it is for this reason native gentlemen wear elastic-sided boots), and it was a much subdued swashbuckler that, after this, appeared before the Prince. But it may possibly be that the recollection of this scene played a part in the tragedy of three years later, when the establishment, European and native, at Futtehghur, belonging to the Maharajah, were amongst the number of refugees, about 200 in all, who tried to escape in boats to join the Cawnpore garrison, and were ruthlessly shot down by the Nana's orders !

Lord Dalhousie still continued his private correspondence with my husband after our return to England. On August 10th, 1854, he wrote :

" MY DEAR LOGIN,

"Your letter of 24th June gave me very great pleasure. You have made a most favourable start in your London life, and I have no doubt all will go on agreeably upon the excellent plan you have laid down for the Maharajah. He has made a very pleasing impression on those to whom he has been introduced, several of them having already written to me to that effect. My friend, Sir George Couper,* will, I am sure, do all that his own many duties will allow him to do to help you.

" Sirdar Lena Singh has died at Benares. The Shahzadah's mother has arrived there, and wrote to me lately. It was a very civil letter, and, among other things, she protested that she had never said a word against you in her life ! †

"We are all very quiet here in India. The King of Ava is sending up an envoy to Calcutta, and Dost

---

* Comptroller of the Household to H.R.H. the Duchess of Kent, to whom were written the " Private Letters of the Marquess of Dalhousie," published by Messrs. Blackwood & Son in 1911.

† This has reference to the Ranee Duknoo's petition to the Governor-General, with regard to which he wrote to Login at the Barrackpore Palace from Government House in March, 1854 :

" MY DEAR LOGIN,—Come to breakfast if you can on Monday. There shall be a room ready for you. Of course, this is only if convenient to you. I have sent you a huge memorial from the mother of the brat you have brought, accusing you of many enormities, of which child-stealing is the least !

" Yours very truly,
" DALHOUSIE."

Mahomed is 'ettling' to be well with us at the other
side of the land. I enclose a letter for the Maharajah.

" Yours very truly,
"DALHOUSIE."

Several other letters to the same effect I found
amongst my husband's papers. In one of them written
in January, 1855, Lord Dalhousie speaks of the Queen's
favourable mention of the young Sikh ruler in her
letters to him as Viceroy.

" I have no right to consider you under my authority
at present; but you may be assured that the unrestrained correspondence between us is a real pleasure
to me. . . . If this young lad does not grow up with
right notions and principles, and well-directed sentiments,
it certainly will not be your fault ! I am very shaky,
and nearly done," he adds at the end. " I beg to offer
my most sincere congratulations to Lady Login, which I
omitted to do before, when I wrote to congratulate *you*.*

" Believe me, my dear Login, yours, etc.,
"DALHOUSIE."

When Lord and Lady Dalhousie were with us at
Futtehghur in December, 1851, shortly after the birth
of my youngest boy " Harry," and learnt that the boy
was god-son of, and named after, Sir Henry Lawrence
(between whom and the Governor-General, though
both men of undoubted piety, strong character, and
intense patriotism, there was a strange sentiment of
antagonism), the Viceroy turned to my husband with
the remark : ," Now, remember, Login, *I* am god-
father to the next child ! "

It was not till a long time after that occasion arose
to remember this mandate of the Governor-General

* Dr. Login had received the honour of knighthood from H.M. Queen Victoria
in November, 1854.

—when given, tantamount to a royal " Command ! "— and by then we had been some while domiciled in Scotland, and the Maharajah, a Christian of some years' standing, asserted his superior claim to stand sponsor to the infant, as born absolutely in his house ! Moreover, just to complicate matters, instead of the expected boy, which would have permitted of two god-fathers, the new arrival had the effrontery to make her appearance in the feminine gender ! I can tell you, we were a little nonplussed how to get over the difficulty, which was finally adjusted by making the Maharajah Duleep Singh the god-father, and giving to the little girl the *names* of her self-nominated sponsor, the Viceroy, and of his younger daughter, Lady Edith Christian Ramsay, who afterwards married Sir James Fergusson of Kilkerran—viz., " Edith Dalhousie Login." The godmothers were the Countess of Leven and Melville, and Lady Hatherton, from whose house at Teddesley the christening took place, in Penkridge parish church, Salop.

I think the last letter that my husband had from Lord Dalhousie was written from Moore's Hotel in Edinburgh, on October 3rd, 1857, when he was on the point of sailing for Malta in search of a warmer climate for the winter. He speaks of the tidings from India as being " too distressing to write of, though they occupy one's thoughts by day and by night," and signs himself " ever yours very truly, DALHOUSIE." *

---

* It was naturally with the greatest interest that I watched for the publication of Lord Dalhousie's Private Letters, which it was known were by his directions not be to published till fifty years after his death. There are direct allusions in it to Sir John Login, and other subjects mentioned above, and one or two other references, under an initial only, which to one acquainted with dates and particulars are unmistakable.

CHAPTER IX

WE saw Egypt under very advantageous circumstances on our way home, as, by Lord Dalhousie's directions, Mr. Bruce showed every attention to the Maharajah's party, and the Viceroy, Ibrahim Pasha, placed carriages and horses at our disposal to view the sights. Nothing would serve Duleep Singh but to organise a race to the top of the Pyramid with his companions, much to the disgust of the Arab guides, who had scented unlimited *backshish*. They had their innings, however, when he inspected the interior; mauling, dragging, and hustling him to their heart's content in the pitchy darkness of the tomb; so that, what with heat, foul air, smell of the torches, and swarms of ill-odorous followers of the Prophet, he was relieved to find himself emerge whole, and with all his pearl necklaces intact !

Those same necklaces were a source of constant anxiety to himself and his attendants. He had long adopted a semi-European style of dress, and wore his full native dress, with all its splendid jewels, only when he went to Court. He still continued, however, in his daily attire to wear the Sikh turban, generally with a jewelled aigrette and other jewels, and was never without the three rows of enormous pearls round his neck, and a pair of large emerald and pearl earrings. It was not till some years later that he fully adopted English dress.

Unlike the usual conception of an Asiatic, the Maharajah had a keen sense of the ludicrous, and used to give way to extraordinary paroxysms of laughter, in which he threw himself about, and indulged in violent antics. Again and again, in these convulsions, has he broken the strings of his necklaces and sent the pearls flying all over the room, so that one of the most arduous and unpleasant duties of his confidential servant was to enter the apartment on these occasions, after his master had retired, and search under every chair, table, and sofa, for the stray gems, the value of which might have even tempted a fair lady to conceal one under her spreading crinoline !

While still in Indian waters, the regulation official salute was given him, by the Governor-General's orders, on the vessel conveying him dropping anchor ; but there was unconcealed satisfaction visible in his countenance when he found the full twenty-one guns awarded him by the military authorities at Malta and Gibraltar, —the first Indian prince to be so acknowledged by the English Government.

This subject was finally set at rest after he had been some little time in England, and received at Windsor, by Her Majesty deciding that his rank was to be the same as that of a European prince, and as chief of the native princes of India, he took precedence next after the Royal Family.*

Just before this announcement was publicly made, a large dinner-party had been arranged in honour of Duleep Singh at the house of Sir Robert Inglis, the Primate (Archbishop Longley), Lord Shaftesbury, and

* Letter from Sir Charles Phipps, Private Secretary to Queen Victoria, to Dr. Login :

" OSBORNE, *August* 14*th*, 1854.
"You are probably aware that, after deliberation, Her Majesty has been advised that the Maharajah is entitled in this country to the same rank and precedence as an European prince."

other notables being invited to meet him. Poor Sir Robert was greatly exercised how to settle the knotty point, and came in great distress to consult my husband on the matter. With what a shout of laughter did the Maharajah receive the suggestion of Sir Robert, that he and the Archbishop should proceed arm-in-arm to the dining-room, and how eagerly he offered to give the *pas* to the Primate, with the remark: "I shall be delighted! *Now* the Archbishop will have to take the *oldest* lady present, and this time surely I may please myself? I always get such old ladies!" His face of dismay when, on arrival at the house, a *second old lady* was brought up to him was truly comical!

Sir Robert, no doubt, had anticipated more difficulty, knowing what sticklers for precedence and etiquette are the native potentates—and indeed all the official classes in India—where these matters are very rigidly legislated for. Anyhow, Duleep Singh came out of the ordeal more gracefully than a certain lady—known to me by name—in one of the large stations there. The story was one well known in Government circles when I was in India, and was told me by more than one within earshot of the incident. Her husband was an official of such high position that, in spite of her want of breeding, she was assigned to the Governor-General as partner for the supper at a ball given in his honour. This selection aroused the ire of the lady appointed to the next official in rank present, who, thinking to abash her rival, said sneeringly, in a stage-aside to her companion, as they followed close behind: "Doesn't the *honest woman* look proud of her exalted position?" But the furious retort launched at her instantly, in strident tones, overwhelmed both her and the company. "No more an 'honest woman' than you are—so *there!!*"

His zeal for truth, and disapproval of " polite lies,"
were sometimes unsparingly displayed at this time. At
a large dinner given in his honour by a General just
returned from high command in India, where he had
already met Duleep Singh, the hostess pressed the
Maharajah to take some curry she had had specially
made for him. She went on to say that no doubt it
was very inferior to what he was accustomed to, but she
trusted, in that case, that he would honestly tell her
if it was not good? The poor boy had been politely
endeavouring to swallow a little of the mixture, which
was certainly very unlike an Indian curry ; but when his
hostess said this, he believed she *meant* it, and, putting
down his fork and spoon with a sigh of relief, he ejacu-
lated : " Oh, you are quite right ! It is horrible !
Take it away ! " The dismay of the hostess may be
conceived ! She thought herself an authority on
Indian dishes, and this was the *plat* of the occasion !

His candour and straightforwardness made him a
great favourite with Queen Victoria and the Prince
Consort, and his outspoken comments on things in
general seemed especially amusing to the Prince, who
delighted in drawing him out, and making him talk
freely to him. He was very frequently invited to Windsor and Osborne, the first visit to the latter residence
taking place in August, 1854, and intercourse and
correspondence encouraged between the royal princes
and Duleep Singh. They frequently exchanged drawings to show their progress in this accomplishment, and
compared notes about their studies, and I have in my
possession now pencil sketches done at this period by
the then Prince of Wales (King Edward VII.) and
Prince Alfred, Duke of Saxe-Coburg-Gotha. The very
greatest interest was always taken in the Maharajah's

education and well-being, by the Queen and Prince Consort; the latter recommended the teachers and professors he was to have—Professors Bentley and Becker for science and German, Dr. Edward Rimbault and W. G. Cusins for music, for which the Maharajah showed an undoubted aptitude, and an enthusiastic devotion. He was engaged in writing and producing an opera just before his final departure from England, and presented me with the libretto.

The Queen showed her solicitude for his health in many ways, and I shall not easily forget the concern she exhibited when she learnt from me that the Maharajah, in spite of our entreaties, and the representations made to him of the danger in our English climate, stoutly refused to wear woollen underclothing. " I shall speak to him myself, Lady Login ! " she said, when I urged that perhaps he might consent if he knew it was her wish, and she called him to her across the room. But, no ! Even to her he was adamant on this point, and she had to waive the point finally on his reply : " Indeed, Ma'am, I cannot bear the feel of flannel next to my skin. It makes me long to scratch, and you would not like to see me scratching myself in your presence ! ! " Her Majesty's face was a picture, but the boy (for he was nothing more) had no conception *at that time* how his words sounded in English ears—he, who was in every way the pink of good manners ! But it will be conceived that after that remark of his the subject was hurriedly dropped !

Presents were exchanged on their birthdays between him and the Royal Family, and many letters of the princes' tutor, Mr. Gibbs, refer to this. A cage of fifty birds was sent on one occasion by the Maharajah to the Prince of Wales, and a trick-ring to Prince Alfred

Presents of Sikh armour, native dresses and hangings, richly embroidered in gold and silver, were sent also by Duleep Singh, and in these costumes the princes were photographed by their father, who was one of the first and keenest of amateur photographers, and imbued the Maharajah with the same hobby. In return, the Queen and princes sent gifts, including a horse from the royal stables, a clock, Christmas-pie, game, and case of Tangerine oranges, at Christmas, from Her Majesty, a roe deer shot by himself from the Prince Consort, and a silver-mounted microscope from the two elder Princes. It was with reference to this last present that Mr. Gibbs was commissioned to write to my husband, to ask for a sketch of the Maharajah's *coat-of-arms!* *
His arms were in the end worked out for him by the Prince Consort, who was an authority on these matters, though Continental heraldry differs from English in many points.

Duleep Singh was very much charmed and gratified by the delightful *camaraderie* of the young princesses. They invited him, with their brothers, to make proof of their skill as cooks at the Swiss Châlet in the Osborne grounds, where a very complete kitchen was fitted up for them. The young princes, however, after the manner of boys, spurned the idea that a girl could cook a potato ! and in order to exhibit their superiority, in that line, installed themselves in the kitchen, turning the key on the real proprietresses, who were reduced to hurling contemptuous criticisms, in dumb show, through the bolted windows ! · Duleep Singh basely revelled in this

* I see that Lord Dalhousie ("Private Letters &c.," p. 320) made great fun of the idea of an Eastern monarch having Western armorial bearings ; but as a matter of fact, most Orientals have a hankering after the symbols of heraldry, and both Runjeet Singh and Shere Singh, Duleep Singh's father and brother, had blazoned coats-of-arms made out by French heralds. Of these I possess authentic copies, as well as that of the King of Oude.

HIS ROYAL HIGHNESS THE PRINCE OF WALES (HIS MAJESTY KING EDWARD VII.).

very ungallant escapade, and as he loved above all
things to dabble with pots and pans, so he was proud of
the fact, that it was *his* practical knowledge that made
a perfect success of the disputed *plat!*

The extraordinary kindness of heart and thought-
fulness for others of the Prince of Wales (our late
lamented sovereign) was seen even in these early years.
It was about this same period that he came, with Prince
Alfred and Mr. Gibbs, to visit the Maharajah at Ash-
burton House, Roehampton. They were all keen on
playing cricket, when the Prince of Wales learnt that
my eldest son, an Eton school-boy, was confined to his
room with a cold, and bitterly disappointed at not being
able to play with the princes as he had hoped to do.
Nothing would serve His Royal Highness but to leave
the cricket field immediately, and, since he was not
permitted to visit the invalid in his room, stand for
half-an-hour under his open window, exchanging
opinions and school-boy confidences. Is it any wonder
that, in after days, his people loved him so ? Moreover,
to give pleasure to the enforced prisoner, the royal
brothers arranged to submit themselves to be photographed by Duleep Singh on the lawn, in full view of the
windows ; and those photographs, you may be sure,
are now treasured possessions with me ! Duleep Singh
had already, with the Prince Consort's assistance, taken
several negatives at Osborne of the royal children,
in fancy dress and in his Indian costumes. ·

H.R.H. Prince Alfred (Grand-Duke of Saxe-Coburg-
Gotha) was shyer than his elder brother, and, on one
occasion, considerably nonplussed by my little boy,
Harry, aged five years, who marched boldly up to him,
on being presented, exhibiting a pair of new shoes, of
which he was inordinately proud, and demanding

pointedly—" Does *your* mama give you as nice shoes as these ? "

It was that same eldest boy of mine—also named " Edward "—who, a year or two later, was always twitted by the family for the extraordinary manner in which he did the honours to royalty, in the person of the Princess Mary (the late Duchess of Teck) in his father's absence. We were then all living in one of the Queen's houses at Kew, next door to Cambridge House. An epidemic of " mumps " broke out, and the whole family, except Sir John, who was away, and my boy Edwy, were laid low with it. One afternoon unexpectedly Princess Mary came to the door, and the butler was ushering her upstairs when, knowing the horror of the Royal Family for any possible infectious disorder of the throat, and in quarantine myself, I bade Edwy fly and meet her at the door, to give her warning. He tore down at break-neck speed, but was so flabbergasted at meeting her face to face on the stairs, that all his manners, and his carefully prepared message, fled from him, and he could only gasp out : " M-m-m-mumps, your Royal Highness ! " For an instant she gazed in consternation, thinking the boy had lost his wits ; then his meaning flashing on her, she turned and fled incontinently, down the stairs and out of the house, while peal after peal of that cheery, ringing laugh of hers, that all who had ever heard never forgot, came in gusts from the far distance ! The very sight of the boy after that was enough to restart her laughter !

Church House and Cambridge House adjoined so closely that the windows of one wing of the former actually overlooked the royal garden, and though I strictly forbade any of our household to look out in that direction, we could not help hearing our dear

Princess Mary's voice and laugh, when romping and playing with her nephews and nieces, and her constant calls for " Dolf ! " or " Dolly ! " her favourite—the present Grand-Duke of Mecklenburg-Strelitz, I believe ? —rather a preternaturally solemn and stolid child. All the royal residences had private doors into Kew Gardens, and at the hours when the public were excluded we used them as if they were our own grounds. Often did we meet Princess Mary racing round with a nephew carried pick-a-back, and the old Duchess of Cambridge taking her airing in her pony-chair. She was once greatly diverted by my little girl, aged three, whom she stopped to speak to. The child made her curtsey dutifully, as bidden by her nurse, but stoutly refused to relinquish the slice of bread-and-butter she was at the moment engaged upon, and with great solemnity waved it in the Duchess's face, while going through the evolution !

A coachman who was in our service at Kew, and afterwards in London, named William Turley, was recommended by my husband to Sir Dighton Probyn, V.C., and ultimately became private coachman to the Princess of Wales (Queen Alexandra).

He was a very honest, trustworthy man, but I often wondered whether, in the royal service, he made out his accounts in the original fashion he used to do with us ! He had an unbounded talent for phonetic spelling. His first monthly stable bill puzzled my husband not a little ! On the left-hand side of the paper appeared a column of figures, and on the right-hand side a row of capital " A " 's !

" What does this mean, Turley ? " asked Sir John.

" That's A, Sir John ! "

" So I see. But what is ' A ' for ? "

"'Ay for the 'osses, Sir John!'" said honest William, with an inflection of reproachful surprise at his master's denseness.

If Princess Mary's laugh was infectious, no one had a keener sense of the ludicrous than my beloved mistress, Queen Victoria. I shall never forget the first drawing-room after the Duchess of Kent's death. For my sins, I had to present a certain Lady D——. Scarcely had I entered the throne-room, and heard her name announced in front of me, when, to my horror, I saw her whisk round in Her Majesty's face, and tear back the way she had come, into the gallery behind, of course turning her back on the Sovereign and everyone! all present staring in petrifaction, the pages racing after her with their staves, frantically trying to hook up her train, as it swung from side to side, nearly upsetting the bystanders, while a long tail of false hair, which I had vainly striven to pin up for her in the entrance hall, became again unfixed and streamed wildly in the air, making her look more than ever like a madwoman. Picture my consternation and annoyance!

But how the Queen and the Prince Consort laughed! As, overwhelmed with confusion, I was making my curtsey, Her Majesty, shaking with merriment, whispered: "What is the matter with your friend, Lady Login? What did she take us *for*?" And the only excuse the silly idiot could offer, when I asked her what she meant by her behaviour, was, "Oh, it was so awful to see them all in black!"

Perhaps the most interesting episode in which I was concerned with Her Majesty took place about this time.

The Maharajah, by the Queen's desire, gave sittings to Mr. Winterhalter for a full-length picture by that artist, which now, I believe, hangs in the gallery at

Buckingham Palace. He was then about sixteen or seventeen years of age and a very handsome youth, slight and graceful. Mr. Winterhalter, wishing the picture to be a permanent portrait of the young Oriental prince in his full dress, has given to the sitter the height he judged he would attain when he reached manhood. This calculation unfortunately proved incorrect, as the Maharajah never grew any taller than he then was.

The sittings took place at Buckingham Palace; the Queen and Prince Consort were much interested in the progress of the work, and frequently visited the room arranged as a studio. My husband or I usually accompanied the Maharajah.

On one of these occasions, when the painter was engaged on the details of the jewels that Duleep Singh was wearing, Her Majesty took the opportunity to speak to me aside on the subject of the Koh-i-noor, which had only recently been returned to her out of the hands of the Amsterdam diamond-cutters, and, of course, was greatly changed in size, shape and lustre. She had not yet worn it in public, and, as she herself remarked, had a delicacy about doing so in the Maharajah's presence.

" Tell me, Lady Login, does the Maharajah ever mention the Koh-i-noor ? Does he seem to regret it, and would he like to see it again ? Find out for me before the next sitting, and mind you let me know *exactly* what he says ! "

Little did Her Majesty guess the perturbation into which her command threw a loyal subject! How thankful I was that the second query followed close on, and covered up the first, which would have been most embarrassing to answer truthfully, as there was no other subject that so filled the thoughts and con-

versation of the Maharajah, his relatives and dependants! For the confiscation of the jewel which to the
Oriental is the symbol of the sovereignty of India,
rankled in his mind even more than the loss of his
kingdom, and I dreaded what sentiments he might
give vent to were the subject once re-opened!

The time passed, and no good opportunity arose of
sounding him on the matter, till the very day before the
next sitting was due, when, as we were riding together
in Richmond Park, in desperation, I ventured to turn
the conversation round to the altered appearance that
the cutting was said to have given to the famous
" mountain of light," and remarked, as casually as I
could, " would he have any curiosity to see it now in its
new form ? "   " Yes, indeed I would ! " he affirmed
emphatically ; " I would give a good deal to hold it
again in my own hand ! " This reply, knowing how
keen were his feelings on the matter, startled me considerably, and it was in much trepidation that I asked
the reason for this great desire on his part ? " Why ? "
was his answer. " Why, because I was but a child, an
infant, when forced to surrender it by treaty ; but now
that I am a man, I should like to have it in my power to
place it myself in her hand ! "

I cannot tell you my delight and relief at his answer,
and, lest he should add anything that might qualify
or spoil such a charming and chivalrous sentiment, I
hurriedly turned the conversation, and with a light
heart awaited the morrow's interview with Her Majesty.

She came across to me at once on entering the room,
the Maharajah being on the platform, posing for the
artist, asking eagerly if I had executed her commands ?
and right glad I was to be able to give his answer. The
Queen seemed as pleased as I had been at Duleep Singh's

response to my question, and, signalling to the Prince
Consort, who was engaged in conversation with the
painter at the other end of the room, they held a hurried
consultation in whispers, despatching one of the gentle-
men-in-waiting with a message. For about half-an-
hour they both remained, watching the progress of the
portrait and conversing with those present, when a
slight bustle near the door made me look in that direction, and behold, to my amazement, the gorgeous
uniforms of a group of beef-eaters from the Tower,
escorting an official bearing a small casket, which he
presented to Her Majesty. This she opened hastily,
and took therefrom a small object which, still holding,
she showed to the Prince, and, both advancing together
to the daïs, the Queen cried out, " Maharajah, I have
something to show you ! " Turning hastily—for, in
the position he was in, his back was towards the actors
in this little scene—Duleep Singh stepped hurriedly
down to the floor, and, before he knew what was happening, found himself once more with the Koh-i-noor in
his grasp, while the Queen was asking him " if he thought
it improved, and if he would have recognised it again ? "

Truth to tell, at first sight, no one who had known it
before would have done so, diminished to half its size, and
thereby, in Oriental eyes, reft of much of its association
and symbolism. That this was what he felt I am inwardly
convinced ; yet, as he walked with it towards the
window, to examine it more closely, turning it hither and
thither, to let the light upon its facets, and descanting
upon its peculiarities and differences, and the skill of
the diamond-cutter, for all his air of polite interest and
curiosity, there was a passion of repressed emotion in
his face, patent to one who knew him well, and evident,
I think, to Her Majesty, who watched him with sym-

pathy not unmixed with anxiety—that I may truly say, it was to me one of the most excruciatingly uncomfortable quarters-of-an-hour that I ever passed! For an awful terror seized me, lest I had unwittingly deceived Her Majesty as to his intentions, seeing him stand there turning and turning that stone about in his hands, as if unable to part with it again, now he had it once more in his possession !

At last, as if summoning up his resolution after a profound struggle, and with a deep sigh, he raised his eyes from the jewel, and—just as the tension on my side was near breaking-point, so that I was prepared for almost anything—even to seeing him, in a sudden fit of madness, fling the precious talisman out of the open window by which he stood ! and the other spectators' nerves were equally on edge—he moved deliberately to where Her Majesty was standing, and, with a deferential reverence, placed in her hand the famous diamond, with the words : " It is to me, Ma'am, the greatest pleasure thus to have the opportunity, as a loyal subject, of *myself* tendering to *my Sovereign* the Koh-i-noor ! " Whereupon he quietly resumed his place on the daïs, and the artist continued his work.

Of all those present on that memorable occasion, I believe that I am the sole survivor, for the late Lady Ely, the Lady-in-Waiting, was the only other lady there, and both Sir Charles Phipps and the equerry are dead. The officer and escort from the Tower had already left the room.

In 1889, one of my daughters, when in Amsterdam, had the privilege of being taken over the factory of the diamond-cutting firm that did the work, having an introduction to the partners from a leading financier in the Dutch capital, and heard from them all the details

HIS HIGHNESS THE MAHARAJAH DULEEP SINGH.

f the process. Her introducer, Monsieur O——, who
vas really only a chance acquaintance, gave her the
mpression of being, for a man of such mark in the world
f finance, extraordinarily incautious and outspoken to
. stranger and foreigner, such as she was. The Boer
Republics were already giving trouble, and he spoke
quite frankly of the support given them in Holland,
ven to mentioning his own share in it. But when he
vent on to boast of how he had induced Prince Bismarck
o put pressure on the Portuguese Government, some
wo years back, to seize the Delagoa Bay Railway, even
o the naming of dates, and quoting of the words of
he telegrams that passed, she began to wonder if it
:ould all be "bluff," or whether he was actually pre-
uming on her supposed ignorance of foreign and
:olonial politics, since it explained much that she knew
lad puzzled our Foreign Office at the time ? As it
lappened, she knew about the Delagoa Railway busi-
1ess, and the muddle England had made of all her
nterests in that part of Africa. My friend Colonel
Malleson was executor for the late South African
nagnate who had financed the project, and he was
greatly bewildered at Portugal's sudden *volte-face*.
This information, when passed on to him and then
:o the Foreign Office, laid bare the whole intrigue.
Monsieur O—— was a strange mixture ! In the same
:onversation he spoke of Germany's deliberate policy
(even then) to absorb Holland, and gravely assured her
:hat the Dutch people were only longing for England
:o counter this by annexing them herself ! It was their
)nly hope ! And all this to a chance acquaintance at
1n hotel *table-d'hôte !*

Castle Menzies, in Perthshire, the property of Sir
Robert Menzies, was taken as a residence for the

Maharajah, and he was there able to entertain as his guests many distinguished persons, among them the chief officials at the India House, and many of the Cabinet Ministers and members of the Opposition in Parliament.

Taymouth Castle was within a short distance, and constant intercourse was kept up between the two houses. Lord Breadalbane was at that time Lord Chamberlain, and entertained a succession of eminent personages to whom the Indian prince was a great object of interest. In this way we met Archbishop Tait (then Bishop of London), Dr. Samuel Wilberforce, Bishop of Oxford, Lord Clarendon, Lord Stratford de Redcliffe, and Mr. Delane, Editor of *The Times*, with whom and his successor, Mr. G. W. Dasent, my husband kept up an interesting correspondence during and after the Mutiny.

With the Earl of Shaftesbury, the philanthropist, Login was on very friendly terms, and many were the notes inviting him to St. Giles for " Indian talks," as Lord Shaftesbury called them, when they discussed the best policy to be pursued in that dependency of the British Crown, including the famous " Oude Proclamation," and the question of education for the natives.

I mentioned, some time back, Sir William Sleeman's injunctions to the Maharajah to remember, if ever he visited the county of Kent, that the inhabitants of that part of England were of the same race as the Jâts, who people the Punjab, and that he and they equally descend from the *Getae* of the Greeks and Romans. He had an opportunity of bearing this in mind when the Ex-Governor-General, Lord Hardinge, who had treated him and his people with such generosity and consideration in the First Sikh War, asked our whole party to stay with him at South Park, near Penshurst. The Maharajah's horses were sent down beforehand, so that we were able to take many rides about, and thoroughly explore the whole neighbourhood.

Lord Hardinge was then Commander-in-Chief in England, in succession to the Duke of Wellington, and a fine, hale-looking old man, with the remarkable bright-blue eyes peculiar to his family. He received with a grand, old-world courtesy, the ex-Sovereign, whose armies he had vanquished in three bloody and hardly-contested fights, in which the British troops were perilously near defeat, yet whose crown and kingdom he had magnanimously spared.

This had been Duleep Singh's first impression of English country life, while he was still residing at Roehampton; but later on he accompanied us to Scotland for a short visit, before his residence at Castle Menzies was decided on, and from Edinburgh, we went for a few days to stay with the Earl and Countess of Morton at Dalmahoy, and, on the return journey, stopped at Hickleton Hall in Yorkshire, with Sir Charles Wood (afterwards Lord Halifax), aslo at Wentworth, with Earl Fitzwilliam, and at Teddesley, Lord Hatherton's place in Staffordshire, so that he very soon became acquainted with the homes of the English nobility.

Later on, both he and ourselves were to pay many visits to Teddesley, and on one of them, on the occasion of the christening of my little daughter, we were much amused at the arrangements in the family pew at Penkridge Church, which was furnished as a *drawing-room*, with easy chairs and a regular fire-place! As soon as the sermon commenced, to the scandalised horror of my children, his lordship got up, carefully drew all the curtains round, so that the congregation could not look in (the clergyman alone, mounted in the pulpit, had a view over the top of the screen), poked the fire vigorously, took his stand on the hearth-rug with his back to it, pulled *The Times* out of his pocket, and read it steadily throughout the discourse, turning over the sheets with a great rustle when he thought the preacher ought to come to an end !

This sort of arrangement was not unusual in those days, for Sir Edward Cust, when proposing to show the Maharajah Claremont House, in April, 1856—" The French Royal Family are away, and I am sure the King of the Belgians would be pleased "—suggested that he should go down on the Sunday to Esher Church to attend the morning service at eleven o'clock. " The Royal Closet might interest the Prince, as it is all panelled in cedar and painted, and is entered by a separate door and staircase, so that H.H. might arrive at any time of the service (!) "

The Royal pew at Kew, where later on we were allotted one of the Queen's houses, was very much on the same lines. A special staircase led up to a corridor, off which opened three doors, the centre—folding ones, surmounted by the Royal coat-of-arms—led into the Royal pew, occupied by the late Duchess of Cambridge and her children. The one on the left was given to H.R.H.'s equerry and family, and the other to ourselves and party. These three formed the gallery at the west end of the church, and were exactly like the boxes now in the Albert Hall, separated by low balustrades upholstered in crimson velvet, over which, I regret to say, my children were frequently detected climbing !

Our residence at Kew was not in consequence of my husband's position as Guardian and Superintendent of the Establishment of the Maharajah, but connected with an appointment which I held personally from H.M. Queen Victoria, and of whcih I shall have more to say presently.

We were there under the *ægis* of the Lord Chamberlain's Department, by whom the house was furnished for us, down to the details of glass and crockery.

Church House, Kew, was next door to Cambridge House, the residence of Queen Victoria's aunt by marriage, and numerous were the neighbourly kindnesses we received from her household, and the acts of consideration shown by the Duchess and the Princess.

I was still an invalid when we first went into residence, and immediately Baron Knesebeck was commissioned by H.R.H. to invite Sir John to dinner that evening, conditionally " on his being able to leave Lady Login without anxiety." Sir George Couper, the Duchess of Kent's equerry, was known to us from the first through the kindness of Lord Dalhousie. We therefore were the recipients of many invitations to Frogmore, and also to " small musical parties " at Clarence House, at which the Queen was sometimes present. Sir George Couper was one of those who fell a victim to the Maharajah's passion for taking portraits of all notabilities who fell in his way, though in his case the likeness was pronounced a not unflattering one.

Although Duleep Singh, to his credit, appeared to prefer the plain-speaking of his friends to the flattery of unthinking people, he would not have been human if his head had not sometimes been turned by the adula- · tion often lavished upon him by women of rank in English society. His character at this time was above reproach, and though amiable in disposition, there was naturally still underlying all a strain of indolence and indifference to suffering which is innate in the Oriental,

K 2

and which Western education only overcomes with difficulty.

An incident which occurred when the house at Castle Menzies was full of guests for the shooting brought this out in a somewhat amusing way.

There had been a great deal of " chaff " at dinner about a cat, which someone of the party had shot when discharging their guns on the way home, near the village of Weem. My husband had " hoped it wasn't a poor woman's pet ! " Duleep Singh " didn't care if it was ; it had no business there ! "

In the drawing-room afterwards, some of the ladies, discussing the affair, declared that the Maharajah had shown symptoms of a cruel disposition ; whereupon Lady Hatherton, who had an intense admiration for him, undertook to combat this idea by proving his positive gentleness and amiability, and as she was an excellent amateur actress, dressed herself for the part of the " poor woman who had lost her cat," convinced that she had only to present her story immediately to arouse his compassion.

On the entry of the gentlemen, therefore, a poor, weeping woman was found in the billiard-room, " waiting to see His Highness." So pathetically did she relate the story of the loss of her favourite and only companion, her " puir cattie," that young Alec Lawrence, Sir Henry's son, was moved almost to tears, and stepping forward, entreated her to " cry no more ! It distressed him to think of the accident. Would she accept ten shillings from him as a small compensation ? etc." This was not what Lady Hatherton wanted, so she redoubled her efforts to gain some sign from the Maharajah.

He stood unmoved, save that his eyes blazed the

while with anger. At last, losing patience, he burst out, shaking his billiard-cue in her face : " Yes, cry ! Cry till you are tired ! Don't let your brutes cross my path. Not a penny shall you get from me ! " Then, laying no gentle hand on her arm, " *Begone*, I say ! "

At this moment Lord Hatherton, recognising his wife, and thinking the joke had gone quite far enough, addressed her by name, and she, to the Maharajah's consternation, dropped her disguise, which had been so perfect that none had suspected it.

Possibly the contrast between his own conduct and that of young Lawrence, might have been more apparent to Duleep Singh had he not been assured by her ladyship, when he tried to apologise for his discourtesy, that she " had only admired his princely air of command," and felt " he was every inch a king, when pointing her to the door, etc. ! "

Charades and round games were very favourite diversions in the evening, and occasionally the younger spirits indulged in regular romps. On one occasion, when I was confined to my room, and had asked a *very* elderly, and, as I imagined, most staid and proper, lady to act hostess in my place, I heard a tremendous commotion in the drawing-room after dinner ! I was told afterwards that the ladies found the dinner so boring, and the men so dull, that after the latter remained when the cloth was drawn, the former relieved their spirits by a game of " follow-my-leader " over the chairs and sofas, instigated by the aforesaid deputy of mine, Mrs. Partridge, wife of the Queen's portrait painter, who must have been well over sixty at the time, but very light and agile ! She had vaulted over the back of a wide " Chesterfield " with ease ; but Lady Gomm, wife of the Field-Marshal, an enormous

woman, and of a masterful disposition, had attempted
to follow, got stuck on the top, and it required the
united efforts of the whole party of ladies to get her
hauled off again, just as the door opened and the
gentlemen solemnly stalked in !

A year or two after, I looked down from a gallery at
St. James's Palace, having the *entrée* for the drawing-
room, on the mob of ladies and their attendant squires
who had come in by the ordinary entrance. They were
herded together in a series of roped enclosures. Suddenly
we saw a lady (whom I recognised as Lady Gomm), in
defiance of the gentlemen-at-arms, gather up her train
and fallals most skilfully, take a run, and deftly clear
one of the barriers, all standing ! her diminutive husband, in full uniform, creeping under the ropes, unable
to emulate the hardihood of his " Commander-in-
Chief ! " The incident was portrayed in the following
week's *Punch*. Evidently her ladyship had gone into
training since her former performance !

CHAPTER X

You can imagine what the news of the Indian Mutiny
meant to us! All our dearest friends were involved,
and we had been for so many years, and so lately,
living in the very district where it showed itself in its
worst form. With what breathless interest we watched
the struggle for the defence of the Residency at Lucknow, every foot of which was so familiar to us!

Thinking we were to be only for two years, at the
most, in England, we had left, as had also the young
Maharajah, much valuable property and furniture
at Futtehghur, in the charge of the European steward,
Sergeant A. Elliott, of the Bengal Sappers, who had
been one of my husband's assistants in the Toshkhana
at Lahore.

Elliott's letters at the outbreak of the Mutiny gave
such graphic accounts of all that occurred, that Login
forwarded one or two of them to Colonel Phipps, for
the information of the Prince Consort, he being then
Private Secretary both to H.R.H. and also to H.M.
Queen Victoria. His brother Edmund had married my
first cousin.

Colonel Phipps wrote to Login, July 24th, 1857, that
these letters had aroused such interest that he was to
request that they might be forwarded as they came,
" as he could not do him a greater favour in the present
awful crisis in India, than give him the benefit of the

views and opinions of one so well acquainted with the
country as himself." Suddenly poor Elliott's letters
ceased, however, and our worst fears were confirmed!
He, his wife and children, Mr. Walter Guise, the Maharajah's tutor, together with the other European residents of Futtehghur, to the number of over two hundred,
had started in boats for Cawnpore, just a few days before
its capitulation and the Massacre, and were fallen upon
and slaughtered by the Nana's men before they got
there. All our subsequent knowledge came from
Bhajun Lal, the Brahmin, who remained loyal to the
British Government, and did his utmost to save the
residue of the Maharajah's property and servants. From
him and from our friends amongst the native nobility,
we had information not easily accessible to most
Europeans.

I can never express the grief we felt when the tragedy
culminated in the loss of that brave and gentle spirit
Sir Henry Lawrence, whose wisdom and strength of
purpose was the rallying-point of the defence of the
British Government, in Oude and the North-West
Provinces, and who had been named by the Home
authorities (such was the confidence felt in his personal
magnetism and sway over the minds of the natives),
though the order never reached his hands, provisional
Governor-General of India, in the event of any misfortune overtaking the actual Viceroy. Struck by a
stray bullet at the post of danger, he was carried in to
die in the very house in which he had so often been our
guest, and on the verandah of which he and my husband
had used to pass hours elaborating schemes for the welfare of the native regiments, and the better government
of the Indian Empire!

Much of Login's time was taken up in answering ques-

tions from public men and officials in England, whose
ignorance on Indian affairs often made them estimate
wrongly the consequences of the different measures
taken by the military and civil authorities. In particular he was at much pains to disabuse Mr. John Bright,
whose interest he specially desired to arouse, as an
advocate for sympathetic legislation, and better educational advantages in India, of certain misconceived
ideas he had formed of the native character, and also
of a circumscribed and commercial view of the object
of our rule in India.

John Bright wrote from Rochdale in September,
1857, that he was " oppressed by the magnitude of the
Indian question. The cruelties perpetrated by the
Sepoys, and the scarcely less horrid cruelties inflicted
by our countrymen, under the name of punishment or
vengeance, will leave a desperate wound, which time
can never heal. . . . The loss of India would not ruin
England, but the effort and the cost of keeping it may
do so ; and the crimes we have committed there must
be atoned for, in some shape, by ourselves or our children. . . . " He signed himself, as ever in his cordial
way, " always very sincerely yours, JOHN BRIGHT."

My husband, in reply, pointed out that these atrocities
were not of uncommon occurrence in the East, in countries to which our influence had not extended, and
although the dread of consequences under our rule had
prevented their manifestation in our own dominions,
there was scarcely, he averred, a man, woman, or child
among them· to whose imagination they were not
perfectly familiar.

But he was more anxious to induce Mr. Bright, instead
of bewailing past and gone misdeeds of the Indian
Government, to concentrate his energies in, and out of,

Parliament, on correcting existing evils, of which he considered the faulty system of education, or rather *no* education, of our native subjects, and especially of the absurdly large native army we maintained, was one of the chief.

In the same way, we had evaded our responsibilities with regard to the princes and chiefs of India, paying them pensions greater than the revenues of many European States, which we allowed them to squander in all forms of extravagance, idleness and vice, and never insisted that their children and dependents should be properly educated, and they themselves fulfil their duties as rulers. It was thus we had bred up for our own undoing the infamous Nana Sahib, the miserable old Mogul Emperor, and swarm of Delhi princes. We had had in our hands, as Paramount State, but had never exercised, the "right of presentation," whereby the Delhi Emperors claimed to control the succession in all the minor principalities, only allowing a fit person (generally a son, though not always the eldest) to occupy the "guddee" on the death of any reigning prince. Doubtless this right had in later times been regarded chiefly as a source of revenue, by making it possible to exact a heavy *nuzzur*, or tribute, from the successor who received the *sumnud* of election ; but it also made it simpler for the Padishah, if he chose, to absorb into his own dominions, with no further formality, the territory of any ruler without direct heirs.

The friendship with John Bright continued through the remaining years of my husband's life, and after his death I had frequent evidences of it on my own and my children's behalf, even up to his own last illness, when he wrote expressing his disappointment that weakness prevented his writing, as he had wished, a preface to the account of my husband's life and work, which I was then publishing.*

Amongst other people whose good offices he at this time tried to enlist in the cause of India was Mr. Delane, Editor of *The Times*, and later, Mr. G. W. Dasent, of the same paper. To the former he wrote on the subject of the use of the Roman character in Oriental languages, in which Lord Shaftesbury and Sir Charles Trevelyan were much interested, and on Indian finance and other matters.

At that period, you must remember, no other officer of the East India Company had been brought into such constant and personal contact with the Court. In consequence of this, and of his intimacy with Colonel the Hon. Sir Charles Phipps, my husband became the medium of communicating unofficially various views and opinions of Indian officers on the crisis.

It was thus that there originated a long, and very confidential, correspondence on Indian affairs between my husband and Her Majesty's Private Secretary, which led to his being asked for hints as to future policy and the need of reform in various departments. Login warmly defended the civil administration of the Company's government, urging that under it 'the native population were more contented and had enjoyed more peace and prosperity than ever known in their previous annals, and contended that the attacks made upon it in Parliament by men capable only of seeing things from an English point of view, and full of prejudice against the Company's rule, had so aroused the loyalty of the Company's servants that they were inclined to screen *any* defects that admitted of improvement, while the *really* weak point in the Company's adminis-

* " Sir John Login and Duleep Singh."

tration, which was at the bottom of all the trouble, viz., the false policy pursued towards the native army, was hardly ever alluded to by these Parliamentary critics !

He suggested the reduction in numbers of native, and the increase of European, corps. That the latter should not be solely dependent on native commissariat contractors, and should be placed in charge of the arsenals, that camps for them be formed at hill stations, where they might be fully equipped to take the field at short notice. That the native army should contain a due proportion of men of all castes (not high-caste *only* as heretofore), and that in every company there should be an admixture of Sikhs, Goorkas and Mahommedans, and that service beyond seas and performance of fatigue duty be included in the terms of enlistment.

It was on receiving these suggestions that Sir Charles Phipps wrote :

" Though overwhelmed with business, as you may suppose, during the visit of the Emperor and Empress "— his letter is dated August 7th, 1857—" I must write one line to thank you again for your *most interesting* letters, and to beg you will continue to enlighten me upon Indian affairs, which I know that you understand better than most people. . . . Have you ever turned in your mind what will be the best plan for the future formation of an efficient army in India ? "

Acting on this, Login prepared a memorandum on the re-organisation of the Indian army, which provided for the formation of a staff corps. European officers who have not passed the examination in Urdu, or who are under twenty-one years of age, to be posted to European regiments first for two years, to be well grounded in drill and discipline. Pensions to be liberally offered to induce the retirement of all officers over 35 year's service. The dress of the whole native army to be made more suitable to the climate and habits of the men, and better educational advantages offered to both the children of European non-commissioned officers and men, and to the Sepoys, if they were disposed to avail themselves of them.

Of the scheme suggested, Sir Charles made one or two criticisms, in a letter of August 18th, and remarking that it seemed to him now impossible to justify the raising of a British army in India to serve anybody but the Queen, added : " I feel confident, from what I hear and see around, that the rule of the Company is doomed . . . and I am equally convinced that the only problems now to be solved are the how and the when ! . . ." He then asks for Login's own opinion on the real origin of the Mutiny itself ?

Login, in replying to this query, pointed out that though we had in every way pampered the Sepoys, and rigorously refrained from interfering with their prejudices and caste observances, we had rigidly opposed all idea of educating their minds. The real cause of the Mutiny was, in his opinion, that the native troops were convinced that the introduction of education, railways, and telegraphs, into India, and the suppression of immoral practices, would *in time* interfere with caste customs, and that now, before it was too late, was the moment to make their stand, since they were persuaded that their loyalty was of supreme importance to the Government, who held dominion in India on their sufferance alone ! " Greased cartridges " was only a rallying-cry, serving for Hindoos and Mahommedans alike ! The older Hindustani Sepoys also resented the enlistment of new recruits for general service, and of Sikhs and Punjabis ; while the finishing stroke was the annexation of Oude, since as long as Oude was a native state, by special agreement, British Sepoys were exempt from taxation, but this grievance was not one to be put forward to the general community, and the cry of "greased cartridges" answered their purpose better !

When Sir Charles Phipps next requested my husband to state his views on the best form of Imperial Government for India, he, in obedience to this desire, drew up an elaborate scheme which provided for a department of State at home, under a Cabinet Minister, assisted by a Council, for whom he should be spokesman and responsible to Parliament, and specifying also the composition and functions of this Indian Council of State. Other details referred to the composition and powers of the Legislative Council in Calcutta, and of the reports to be laid periodically before Parliament, one of which should be "on the moral and material progress of India."

"You will not be surprised," remarks Colonel Phipps, in his voluminous reply dated Balmoral, September 14th, 1857, "that I hesitated, and took time to consider, before I attempted to enter upon a subject which you have evidently considered so deeply, and understand so well, as that of the transfer of the supreme power in India from the Directors of the East India Company to the Crown. . . . But I must thank you for the free and unrestrained manner in which you have entered upon the different subjects. Without such sincerity, a correspondence such as ours would be a waste of time. . . ."
"I have never kept copies of *my* letters, and I should be very much obliged to you if you would either let me have the originals to take copies, or have copies taken for me—not for their own value, but because *your letters lose some of their value* without those to which they are in answer. . . . "

While engaged in this correspondence with Sir Charles Phipps, Login wrote to Sir James C. Melvill, secretary to the Court of Directors, explaining to him (for the information of the Board) the circumstances under which the correspondence had arisen, and forwarding copies of all his letters as they were despatched, ending by saying :

" As I think it is not unlikely that these opinions are made known in a high quarter, although I cannot presume to think they are likely to have much weight, I consider it my duty, situated as I am, to let you know what I have done. I hope that you will, whether you approve of my opinions or not, be assured of my desire to do nothing which I cannot freely communicate to you. . . . I have also had frequent conversations with Mr. Bright on the subject of India, whilst he was here on a visit, and have done my best to modify his views. . . . From all the opportunities of observation which I have lately enjoyed, I am satisfied that the transfer of the Indian Government to the Crown has been *determined upon*, and that the *how* and the *when* have only to be considered. I have, therefore, thought it my duty to meet Colonel Phipps's wishes, by giving such information as I am able to do on various points connected with the transfer. . . . I have no doubt that I may be considered very presumptuous in all this ; but the opportunities afforded me of expressing my opinion have not been of my seeking, and I think I do right to avail myself of them."

It is gratifying to note, from the following quotation from the " Life of the Prince Consort," that the Queen attached value to Sir John Login's opinions on Indian affairs. Writing to Lord Derby (then Prime Minister) in reference to Lord Ellenborough's secret despatch to Lord Canning, April, 1858, and of his second despatch, May 5th, Her Majesty says :

"The despatch now before me, for the first time, is very good and just in principle, but the Queen would be most surprised if it did not entirely coincide with the views of Lord Canning, at least as far as he has hitherto expressed any in his letters. So are also the sentiments written by Sir John Lawrence (in a private letter which Lord Derby had sent for Her Majesty's perusal) in almost the very expressions frequently used by Lord Canning. Sir John Login, who holds the same opinion, and has great experience, does not find any fault with the proclamation, however seemingly it may sound at variance with those opinions ; and he rests this opinion on the peculiar position of affairs in Oude."

The correspondence with Sir Charles Phipps at this period was almost entirely on Indian matters. But occasional remarks on current affairs and other little pieces of information crop up. Thus, with reference to Lord Canning's Oude Proclamation, comes in this paragraph on a point of constitutional law (September 2nd, 1858) :

"In this country the Sovereign can only go a certain distance in the control or contradiction of the Government. A measure discussed and agreed to in Cabinet *can only* be rejected by the Sovereign upon such grounds as would justify a change of Ministry, which must be the result, in the event of both parties adhering resolutely to their opinions. The Government is the responsible body upon the issue of all Proclamations."

Again, on February 17th, 1857, he announces the probable date of Her Majesty's accouchement, and continues :

"There is great talk to-day of the attack upon Sir C. Lewes' budget which is to be made upon Friday by *D'Israeli and Gladstone*. I do not think, however, that the Government appears to be much alarmed as to the

THEIR ROYAL HIGHNESSES PRINCE ALFRED AND PRINCE ARTHUR IN INDIAN DRESS.

result. The visit of the young Princes to India* is only amongst the *possibilities* of future years, but is quite in an unshaped state at present, and may indeed never come to pass, though it would be a very good thing to do."

Readers of the Queen's "Journal" will remember the accident to the Princess Royal,† which occurred about this time, caused by the sleeve of her muslin dress catching fire from the candle which she was using when sealing a letter; and many were the rumours spread abroad of serious injury to her Royal Highness. The following note from the Prince of Wales was written in answer to the Maharajah's inquiries on hearing of the accident :

"BUCKINGHAM PALACE,
"*July 16th*, 1856.

" MY DEAR MAHARAJAH,

"I am very sorry to have neglected writing to you till to-day, but I have been so busy that I have not had a moment's time.

" Princess Royal's arm is a great deal better now, and she thanks you very much for having inquired after it. She really has borne it very well. A minute more and it must have proved fatal.

"I saw Sir John Login the other day, who gave me very good accounts of you. Will you remember me to him. We are going to spend two nights at the camp of Aldershot, and are then going on to the Isle of Wight.

"I remain,
"Yours affectionately,
"ALBERT EDWARD."

Shortly after the tidings of the Indian Mutiny reached this country, and while all trembled with anxiety as

---

* This is, I think, the first intimation of a project never fulfilled until twenty years had passed, and then not exactly as here suggested.

† H.I.M. the late Empress Frederick of Germany.

to what news next mail might bring, I was one morning
told that two men on horseback had arrived at the
Castle, from Kinloch, and one of them craved a private
interview on matters of importance, which he firmly
refused to communicate to any intermediary. Coming,
as they did, from the home of my childhood, I at once
sent for the man, and, on his entrance, recognised one
of my brother, General Charles Campbell's, tenants,
Donald MacCulloch, an old acquaintance, who, shutting the door cautiously, and speaking in a whisper,
said, " We just thocht we wad come ower the hill, to
see if ye were a' richt, for there's no trustin' thae black
men noo ! "

Seeing I looked puzzled, he asked, in a hoarse whisper,
pointing with his thumb over his shoulder, " Is *he*
keeping quate ? , If there's ony fear o' his brakin' oot,
there's a wheen o' us ready to come ower the hill and
sattle him for ye, gin ye gie the word ! " To his great
relief he was told that the " black Prince " had only
two native servants, and that both he and they were
very peaceably disposed—would he like to see the
Prince ? he had been in that room only a few minutes
ago.

The poor man absolutely jumped ! " What ! is he
loose ? I never saw but ae black man in my life, and
that was yer uncle Sir Patrick's naygro, carrying his
bag on the moors. I was but a laddie then, but I
still shake when I mind o' the Admiral cryin' on me,
'Donald, here's *auld Clootie* wi' his poke come for ye ! ' "

Knowing how the Maharajah would appreciate the
joke that fifty Highlanders were preparing to " stalk "
him, in the event of his showing symptoms of " rising "
on his own account, I went in search of him, to break
to him what was in store, and to request him to assure

the man, by his peaceable demeanour, that he had for the present no intention of running *amok*, and single-handed attempting to massacre the forty-odd other inmates of the Castle! He promptly fell into such convulsions of laughter that he could hardly speak, and really nearly gave the man a fit in sheer terror, by tumbling headlong into the room, rolling his eyes, and gnashing his teeth at him, in the interval of his explosions of mirth, while he kept on reassuring him in faultless English, far better than his own, that "he really wasn't a cannibal! and was quite harmless!"

The brave Donald gradually recovered his equanimity when he discovered that the Prince was very little "blacker" than himself, and finally went off home quite happy, *on foot*, having made a capital bargain and sold his sturdy little black mare to the Maharajah for an excellent price.

CHAPTER XI

My husband found that as, according to native ideas, Duleep Singh was already of marriageable age when he first came under his care, it behoved him to lose no time in setting on foot enquiries for a suitable *partie* for his ward.

In June, 1850, he heard of a native Princess who appeared to be just the very thing he was seeking. The ex-Rajah of Coorg, who since his deposition had been residing at Benares (even then a sort of head-quarters for political prisoners of rank), had two or three daughters, one of whom—the child of his favourite wife, now dead—he was especially devoted to ; and as he was a great admirer of English manners and ways of living, and had complete control over the child's up-bringing, she being motherless, he had asked for and obtained permission to send her to England for her education.

From many quarters, including Major W. M. Stewart, Agent in charge of the native Princes at Benares, Sir C. Macgregor at Lahore, and members of the Viceroy's staff, Login heard eulogistic descriptions of this little Princess of eight years of age ! He was told she was of very fair complexion, and extremely good-looking (her mother had been of Circassian extraction), with every indication of high lineage, and intelligent. She was habitually attired in English dress, and looked exactly like an European. She had not been brought up in caste observance, and was accustomed to take meals with the English officials and their families. Lord Dalhousie himself had been rather attracted by a younger sister of hers, only six years of age, who was an exceedingly pretty child. But she was being brought up in native style, and wore native dress, and ultimately became a wife of Jung Bahadour.

The Rajah of Coorg was himself much liked by Englishmen, for whom he had a great admiration ; but for that very reason was regarded with disfavour by his own countrymen. He was considered to have failed in his duties as a parent, according to Hindoo ideas, as he had not yet married off an elder daughter, who was already twenty years of age, and though popular with the civilian officials, they considered him " a mere child in the ways of the world," because of this openly-avowed intention of his of having this daughter educated in England, presumably as a Christian, in order that she might marry an English *nobleman !* for he quite recognised that by crossing the " kala-pani," and breaking her caste, she would be entirely debarred from marriage in India. Such a notion, it was thought, was proof of mental aberration !

Coorg is a mountain principality in the south-west of India, of which the capital was known as Mudda-. kerry, or Mercara, and the Rajah had a private and special reason for making his way to England, which he very wisely did not put forward. His predecessors, who had been for some generations friends and allies of the British in India, and advanced them considerable sums of money, held a good deal of the H.E.I.C.'s stock on which annual interest was paid by the Madras Government. After his accession in 1821, owing to some asserted contumacy on his part, this stock was seized and no interest paid. He then defied the Government and threatened rebellion ; but on a punitive expedition being despatched to Coorg, he surrendered to Colonel James S. Fraser, the Political officer, on April 24th, 1834, and had ever since remained a political prisoner at Benares.

Soon after his arrival in England in March, 1852, he instituted a claim in the English courts against the East Indian Government, demanding the restitution of this money. He had been received with much distinction, treated as a royal person, invited to Court, where he handed over his daughter to Queen Victoria's care, who made arrangements for her education, and instruction in the Christian faith, under the charge of Mrs. Drummond, wife of Major Drummond, who had been a fellow-passenger with the Rajah and his daughter on their voyage from India. The baptism of this first Indian convert of royal birth was made a function of some splendour at Windsor, the Rajah himself being a witness, as well as several members of the India House, and of the Government of the day, Her Majesty standing sponsor and giving the child her own name. An allowance was also arranged for the little Princess out of the Indian revenues. It was the ceremonial attached to this christening which Lord Dalhousie had stigmatised as a " tamasha " in his letter to Login at the time of Duleep Singh's baptism.

So the poor old Rajah felt much insulted and humiliated when, on the top of all this adulation, the Indian Government tried to compel his return to India, as a political prisoner, before his suit could come up in the Lord Chancellor's Court !

The Queen, meanwhile, took much interest in the little girl's welfare, and saw her frequently. After we

came to England with the Maharajah, Mrs. Drummond
(with the Queen's sanction) brought her to visit us at
Castle Menzies and elsewhere, and the Rajah conceived
an intense admiration of my husband, who he swore
was his best friend, and consulted him continually
about his affairs, even to naming him, later on, as
executor to his will.

Mrs. Drummond* was an exceedingly intellectual
woman, as I need hardly say to those of our neighbours
who knew her, and our friendship, up to the present
day, and her daughters were gifted like their mother ;
but poor little Princess Gouramma had no special
literary cravings, and I fear took small advantage of
the educational opportunities she enjoyed ! The Drummond girls were growing up, and would soon be fit to
take their place in society ; but the other occupant of
the schoolroom, although nearly seventeen years of
age, seemed still too backward and too childish to take
an intelligent interest in general matters ; and as there
were indications that the native instinct for duplicity
and intrigue were appearing in her character, it was not
surprising that Mrs. Drummond expressed a desire to
be relieved of a charge which was growing to be somewhat anxious and embarrassing.

It was in a letter to my husband from Osborne, dated
September 5th, 1854, not so very long after we arrived
in England, that Sir Charles Phipps first alluded to the
Queen's wishes for an alliance between this young
Princess and Sir John's ward.

"The more I think upon the subject," he wrote,
"the more it appears to me that these two young
people are pointed out for each other. The only two

* After her husband's death, Mrs. Drummond became the wife of Mr. Alexander, the banker, and latterly resided at Cheveney, Hunton, Kent.

Christians of high rank of their own countries, both having the advantage of early European influences, there seems to be many points of sympathy between them. They are both religious, both fond of music, both gentle in their natures. I know that the Queen thinks that this would be the best arrangement for both their happiness, *provided that they were to like each other*—of course, without this no happiness could exist. Of course the Queen takes a great interest in the little Princess, as Her Majesty considers Herself as *more* than a godmother to her."

Then, nearly four years later, on May 14th, 1858, Sir John was consulted about a " successor to Mrs. Drummond " ! Could he suggest anybody ? It was " so difficult to find a person with the desired qualifications," knowledge of the Indian character and habits, accustomed to live with native royalties and enter into their ideas, etc. . . . Finally, finding that hints were not taken up, for frankly, I had no wish to undertake the office, with the cares of a young family on my hands, and my own eldest girl at home in the schoolroom, the question was put to me direct, as a personal request from Her Majesty ; and how could I evade my duty as a loyal subject ?

That my unwillingness in the matter had not been very successfully concealed from my beloved Sovereign and Mistress is evident from a remark of her private secretary, writing on her behalf from Balmoral, on September 16th, 1858, ten days after I received the Princess into my charge. " The utmost consideration is due to you for your certainly most disinterested, and not very spontaneous, undertaking of a most difficult task (!) "

Personally, I found the little Princess most amiable

and engaging, and in no way intractable, while she showed a real affection for both me and my husband, and never resented or disregarded our necessary restrictions.

She had been residing for some time at Ryde in the Isle of Wight, for the benefit of her health, when Mrs. Drummond brought her over to join me at Albany Villas, Brighton, on September 6th, 1858. Previously, they had been living at Kew; and it was to Kew that we were to take her as soon as Church House could be got ready for us by the Lord Chamberlain's department.

I had previously to this received special instructions from Her Majesty that I was " to write freely to Her *personally* anything I wished to say about the Princess Gouramma "; rather an alarming prospect to one unversed in the peculiar style of address customary with the Sovereign in the English Court ! And I had scarcely contemplated the possibility, when I was called upon to put the command into execution, after the Princess had been only four days with me. This august and confidential correspondence continued, at short intervals, throughout the following eight months.

" To Her Most Gracious Majesty,
    " Lady Login desires respectfully to present her most humble duty to the Queen, and her grateful thanks for the gracious permission accorded her of addressing Her Majesty personally on the affairs of the Princess Gouramma.

    " A few days after Lady Login was honoured with an audience by Her Majesty, she had a very private conversation with the Princess, who professed her intention of concealing nothing, but of opening her heart on the subject " (of a foolish scrape into which she had been led some time before, and of which some details had become known to Her Majesty, who had desired me to endeavour to get to the bottom of it, if possible. I elicited that certain acquaintances of the Princess had been mixed up in the matter). . . .

" Lady Login is therefore very anxious to ascertain Her Majesty's sentiments and wishes on this subject, and whether any arrangement can be made that may prevent her again being thrown in contact with these people ? . . . .

" When Lady Login had the honour of an audience, Her Majesty was graciously pleased to express an intention to determine at an early period the Princess's future provision, in the event of an offer of marriage, and . . . it appears . . . that it would be well to have this matter . . . soon decided.

" The Princess arrived here on the 6th ; she seems to be in excellent health, and appeared to have benefited by her residence at the seaside. And from the pleasure she evinces at the new arrangements for her, Lady Login would fain hope that all will go on satisfactorily.

" Lady Login trusts to the Queen's great kindness to forgive her for having trespassed so long on Her attention, and hopes the subject of her letter may be considered of sufficient importance to excuse her.

"BRIGHTON, *Sept.* 10*th.*"

In reply I received the following :

"BALMORAL, *Sept.* 16*th*, 1858.

"DEAR LADY LOGIN,

" The Queen has shown me your letter of the 10th, and has directed me to answer it according to Her Majesty's commands.

" In the first place, I am desired to inform you that Her Majesty is very much obliged to you for writing to Her so fully, and without reserve, upon the subject of the Princess's past conduct, disposition, and prospects, and would wish you always to do so. . . . The only effectual mode of action the Queen can see . . . would be by the original plan of taking her for a short time abroad. New scenes, new pursuits, and new ideas, would be thus created . . . she would be left entirely to the influence of your good sense—in which, I may say, without flattery, I have great confidence . . . and the Queen is disposed to think, that such an entire change of scene, and life, might be attended with the happiest results.

"With regard to the proper, and most important, question which you ask, as to her future prospects, the Queen desires me to say that She thinks that She can arrange that her present provision shall be continued to her by the Indian Government for life. Her Majesty is not sure that the best chance for the Princess of a matrimonial connection, might not be with some foreign Prince, or Nobleman of rank. To this the Queen would not object, provided that the gentleman's position was a creditable one, and that his own character was such, that the Queen might feel satisfied that She had properly discharged the duties for which She has made Herself responsible. . . .

" . . . The Queen begs that upon the first appearance of the formation of any mutual attachment between the Princess and any gentleman, you would communicate all particulars to Her Majesty, so that She might at once give Her opinion upon it.

" Pray tell me what you think of the feasibility of a short tour upon the Continent ? I am sure I need not say . . . that the subject is of too much importance not to call for the simplest candour and unreserved openness. . . ."

. Scarcely had this subject been discussed, and disposed of, when I had again to address Her Majesty personally on October 2nd, in order to inform her that Princess Gouramma had had an attack of internal hæmorrhage and spitting of blood, though apparently at the time in perfect health, and suffering from no cold or cough. I enclosed the report of Dr. Edward Ormerod, of Brighton, whom I had called in at once. He regarded the matter rather seriously, but the Princess had evidently no idea there could be any danger, for she informed me that she had had a slight attack of the same kind at Ryde, but had not thought it necessary to inform Mrs. Drummond !

The interest and the maternal care that Queen Victoria lavished upon her god-daughter, at this, and at all times, was remarkable, and it was marvellous how, amid all her cares and duties, she found the time to examine and comment on all the details sent at short intervals by her desire. As soon as the attack was subdued, the Queen urged the removal of the Princess to the Continent, and I had to point out that some little delay was inevitable, first, in order that the Princess, who had passed the age of *seventeen*, should be prepared for confirmation before she left England, and secondly, that I might see my younger children comfortably settled in the house provided for us by the Queen, at Kew, and which the Lord Chamberlain's workmen had not yet been able to get ready for occupation.

It seemed to me very essential, under the circumstances, that the Princess's confirmation should be no longer delayed. It was desirable to rouse her somewhat indolent will, and spiritual aspirations, to give her more sense of responsibility with her growing years, and to deepen and widen her too frivolous inclinations. I felt that this preparation could best be done under the Rev. Vaughan Elliott, while we were quietly living at Brighton, and that she might easily return there later, to receive the rite from the Bishop of Winchester, when he made his tour of the diocese for the purpose.

I was very, very anxious to do all in my power to avoid any fuss or display in the young girl's confirmation, as had been the case with her baptism. To one of her nature it was apt to obliterate the religious

THE PRINCESS VICTORIA GOURAMMA OF COORG.

solemnity of the act. Unfortunately, I was not entirely successful in my purpose.

The Royal Family, I notice, view the rite of Confirmation largely as a social event, as marking the young boy or girl's entrance into society, and not simply as a religious act, as do most English Church people. I know not if this aspect is German in its origin ?

Her Majesty took a very deep and tender concern in all the instruction, and the arrangements. All Mr. Elliott's questions and examination papers were forwarded for her consideration, and I think, from some remarks of Sir Charles Phipps in his letters, they were regarded as unduly searching and comprehensive. But the suggestion that the young Princess might form one of a band of candidates going up to receive the Apostolic " laying on of hands," was very decidedly objected to. Hers must be a " private confirmation " in so far as she was to be the *single* candidate, but it must take place in public, and in the Royal Church at Kew, and the Archbishop of Canterbury was applied to to perform the rite.

He, however, represented that the Bishop of Winchester, as Diocesan, was the proper person, and that prelate was instructed to hold himself in readiness, and communicate with me, as to the date, as soon as it was definitely ascertained that Her Majesty—who had first announced her intention of coming to Kew for the purpose—had, finally decided that she would not herself be present.. By the Queen's desire, however, Lady Hardinge and Sir James Weir-Hogg, both of whom had acted as god-parents at her baptism (and the latter was her legal guardian on behalf of the Indian Government), were invited to the ceremony, as well as several

friends and members of the congregation, and especially
H.H. the ex-Rajah of Coorg, the father of the young
girl, who had also witnessed her baptism, and—rather
to our consternation—eagerly availed himself of the
invitation ! Truly an odd juxtaposition of incongruous
elements—a Hindoo offering his sanction, and congratulations, to his daughter, on taking upon herself her
baptismal vows as a Christian !

All these notabilities, including the Bishop of Winchester, who arrived beforehand to have a private
interview, and examination, of the candidate, repaired
after the service to Church House for a reception and
refreshments.

Her Majesty had asked beforehand my opinion as
to the most suitable present for her to give her god-
daughter on her confirmation. I was uncertain whether
to recommend some devotional book, or something
which she could have in use at all times, to remind her
of a solemn occasion, and of the Queen's affectionate
and maternal solicitude for her well-being. We were
just preparing to cross to the church on the other side
of the road—the Bishop having already gone to robe—
when a mounted messenger from Windsor, in the Royal
livery, came spurring up to the door, having been delayed
on the road, and handed in a packet addressed to me,
containing a set of coral and diamond ornaments
(necklace and earrings) from Her Majesty to the Princess, and the following letter, written, at her instruction,
by Sir Charles Phipps :

> "WINDSOR CASTLE,
> "*Jan.* 10*th*, 1859..
>
> " DEAR LADY LOGIN,
>
> " I send to you by the Queen's command, a present
> from Her Majesty to the Princess Gouramma, upon the
> occasion of her confirmation.

" The Queen hopes that these ornaments, instead
of gratifying the vanity of the young Princess, may
serve, when she looks at them, frequently to remind her
of the high duties and responsibilities, which she has this
day taken upon her.

" The Queen is pleased to believe that your young
charge feels deep affection and gratitude to Her Majesty,
and that this feeling will be a constant motive to her, so
to conduct herself as to justify the continued regard
and protection of Her Majesty—but the Queen hopes
that, from this day, the Princess will feel the far higher,
and holier aspirations, which should fill her soul with the
desire to please that Almighty Being, whose service
she this day takes upon her, and before Whom the
Queen, and the Princess, will equally have to answer
for the part which they have each taken, in obtaining
for the latter the blessed hopes of Christianity.

" The Queen directs me to send many messages of
kindness to the Princess, and to assure her that it gives
Her Majesty sincere pleasure when you are able to give
a satisfactory report of her.

" Sincerely yours,
"C. B. Phipps."

I could not refrain from quoting this letter in full,
as I think nothing could more clearly show the sense of
personal responsibility which moved the mind of the
Sovereign, in her dealings with this one young girl,
of a different race, from a distant portion of her
dominions, not yet recognised as an integral part of the
Empire, and also exhibit the greatness of heart and
sympathy, mingled with a true Christian humility, of
the beloved Queen whom we have lost.

I greatly doubt, however, whether the recipient of
those jewels did not, owing to their advent at this
moment, have her mind directed less to the ideas with
which her sponsor desired them to be concerned, than

to a contemplation and satisfaction in the " pomps and
vanities " she had promised to renounce ! And that
their arrival afforded unbounded delight to the little
Rajah of Coorg there could be no question ! He plumed
and preened himself, with satisfaction, the whole afternoon, and doubtless felt that, with this signal manifestation of " the Padishah's " favour, and the realisation
of his great wish to see his daughter placed under my
roof, although the Maharajah was now technically no
longer my husband's ward (he had a separate establishment, and house of his own, but continued constantly
to visit us, and we him), he might fairly consider that
his ambitious adventure, in leaving his own country
and braving the perils of the deep, was not in vain !
Poor Veer Rajundur Wudeer ! he was a most amiable
and polite specimen of a native ruler, and appeared
genuinely attached to his little daughter—who, on her
part, I am sorry to say, seemed very indifferent in her
manner to him—but he never could refrain from theatrical posing in the public view, and there was one daguer-
reotype in his daughter's possession, taken specially
as a souvenir to keep him in her memory, which always
aroused in me an access of ribald mirth. The Rajah
was depicted—as it were, in the full limelight—his eyes
raised to Heaven in pious invocation, while his out-
stretched hands pointed to his daughter, seated with
downcast eyes (and with a very sulky expression !)
by his side. This was intended to typify the agony
of a father handing his child over to the protection of
the British people ; but think what histrionic talent
must have come into play, to rehearse all that for the
lengthy period then required to produce a photographic
negative ! He was the father of eleven children, but
I am bound to say, never showed for any of the

others an iota of the affection he lavished on little
Gouramma.

As to the Princess's own character at that time, I
wrote to Sir Charles Phipps that I was fully sensible that
.her "future conduct would exercise a great influence
for good or for evil on the females of India. I am most
anxious," I said then, "with God's help, to do my part
in endeavouring to train her in such a way as shall do
credit to her Christian profession. Should the result
of our experimental tour on the Continent be such as to
lead the Queen to desire that a prolonged residence
should be made, we shall endeavour, at any personal
inconvenience, to meet Her Majesty's wishes, if we can
find a suitable place where we can take our children "
(my eldest girl, two or three years junior to the Princess
in age, though far in advance of her in education and
accomplishments, had been sent to a boarding-school
in Brighton), "though of course my husband is naturally anxious at present to be in England, in case some
work may be found for him in which his knowledge of
India may be turned to account.* It is rather early
yet to give an opinion, but in justice to the Princess
I must say, that I have had every reason to be satisfied
with her since she has been under my charge. She says
that she is very happy, and certainly appears so. She
evidently enjoys riding on horseback, and can ride a
good distance without feeling fatigue. Although Mrs.
Drummond prepared me for it, I am much disappointed
in her attainments, particularly in her music, in which
I had fancied she excelled. It is, like all her other
studies, a great labour to her; however, she seems
quite aware of her deficiency, and anxious to do her

* This of course referred to the correspondence on India with Sir C. Phipps, of
which mention has been made.

best to make up for lost time. I tell her she is too old
to be forced, and unless she works with her own goodwill, all will be useless. She really seems anxious to
please me, and to gain my good opinion, and in this
I fervently hope she may succeed."

I had received Her Majesty's summons to an audience
at Windsor on the 8th November, to give my report on
the Princess, but at the very last moment had to send a
messenger to Sir Charles Phipps, to beg that I might be
pardoned for not appearing, as my baby, about seven
months old, had been seized with serious illness. I
cannot tell you what kind letters—more than one—
were written me by Her Majesty's desire. "One line
to assure you, though I am sure unnecessary, how sorry
the Queen—as well as all of us—was to hear of the
cause of Lady Login's absence to-day." And again,
to the same effect, and to inquire for the child, on
the 11th. On the 15th Sir Charles wrote to arrange
another interview, and to make it all easy, I was to
go first to his apartments, and he conducted me to the
presence.

When the arrangements were in progress for our visit
to the Continent with the Princess, I asked if I might
be allowed a further audience to receive full instructions? This was at once accorded, and I was bidden
to bring the Princess Gouramma with me to luncheon
at 1 p.m. on January 27th, 1859, a memorable date in
the history of Europe as it proved, and I too was, as
it turned out, to have a dramatic announcement—at
first hand—of an event which has had an overpower-
ing influence on the destinies of many millions. It was
in this wise.

After the luncheon, at which Her Majesty talked
in a most kindly and gracious manner with all, and my

interview with her, during which my charge was entertained by the royal children, we took our leave, and the gentleman conducting us—for we had been prevented seeing Sir Charles and Lady Phipps this time, owing to " mumps " in his family—proposed that, as it was early in the afternoon, we might like to see some of the galleries and State apartments? We were passing through an immense saloon, when suddenly there was heard the sound of opening doors, and the rush of hurrying feet, accompanied by a whispered cry, " The Queen! The Queen! " Our guide at once motioned us to stand aside, and, at the same moment, a door at the further end of the apartment was flung wide, and now the cry came in stentorian tones, while the Lord Chamberlain appeared, running backwards with extraordinary agility, to keep pace with the Sovereign whom he was ceremoniously ushering—thus showing that it was an errand of state that she was on.

For the Queen, whom we had so lately parted from in calm dignity, was flying with the eagerness of a young girl, and so rapid was her movement, and so joyous her expression, it was plain that her suite had much difficulty in keeping pace with her speed. Catching sight of me in the distance, as she came up the long room, she suddenly waved aloft a telegraph form that she was holding in her hand—ominous missive usually, in those far-off days — and called out in triumphant tones, unheeding the shocked expression of her attendants at such unconventionality: " Lady Login! Lady Login! *I am a grandmother!!* "

Thus she herself announced to me the birth of her first grandchild, the first comer in the line of succession to the British Crown, whose advent she was hastening to communicate, with all due etiquette of Minister in attendance, to her Consort, Prince Albert, in his apartments. I actually was, in this way, a recipient of the news from her own lips, before the grandfather knew it, and within an hour of the actual event, which took place, as the Kaiser Wilhelm II.'s horoscope is careful to inform us, at 3 o'clock in the afternoon of January 27th, Anno Domini 1859 !

Many a time since has that scene recurred to my mind, more especially on a brilliant summer's day, thirty years later, when I stood on the after-bridge of my son's ship, H.M.S. *Anson*—his first as Commander—at the head of the line of the Channel Fleet, lying out at Spithead, ready to receive the new German Emperor on his first State visit to his grandmother. I heard the muttered criticisms of the group of naval officers of high rank who stood around, as the original *Hohenzollern*—followed by her escort of two old-fashioned German cruisers, standing high out of the water, black, and with open ports bristling with guns, in contrast with the grey hulls and low freeboard of our own ships—swept round across our bows, close alongside, and under our counter (to avoid an idiotic yacht that got right in the way, in defiance of orders), piloted by the Trinity Yacht and the *Enchantress*. I marvelled to see the German seamen stand shoulder-to-shoulder round their vessels, whilst ours barely manned the sides with hands clasped and arms extended, and asked if the visitors had not extra complements on board ? I remember the Flag-Captain's answer. "Double-manned, did you say ? Why, they're *treble*-manned ! If they attempted to fight those ships, they would be tumbling over each other ! "

Ours was the first ship to greet the Emperor on that

occasion, as he stood smiling with gratification on the bridge of his yacht, returning the salutes of officers and men, of the guns, and of the ensigns, our band meanwhile playing the " Heil ! Dir in Siegerkranz ! " while the blue-jackets gave the regulation cheers. Well I know how, even in those days (1889), there was present a feeling of antagonism, a certain grim repression amongst us all, owing doubtless to his known unfilial treatment of his mother, the Princess Royal of England ! Among the many guests on board the second Flagship were some foreign diplomats, and I remember how one lady, wife of an English politician, noticing the somewhat cold and supercilious air with which the naval men on board scanned the warlike aspect of the foreign warships, observed in rebuke to the company in general : " Why do you criticise, and make remarks, as if they could be anything but our friends and allies ? " and the chilling silence, and looks askance, with which the observation was received.

My husband's gallant old friend and colleague of the first Afghan War, Sir Frederick Abbott, was one of our party on board ; and returning to Ryde in the torpedo boat that had taken us out to the ship, one of the petty-officers put into words, in answer to a question of Sir Frederick's young son, the under-current of sentiment prevailing, at that period, in the British Fleet. " Look like business, do they, sir ? Fully armed, eh ? My word, sir, *won't they make rattling good targets ! !* "

This was Kaiser Wilhelm's first view of the new *Anson,* a ship which was the object of his liveliest curiosity, being of an entirely new type in those days, and the first built with only military masts. Later on, he was to inspect her most exhaustively, in his own

harbour of Kiel, descending to the lowest depths of the
engine-room and torpedo-flat, rather to the terror of
his suite, who knew the danger of a slip on the steep
steel ladders, his imperfect left arm giving him no grasp
on that side. To diminish risk, by Admiral Sir R.
Tracey's direction, my son, as Commander, was deputed
to immediately precede, and act as cicerone, to H.I.M.,
in order that, in case of accident, his bulk and strength
might interpose and avert a fall. All on board the
Anson, however, knew that the Kaiser, in characteristic
fashion, had taken an opportunity of a close and
private, though necessarily superficial, survey of the
ship already, a few weeks previous, when the Channel
Fleet entered Bergen harbour, at a time when the
Emperor's yacht also lay there, on one of his earlier
flying trips to Norway.   Scarcely had the *Anson*
anchored, when a boat put off from the *Hohenzollern*,
containing the commanding-officer of the latter, come to
visit the Rear-Admiral and Captain. He was of course
received with all the honours, and went below to the
Admiral's quarters, leaving his galley's crew in their
craft alongside. These pulled very slowly to and fro
about the ship, scanning her build and armament with
attention, while a cluster of disrespectful and irrepres-
sible youngsters, from the *Anson's* gun-room, hung over
the side, making observation of the visitors in their
turn, and some audible remarks as to "cheek"; for too
close scrutiny "à l'imprévu" is not regarded as good
naval manners !

Suddenly the attention of a "reefer," rather smarter
than his fellows, was attracted to the presence of a
gentleman in blue serge yachting dress, sitting in the
stern-sheets of the galley, smoking silently in a non-
chalant attitude, but unmistakably making good use

of his powers of vision, aided by binoculars, in the position he was in. A quiet hint brought all the boys' eyes to bear on this individual, and their sudden silence attracted the officer of the watch, when an unguarded movement on the part of the observed, revealed the well-known lineaments of " William the Unexpected ! "

CHAPTER XII

WE went abroad with the Princess in the February of 1859, and travelled through Italy, making little stop till we reached Rome. We were, of course, furnished with introductions to many people of note, and to our Ambassadors at the different Courts ; but as this was our second visit—having made an extended tour with the Maharajah in 1856—we had already many acquaintances in various parts of the peninsula.

The Maharajah had left England a little while before, having as companion a very distinguished traveller in the East, who afterwards made a great name for himself as a discoverer in the upper regions of the Nile, being rewarded with a knighthood. They were to go first to Vienna, where letters were written to the Ambassador on H.M.'s behalf, to show all attention to the Maharajah, and Baron Kügel sent by my husband's request the name and address of a bird-fancier in Vienna the Maharajah wanted to look up. For the idea of the trip was a shooting excursion in Hungary, Transylvania, and all down the Danube to Constantinople ; and, as ever, his great craze was for all sorts of sport, especially shooting birds, wherever he went, he wanted specimens of each kind, to rear, and study their habits.

Her Majesty had been very anxious that he should take a gentleman with him, as some sort of equerry or attendant, but this, in spite of strong hints through Sir Charles Phipps, he steadily declined to do.

Feeling thus quite free to devote ourselves to the welfare and encouragement of Princess Gouramma, and to the developing of her mind and interest in various pursuits, it seemed to me that it would be more amusing and lively for her to take my young daughter with us, who, though some years her junior, was a clever child, had a great talent for both music and drawing, and would take full advantage of the opportunities of studying these, and the languages of the countries we should visit. Thus she would gain as great educational advantages as if she had remained at home at school—whither it had been a great wrench to send her, as I had done, never having, in any other case, parted with my daughters for that purpose—and at the same time, the young Princess, finding her junior so far ahead in application, would be spurred into emulation and interest on her own account. The plan answered admirably, and as she was really fond of my " Lena," and pleased to be treated as a grown-up, while the other was a school-room girl, she seemed to thoroughly enjoy the changes of scene, and improved immensely in intelligence and deportment. During part of the time, my eldest son, then an Eton boy, was also of the party, so that occasionally the liveliness of our company might be termed exuberant, not to say boisterous, which condition of affairs chimed in exactly with what the little lady revelled in !   '

On arriving in Rome, we took an apartment at No. 56, Capo la Casa, and many old and new acquaintances came to see us. Amongst others, H.R.H. the Prince of Wales, who was in Rome that winter, with his governor, General Bruce, honoured us with a visit, and invited my husband to dine with him at his hotel. During the Carnival, he came to our balcony in the Corso (we had

hired one there for the three days, as was the custom),
with a bouquet for the Princess Gouramma, and after
watching the procession for some time with us, passed
on to the balcony of the next house, which was occupied
by the Prussian royal family.

Very much to our surprise, we found that the Maharajah Duleep Singh had hurried away from Constantinople and was here in Rome awaiting our appearance !
His expedition had been rather a fiasco, his guide—an
old *habitué* of Oriental cities—had not proved a wise
counsellor to a young and inexperienced charge. The
Maharajah was not happy, and seized the first opportunity to come and join us in Rome, and we, seeing
him thus, had hopes that he came with the intention
of seeking the society of the young Princess, with
whom, he well knew, there was a wish he should ally
himself. He had expressed himself to me in July, 1858,
as "so very glad to hear that the Queen has asked
you, and you have agreed, to take charge of the young
Coorg Princess. I am sure," he continued, "that you
will make her very happy, and treat her with that
motherly kindness which I myself have had the good
luck to experience. . . . Tell me when to expect
Edwy ; he will enjoy fishing, . . . " ending, as usual
then, and for many years, "Love to all. Yours affectionately, DULEEP SINGH."

All seemed to promise therefore that matters were
proceeding even better than could be wished, and,
towards the end of March, I sat down to write
to Her Majesty, as directed, for her personal consideration, the following report on the Princess's
conduct and doings. I give a few extracts only, as
the correspondence had to be detailed, and is rather
voluminous :

" MADAM, . . .

" . . . I think I may venture to say that the object Your Majesty had in view in sending the Princess abroad for a short time has been, in a great measure, obtained ; for she is, in a pleasing way, acquiring knowledge on subjects of which she was deplorably ignorant, and about which she felt before quite indifferent. There remains still much to be desired, but as the Princess is very docile, and really does her best to improve herself, and seems most desirous to please me, I feel that the time has not been lost since she left England.

" She is very much steadier than she was, and conducts herself, when in society, with great modesty and proper dignity. I have only once had occasion to reprove her seriously for levity of conduct. Her manners at the Carnival were excellent, though she enjoyed it heartily, and regretted its short duration. We made arrangements that she should see all that it was desirable that she should see without attracting much attention, and I think she was little known or observed, except in an unobjectionable manner. I have engaged the services of a Parisian lady as French teacher during our stay here, and the Princess is very industrious. As she seemed anxious to learn sketching from nature, so as to be able to sketch like our little girl, I have got the best English drawing-master here to go out with her. . . . Though she has little or no talent for drawing, . . . it is as well to cultivate it if possible.

" She seems to have enjoyed her sojourn here thoroughly, and I regret much, for her sake, that it will soon be over, for I feel that her mind and interest are opening, and although it is rather harassing to have to instruct her by constant explanations, and by trying to emphasize facts on her memory (for she cannot read for herself), yet I am encouraged to go on by seeing a visible improvement.

" The Maharajah Duleep Singh is with us constantly.

and although I should wish to be very careful in taking up an impression regarding his feelings towards the Princess, I cannot be blind to the fact that he entertains very different sentiments, in many respects, to his former ones.

" I have avoided throwing the Princess in his way, and quite agreed with the determination he at first expressed, of not getting their names mixed up together. But by degrees he has come back to us on the old footing, and constantly spends his evenings with us in familiar intercourse, without any invitation, and the circumstance of our boy and girl being with us brings him more into contact with the Princess. He has been talking to me more than once of his future prospects, marriage, etc., . . . and seems fully alive to the difficulties in his way of marrying an Englishwoman of the birth and rank to support his position. The great interest that Your Majesty takes in the Princess is not without its effect upon him, and even the kind attention shown her and us by the Prince of Wales is remarked. upon by him, as proof of Your Majesty's favour. . . .

" . . . I am anxious to receive Your Majesty's commands upon the manner in which Your Majesty wishes the Princess to be introduced into society on her return home, as this will naturally influence the period of our stay abroad. When I had less hope of the Princess becoming a credit to Your Majesty's gracious kindness, I was disposed to think it would be well to make as little exception in her favour as possible, with regard to the manner of being received at Court. But circumstances have considerably altered, and, as I see that any distinction conferred on the Princess has great weight with the Maharajah, it only remains for Your Majesty to determine whether she is to go through the formality of a presentation or not. . . ."

How all these fair hopes were totally and unexpectedly dashed to the ground, and a most bewildering and uncomfortable *dénouement* revealed itself, will best appear if I venture to quote from a letter with which I found myself compelled to follow up the preceding, only two or three days later.   At the period at which it was written, naturally, its contents could only be regarded as exceedingly private and confidential, but the many decades that have since elapsed, make it possible, without indiscretion, to make known some portion of them.

"TO HER MOST GRACIOUS MAJESTY THE QUEEN.
"MADAM,

"When I had the honour to address Your Majesty so lately, I did not anticipate the necessity of so soon again doing so, but as I am very greatly concerned at the purport of a conversation I have just had with the Maharajah, I am desirous of losing no time in making it known to Your Majesty.

"The Maharajah had met the Princess Gouramma, a few evenings ago, at a small party, and I observed that he sat by her talking for some time.   The next day he asked for a private interview with me, and, after saying that he thought the Princess much improved in manner and appearance, and that he felt a sincere interest in her as his countrywoman, he said that he considered it only right and honourable on his part to tell me at once that he could not ask her to be his wife ; that, from what he had observed of her lately, he had made up his mind that she was not calculated to make him happy, as he did not feel the confidence in her . . . he would in an English girl.

" I was much distressed at this, for I had hoped that she was conducting herself so as to make a favourable impression, . . . but he said repeatedly, ' I could never marry her !   I could never feel more than pity for her ! She would not be a safe wife for me ! I don't seem to trust her ! and I dread so any trouble after marriage ! '

"He then went on to say that he felt very unhappy

about himself, that he saw the necessity of altering
many things in his own conduct, and of endeavouring
to live more as became his profession of Christianity,
and his position in society ; but that his temptations
were so great, and he felt himself so weak to withstand
them, that unless he could have some definite object
in view, and some reward to strive after, he feared for
the future ; . . . that up to this time his life had been
aimless, that he felt he had no ties to bind him, no home
or kindred that he could claim as his own, but that
if this could be altered—if a hope could be held out to
him that he might, at some future period, be permitted
to try and win the love of one whom he had known and
loved from her childhood, he would undergo any probation it was thought fit to impose on him, and strive,
with God's help, to make himself worthy of her ! . . .
(Here he named a young relative of my husband, who
had her in his care and charge.) . . .

"On observing the effect this utterly unexpected
announcement had upon me, he became so confused and
nervously excited, that he could not express his meaning
clearly, and therefore begged I would give him no
reply at present, but allow him to come next day and
talk it over calmly, and, in the meantime, if we should
feel . . . inclined to reject his desire (as he feared
might be), that we would reflect deeply on the effect such
a decision would have on him.

"I hope I need not assure Your Majesty that neither
my husband, nor myself, had the slightest suspicion of
the Maharajah's sentiments towards ——, and that we
were quite unprepared for his request, which caused
us the greatest anxiety and pain on her account, even
more than on the Maharajah's ; and though we felt
ourselves in a very peculiar position towards him, as
his only Christian parents, and in a great degree bound
to give him every aid we could, still, at the same time,
this young girl's happiness and welfare must be paramount with us.

" When he came the next morning, he said much of
the great difficulty he should always find in becoming
acquainted with the real disposition and character
of any young lady he might meet in society;
that in no other family could he be domesticated as
he was with us; that he had known ——'s temper and
disposition thoroughly, and watched her closely, and
had long felt that . . . she was in every respect what
he wished for in his wife; her truthfulness and purity
he could rely on, and her religious feelings he reverenced.
But if we, whom he trusted and regarded as parents,
could not accept him into the family; if we, who had
taken him from his own country and people, and cut
him off (though at his own request) from all prospect
of mixing with his own race, should refuse to regard
him as one of ourselves, to whom could he look?

" I earnestly hope that in the reply that we have
given we have been rightly directed, and that, with
God's blessing, the event may result in good. We have
told the Maharajah that in our peculiar situation, and
as Christians, we cannot altogether refuse his request,
though we must adopt such measures as shall, as far
as possible, render our present concession harmless to
the other person involved, . . . as she must be our
first consideration; that in the earnest hope that this
may lead him to higher views of the duties of his position,
and of his Christian profession, if it was found that for
the next three years his conduct gave us confidence in
his sincerity, and in the depth of his present feelings,
and in the event of his obtaining Your Majesty's gracious
approval, we would allow him to plead his own cause
with the young girl, who would then be of age sufficient
to make the decision for herself. In the meantime, he
bound himself, on his honour, not in any way to make her
aware of his sentiments—we, on our part, being careful
that they shall see as little as possible of each other in
the interim.

" We have told him that we make this promise, and

hold out this inducement to him, solely in the hope that, before this period expires, he will see his true position more clearly, and meet with someone more suitable in every respect, . . . as we in no wise covet such a destiny for our charge. . . . We felt that to deprive him of all hope, considering the position we have held towards him, would have been both unchristian and injudicious, and might have led him to become utterly careless.

"There were many circumstances which I cannot detail by letter, which have strengthened us in resolving on this reply. My first impulse was to return straight to England, instead of going on to Naples, in the hope of being permitted personally to lay everything before Your Majesty. On second thoughts, knowing how much Your Majesty desired that the Princess should be as long abroad as possible, and that her health would be benefited by a stay at the seaside, I have decided to adhere to our first intention. Need I express to Your Majesty with what deep anxiety I shall await at Naples the expression of Your Majesty's opinion on the course we have thought it our duty to pursue with respect to the Maharajah ?

" I have the honour to be, Madam, with most dutiful and grateful respect,

" Your Majesty's most humble and most devoted servant,

" LENA LOGIN.

" ROME, *March* 31*st*, 1859."

I will not attempt to describe our utter consternation at the bombshell thus exploded by the Maharajah, shattering all the ideas and arrangements formed in the minds of exalted personages interested in his future ! It was so entirely unlooked for as to leave us almost speechless with astonishment ; and, as I expressed it, in writing privately to Sir Charles Phipps at the time, " he would readily believe that such an alliance was not what we would seek " for the young lady in question. Hoping that the period of probation would give time for him to change his mind and look elsewhere for a wife, we refused to allow him to consider himself bound in any way by anything he had said, and stipulated that all that had passed must be kept entirely secret.

This, of course, made it more difficult to account to our acquaintances for the extraordinary vagueness that suddenly enveloped all our plans and movements, until we received instructions from England. One step only I thought it right to take at once, and that was to inform the poor little Princess of the unfortunate impression that her manner had conveyed to the Maharajah. I really felt quite sorry for her; she was so abashed to find what a gentleman's opinion of her really was, that I felt every hope that the lesson might prove an effectual cure. It had a most salutary effect upon her in many ways, and the improvement in her dignity was noticed by everyone. I was extraordinarily pleased, and touched, by the humility with which she received my lecture.

Naturally, I felt it my duty to inform the Queen that, as one of the chief reasons for my selection as the Princess's chaperone was removed, since there could no longer be a question of marriage between her and the Maharajah, I was quite prepared to meet Her Majesty's wishes, should she wish to place her in other care; but had no desire to relinquish the charge I had undertaken to fulfil. I also suggested that, if the Queen wished it, I could arrange to make the acquaintance of some of the members of the Prussian Court, in attendance on King Frederick William IV., then staying in

Rome, as the Queen had before hinted that a foreign nobleman might make a suitable match in her case? It is easy to imagine with what trepidation I awaited Her Majesty's reply to my communication, which, owing to some delay, did not reach me until April 24th, by which time we had left Naples and were staying at Sorrento !

" BUCKINGHAM PALACE,

"*April 8th*, 1859.

" MY DEAR LADY LOGIN,

"The Queen has received and read with great interest your letters of the 26th and 31st March.

" Her Majesty fully comprehends, and sympathises with, the conflicting feelings with which you must have received the unexpected declaration of the Maharajah, and Her Majesty thinks that, considering all the circumstances, the decision at which you arrived was not only the soundest and most prudent, but also the kindest and the most likely to be beneficial towards the Maharajah.

" . . . If his attachment to this young lady is deeply-rooted and really sincere, it may afford him a sufficient object to strengthen and render permanent his good resolutions, and thus establish a strong motive for good, so much wanting in an indolent and self-indulgent, though generous, honourable, and upright nature, such as his. The Queen has therefore no doubt that you answered him both wisely, and in accordance with that affectionate regard which you and Sir John have ever shown him. . . .

" Her Majesty hopes that the conversation which you have had with the Princess . . . may have a good effect, and that a marriage with some other eligible person may be effected. It would be desirable that any such prospect, with a person whom you would approve, should be in every way encouraged. It is most probable that union with a sensible and kind husband, whom she could respect and look up to, might have the most desirable effect upon her character. The Queen entirely approves of your decision not to return home immediately, and is quite of opinion that a little longer stay abroad is likely to be, in every way, the best plan for her.

" With regard to her presentation at Court, the Queen thinks that whenever it shall be decided that she is to come out in London, it will not be necessary for her to be *presented* at Court at all. Having been for many years under Her Majesty's protection, such a ceremony would not be required ; but the Queen thinks that the decision as to her coming out at all this year, must depend very much upon the report which you are able to make upon your return to England. It does not, at present, seem improbable, that it may be thought prudent to delay for another year her general introduction into Society. As, from her rank, and the peculiarities of her position, she will be very much watched . . . anything unusual in her manner would be made subject of general remark, and might have a most prejudicial effect upon her prospects, which must, for her happiness and future welfare, be directed to secure a suitable marriage.

" It gives me great pleasure to be able thus to convey to you the entire approbation of the Queen of the course you have pursued, under circumstances of certainly unusual difficulty.

" With kindest remembrances to Sir John,
" Believe me, dear Lady Login,
" Very sincerely yours,
" C. B. Phipps."

At the same time Sir Charles wrote privately to my husband to the same effect, saying " how completely the Queen approves of the answer returned to the *unexpected* announcement of the Maharajah," with respect to whose character he enlarged at some length.

"With regard to the Princess, the Queen becomes anxious that she should find a good husband, as H.M. thinks that that is the best chance for her happiness. Whatever way the proposal of the Maharajah may end, I assure you that my first wish is that it may conduce to the real happiness of yourself, Lady Login; and your family, and that you may all reap the reward of all the kindness and benevolence that you have displayed."

I replied to Sir Charles Phipps' letter conveying Her Majesty's approval of my conduct, on April 25th, and told him how " I could not express my gratitude for the condescending kindness with which Her Majesty had entered into our feelings, and so fully appreciated the motives which had influenced us." The Maharajah had written me a letter from Rome (where he had remained on our departure for Naples) full of penitence and good resolutions, saying that he meant to return to England, and apply for permission for a short tour in India. I had great hopes, I told Sir Charles, that the Maharajah's plain speaking had had a most salutary effect upon the Princess. . . . " She is, in many respects," I wrote, " so amiable, and so easily made happy, that there seems a very fair prospect that she will turn out well. We hope to be in England within a fortnight," I added, " and I trust I may shortly afterwards be permitted the honour of explaining in person, to Her Majesty, my reasons for thinking that the introduction of the Princess should not, if possible, be delayed for another year. I fear her father's presence in England will be a great obstacle to her making a good marriage ; but perhaps his affairs may be arranged by the Indian Council, so as to admit of his speedy return to India.

" I have the honour to enclose a letter from the

Princess Gouramma for the Princess Alice, and I have also taken the liberty to enclose one or two letters to be forwarded by post to their addresses." *

A letter from the Maharajah reached me at Sorrento, in which he referred with enthusiasm to its being "the happiest time of my life when I am married," and asks to be told the Queen's reply to my letter as soon as received. He makes a little pathetic reference to his lonely life, and having "no one who cares for me," and then goes on : " As there is no Miss P. this year to buy a bracelet for, perhaps you will buy a pair of ear-rings and bracelet . . . for someone else, whose name, I fear, I dare not mention ? " This was the only effort to break the conditions laid down, save once again, four months later, when he sent a note to be given to the young lady, and when it was returned unopened, remarked, that he had written to ask permission and I had said nothing, so he " took for granted he might ! " He then coolly suggested that to make up for his disappointment I should bring her with me when I went to stay with him at Mulgrave Castle, and promised that I should " see nothing in his conduct that would give me the slightest suspicion " (whatever he meant by that !), and, as he put it, " if I do anything that will not please you, surely you can tell me ? " A post-script at the end requested a lock of hair ! though he adds naïvely : " I ask this although I don't expect to get it ! "

This was by no means, I may state here, the first occasion on which the Maharajah's matrimonial pro-jects had caused perturbation in our minds. Our former visit to Rome had likewise been marked by a very violent " attack of the heart," and the memory

* Their letters went in the Embassy bag, by Queen's Messenger.

of it actually remained impressed on his recollection for *over a year*, to judge by a letter that he wrote me in May, 1858, referring to another beauty he had been presented to in Sardinia! But, as a rule, his love affairs were so exceedingly transient, that we had every expectation that the period we had placed upon any further reference to this one would, when passed, find him with a fresh object of attraction, and the former image entirely obliterated.

Strangely enough, this did not prove entirely the case. In spite of various intermediate episodes and "affairs," quite openly and naïvely alluded to in his letters—in one case in this self-same year it was the beautiful daughter of a marquis; in another letter, in October, 1862, he writes that he has found "one who will make him a good wife," though he had not yet summoned up courage to propose!—he nevertheless returned to his declared intention from these excursions into other regions, very persistently for over four years, not relinquishing the quest until satisfied that he had his answer personally, and finally! I may truly say, that his various projects of matrimony gave constant and perplexing occupation, and food for thought, to myself and his intimate friends, including, as I need not specify, the highest in the land, up to the time of his actual marriage in 1864.

Already, before our departure for Italy, on January 28th, 1859, the day after our audience, and the birth of the present Emperor of Germany, Sir Charles Phipps, in writing to my husband, said of Her Majesty's impression of her god-daughter : " I am sure both Lady Login, and yourself, would have been pleased had you heard the Queen speak last night as She did, of the improvement, in every respect, which She observed in the Princess Gouramma, most of which She attributed to Lady Login's judicious management." And when she saw her again, on our return to England in the spring, she expressed herself as still more satisfied with her appearance and manner.

I was anxious, however, to be relieved soon of my charge, both on account of the awkwardness of our constant association with the Maharajah, who was continually pressing me to come and act hostess for him, at Mulgrave Castle, and Auchlyne in Perthshire, bringing the children with me, to whom he was very much attached; and also because I felt these latter were now growing of an age to require my undivided attention. I had represented this to Her Majesty, and she graciously accepted my resignation, to take place when she had found another lady suitable for the position. On May 16th I was informed that Lady Catherine Harcourt had consented to undertake the charge, and I was summoned to an audience of Her Majesty two days later.

It was arranged that I was to take the Princess to a State Concert on May 30th, and there make the acquaintance of Lady Catherine, and that the Princess should make her appearance at the State Ball on June 9th, under the *joint* chaperonage of Lady Catherine and myself, and at the Drawing-room of the 11th should be in the sole charge of Lady Catherine Harcourt. The latter, however, was unable to attend the Drawing-room, and the Princess consequently made her *début* in the Royal Circle under my escort, and her transfer to her new chaperone, postponed till June 23rd, had to be again deferred, owing to the fact that her father, the ex-Rajah of Coorg, was then dying in London, and begged that she might remain nearer him for a time, so as to come over occasionally to see him, which would not be so easy if she joined Lady Catherine, then in the Isle of Wight.

I took the daughter over from Kew once or twice to see the poor old man, but it was a very painful business. He was really fond of her, but she seemed to be quite indifferent, and showed very little feeling. He could speak no English, and she seemed to have entirely forgotten her native tongue, so that actually I had to act as interpreter between father and daughter! On one of these occasions, the old Rajah took the opportunity to make over to his daughter the jewels that he had set aside as her portion, and this was the cause of much correspondence afterwards, as Colonel Harcourt thought the terms of the will implied that she was also to share at her father's death; and this, I am positive, was just what the old man meant to avoid.

Her Majesty, however, did not approve of the Princess visiting much her father's abode; in fact, Sir Charles Phipps told me plainly, that intercourse between them had always been discouraged since Her Majesty had taken her under her protection. I was therefore directed that, as the Rajah seemed in no immediate danger, I should hand her over to Lady Catherine at once, as she was now ready to receive her, and she could be sent for when necessity arose, if her father took a sudden turn for the worse. Rather to my dismay, I discovered that it was the intention of Lady Catherine that she should be placed once more under the supervision of a governess, a Miss Sharp, who came to escort her to her new home. I rather feared the result on one of her temperament, after having been treated as grown-up, and allowed to take part in Court functions. It was a hazardous experiment, at her age, to show any want of confidence in one of her race and antecedents.

It was in the latter part of July, 1859, that she left my charge, and on the 27th or 28th I received, by special messenger, the very signal honour of a letter from my beloved Sovereign, written by her own hand—the envelope also directed by herself to " The Lady Login," and endorsed " The Queen." It was couched in the following terms :

" OSBORNE,

" *July 27th*, 1859.

" MY DEAR LADY LOGIN,

" Princess Gouramma having now finally been given over to Lady Catherine Harcourt, I wish to express to you my sense of the great improvement which I find in her since she has been under your charge, and I thank you for all the kind and affectionate care you took of her, and the trouble you gave yourself in watching over this interesting child. May she turn out as we could wish !

" With the Prince's kind remembrance and ours to Sir John Login, believe me,

" Yours sincerely,

" VICTORIA R."

It was sealed with her private coat-of-arms, twin shields of England and Saxe-Coburg-Gotha, and bore the royal monogram interlaced surmounted by the Imperial crown. Well was I repaid by such an honour for any trouble and anxiety I had been put to !

Five days later came another royal messenger with a jeweller's packet and a letter from Sir Charles Phipps :

" OSBORNE,

" *August 2nd*, 1859.

" DEAR LADY LOGIN,

" I am very glad that you were so much pleased with the Queen's letter.

" I have now received Her Majesty's commands to forward to you the accompanying bracelet, as a more durable mark of her appreciation of the readiness with which you undertook a charge, at a time when it was inconvenient to yourself, and of the admirable manner in which you discharged the duties which thereby devolved upon you.

"With kindest remembrances to Sir John,
"Ever sincerely yours,
"C. B. PHIPPS."

The bracelet, a plain gold " gipsy " band, set with three fine stones—emerald, diamond and ruby—is engraved inside : " To Lady Login, V.R., 1859."

I have mentioned the case that Veer Rajundur Wudeer had going on in the English Courts against the Indian Government, and that the latter endeavoured to insist upon his return to India as a political prisoner before the suit could be tried. They had to yield to the agitation their action excited in Parliament. He had appealed to the Queen to be allowed to remain and bring his sons—he had seven, but only one they called " legitimate "—to England, to be educated. Her Majesty referred the matter to the Governor-General for his comments, and Sir Charles Wood (afterwards Lord Halifax) requested the Governor-General, on June 30th of this year, to send a speedy reply on account of the Rajah's health. None came before the Rajah's death, which occurred on September 24th, and on the 30th September, Sir Charles acquainted Lord Canning of this fact, and also informed him that Login had been appointed executor under the Rajah's will. He begged him to lose no time in sending his decision on the provision for the children, and the Ranees and concubines of himself, his father and his

uncle, all living in actual penury at Benares! Two
" female servants," dignified by the English Press with
the title of " Ranees," were over with the poor old man
in this country—which was one reason that the Queen
was not anxious for the Princess Gouramma to have too
close an intercourse with her father's household here.
To our English ideas it would be an extraordinary
" interior " into which to allow a young girl to pene-
trate. We old Indians perhaps grow to view these
things with a more understanding eye, and I could not
help feeling that it was unsympathetic, not to say somewhat unfair, thus to presume on the old Rajah's
voluntary act in depriving himself of the education of
his daughter, for her own good, as he thought. He was,
according to the standard of native ideas, by no means
a bad man, though viewed through English eyes he
might be indeed a hoary reprobate! Still, he remained
her father through all, and she owed to him the fact of
her present opportunities of Christian teaching.

At the moment of the Rajah's death my husband was
in Scotland, and took time to consider before he consented to act as executor. Mr. Montgomery Martin, who
was on the spot, alone acted at the time, placed seals on
all the property, and had the Rajah interred at Kensal
Green Cemetery, a Wesleyan minister, Mr. McArthur,
reading over the body, before it left the house, part of
the Church of England burial service! This extraordinary travesty of funeral rites shocked everybody,
even those who could not help perceiving the grim
grotesqueness of the whole ceremony!

As soon as the intelligence of the Rajah's death
reached Benares, the two principal Ranees immediately
took measures to carry out their expected duty,
promptly swallowed poison, and died before the Civil

Officer in charge arrived with a doctor! The third
remaining Ranee, and one concubine, endeavoured to
commit suicide by starvation, but were prevented, and
recovered. On the arrival of Mr. F. B. Gubbins, the
civilian, to take possession, as directed, of all the late
Rajah's jewels and effects, it was found that all had
disappeared and been buried! They were, however, under
pressure, discovered, dug up, and placed under guard
in the portico of the house. After repeated applications
from Sir C. Wood, Lord Canning apportioned 3,000
rupees per month for the support of the family in
India, who apparently consisted of eighteen or twenty
persons, exclusive of servants, the Princess Gouramma
having already (16th August, 1860) had £1,000 a year
settled on her for life by the India Office in England.
Sir H. Bartle Frere wrote most strongly to the Governor-
General, on "the flippant manner" in which Mr.
Gubbins detailed the occurrences in his despatch, and
the want of consideration shown to a native princely
family. "It is difficult for anyone who does not personally know it, to understand how utterly different
this race is from us," he remarks, "and even from most
Indian races, in all their motives and modes of action;
but there is much, even in these few papers, to illustrate
the wideness of the gulf which separates us, and the
difficulty of judging them by European standards." *

One of the daughters was a wife of Jung Bahadour,
the Prime Minister of Nepal, and, I fear, had anything
but a happy life, but anyhow, she was not in actual
penury, as were the remainder. Occasionally I received

* The whole correspondence, including Lord Canning's despatches and Sir
John Login's representations, were published in the Blue Book ordered to be
printed by the House of Commons, July 21st, 1863. Sir John W. Kaye was then
Political Secretary to the India Office. Sir Roundell Palmer (afterwards
first Earl Selborne), Mr. Leith, and Mr. Schomberg, were counsel for the Rajah
of Coorg.

appeals from them, or their agents, up to the year 1882. In April, 1881, a most pathetic and quaintly-worded missive reached me from Secunderabad, written by one " B. Sashagorri Rai," on behalf of Prince Somasuckni Wadeer, and the family of the late Rajah. It reminded me of " the parental affection and sincere feelings entertained by Sir John Login towards the family," and stated that " ever since the patron's demise the affairs of the family were ceased to bring forward," and they were reduced to " lowest ebb ! Generally dependants appeal to the mercy of their mother, in the absence of their father," the writer continues, " . . . I am impatiently waiting for motherly instructions ! . . . I regret poverty is pinching at the Rajah's family, the maintenance was reduced for few rupees. . . . If anything to be done for them, no other than yourself, Madam, are liberal enough to patronise. The good feeding given to the children by their mother shall be rewarded in double when they are successful (!!). I entirely depend on your early instructions." As I was at that date in constant touch with the India Office, I did my best to urge the case on their attention, but cannot tell, alas ! whether my representations had any effect.

Princess.Gouramma's sojourn under Lady Catherine Harcourt's charge did not prove altogether successful. The girl's temper became sullen and obstinate at what she regarded as an indignity, in being once more relegated to a governess and the schoolroom. She resented also the dulness of her daily life, and partly from *ennui*, partly out of revenge, began once more to indulge in her passion for intrigue and secrecy. Of course her mischievous propensity came to light, and was regarded as abnormally heinous by Lady Catherine and her husband, they not having had experience of the Eastern character, and so asked to be relieved of their charge. She was then put under the care of Sir James Weir Hogg, the guardian appointed by the Lord Chancellor, and moved nearer London, with her governess.

I could not but feel sorry for Lady Catherine, a most conscientious, kind-hearted woman, but could scarcely refrain from smiling at her expression of horrified reprobation of this young girl, in the letters she wrote to me at the time, though I could quite imagine that the culprit's air of stolid indifference would make her appear utterly " callous," and perverse. But my sympathy went out even more to the ignorant child, rigorously punished for faults due to early up-bringing in an Indian zenana, and not wisely corrected when first brought under the influence of Christian morality. There was something so exceedingly attractive, and amiable, in her natural manner, that I for one, regarded her with a very sincere affection, and this I believe she genuinely reciprocated.

About six months after she had left the Harcourts, the Maharajah, who concerned himself a good deal about her future, thought it would be a splendid thing to make up a match between her and one of my brothers, Colonel John Campbell (then a widower with several boys), for whom Duleep Singh had a great admiration. He accordingly made them acquainted with each other —for they had never met before—and he plumed himself greatly on the result when he found them mutually attracted. Sir James Hogg, her guardian, viewed the idea with great satisfaction. My brother, though so much older than the Princess, was still a very handsome, soldierly man, and very popular in society.

Nothing of all this was however known to me and my husband, and we were greatly surprised to hear from Sir Charles Phipps of the engagement, and that Her Majesty had graciously expressed her approval! Sir Charles in his gallant manner informed us that he had not had " the pleasure of Colonel Campbell's acquaintance, but he should expect everything from a brother of Lady Login. "

Well! they were married in July, 1860, and went soon after to pay a long visit to my eldest brother at old Kinloch, whence Gouramma wrote to my husband in a state of ecstatic happiness. She made my brother a very affectionate, devoted wife, and I feel thankful to know that these last years of her unhappy, chequered existence, had their measure of domestic and maternal joy, for a little daughter was born to them in London, on July 2nd, 1861, to whom the name " Edith Victoria Gouramma " was given—of whom more anon.

It was pathetic, the eagerness with which poor Gouramma identified herself with her husband's family ; and of all of them, of course, she knew us best, and turned to us as time went on. I have many of her affectionate letters, written latterly when strength was failing, but when nothing would damp her optimism, or make her take even reasonable care of her always delicate health.

I will just quote here the letter that she wrote to me on hearing of the sudden death of my husband, when she herself was ill already with the last fatal malady, by which she was carried off only five months later. I went to see her at once, in spite of my recent widowhood, when I learnt of her illness, and shall never forget how she received me, sitting up in the drawing-room (though really only fit for her bed !) clothed in the

deepest mourning, and with the little one, a preternaturally solemn, quiet child, of two years, attired
also in black from head to foot! to testify, as she
informed me, how she mourned "for that great, good
man, who had been such a true friend to her!"

"27, PORCHESTER TERRACE,
"*October* 21*st*, 1863.

"MY DEAREST LENA,

"I cannot express how truly distressed I am to
hear of the sudden death of dear Sir John. I loved him
better than any relations I ever knew, and I never can
forget his kindness to me. I deeply feel for you, my
dearest sister. I love you more than I ever did since
you have written me that kind and affectionate letter.

"I am much better than I have been, though still
very weak, and the sad intelligence coming on one so
unawares has made me feel still weaker, and my ideas
so confused that I don't know how to express myself.

"May God bless you and give you comfort in your
great sorrow, my dearest sister! John is much grieved,
and sympathises with you most deeply. I am so much
distressed I can write no more.

"Believe me ever your affectionate sister,

"VICTORIA GOURAMMA."

I at once informed Sir Charles Phipps of the critical
condition in which I judged that the Princess then was,
and nothing could exceed the concern displayed by
Her Majesty in her illness. I was directed to send
constant, and at one time, daily reports, as soon as Her
Majesty became aware that she was in too precarious
a state of health to accept her gracious invitation to
come and visit her, either at the Castle or at Osborne.

With varying fluctuations of strength she lingered
on ; but the fatal disease had taken too firm a hold for
a definite rally, and she died of consumption at the

early age of twenty-three, on March 31st, 1864. Her last pencilled letter when very weak, was written to me on January 15th. Latterly I was much with her, and she implored me to make her the promise that I would take her little daughter into my care, and bring her up with my own children until she was of age.

Princess Gouramma was buried in Brompton Cemetery, and on April 8th the Queen wrote to express her hope " that the poor little Princess' grave will be marked by some suitable memorial. H.M. thinks a marble or granite cross would be the most appropriate, and hopes that, in the inscription, the fact of her having been god-mother to the poor Indian child. may not be forgotten. No one knows better than you what deep interest the Queen took in her welfare. . . . I cannot help thinking of her," interjects Sir Charles in the message, " with the melancholy look which she had, poor thing, when I went down to see her ill and unhappy at the Harcourts'. Still, it is a blessing that she is at rest, and that she was, by your brother's goodness, enabled to die in the hopes of a Christian. I send you the drawing suggested. . . ." Again, later, " I submitted . . . to the Queen the enclosed draft for the inscription on the monument, of which H.M. approved, but said that a text must be added. . . . The Dean of Windsor . . . has not yet found what he likes. . . . Of course the enclosed inscription is only a proposal, and can be altered as Colonel Campbell likes. . . . I should be very glad to hear that Colonel Campbell's petition was successful " (for a continuance of part of the Princess's pension to her daughter), " but I should rather be afraid the Secretary of State would consider the child as his, and that they had done all that they could in giving the allowance for the poor

Princess's life. There can, however, be no harm, in trying, and it would give me great pleasure to hear of his success." *

I seem to have dwelt at such length on the story of poor Princess Gouramma, so tragic in many respects from its changes, vicissitudes and misunderstandings, that I will leave for the present any further mention of the little daughter who bore her name, and who in some ways so much resembled her.

---

* The inscription ran thus : " Sacred to the memory of the *Princess Victoria Gouramma*, daughter of the Ex-Rajah of Coorg, the beloved wife of Lieut.-Colonel John Campbell. Born in India, July 4th, 1841. She was brought early in life to England ; baptised into the Christian faith, under the immediate care and protection of *Queen Victoria*, who stood sponsor to her, and took a deep interest in her through life. She died 30th March, 1864. ' Other sheep I have, which are not of this fold ' (John x. 16)."

CHAPTER XIII

WE made two tours in Italy, in the fashion of the day, travelling in our own carriages, sometimes sitting in them, secured to the deck, when on board the steamer, or on a truck, when travelling by rail, thereby receiving our full modicum of wind, dust and coal-smoke!

The first time we left England, in December, 1856, the Foreign Office passport supplied to my husband (which was visé'd and endorsed at every octroi, guard-house, and town, we passed through, throughout the whole journey) gave permission to travel in a given direction, to " Sir John Login ; his lady ; ' Mr. Login' ; Mr. Ronald Leslie-Melville ; Mr. Cawood, secretary ; Prensanzini, courier ; Thornton, valet ; and Clara Sanderson, ladies' maid." " Mr. Login " was quite frankly stated in parenthesis to be the *nom de voyage* of H.H. the Maharajah Duleep Singh. Mr. Ronald Melville, afterwards the eleventh Earl of Leven, was then an Oxford undergraduate, and close companion of the Maharajah.

We had one or two exciting adventures when driving on this tour ; once, when crossing the Estrelles in the dark, the postillion, who was drunk, galloped his horses down-hill, collided with a post, and decanted the whole party, in a heap, in the middle of the road ! Again, having driven out from Rome to Tivoli with the Brights, for a picnic, on coming home we left the two politicians (Mr. John Bright and Sir John), too deep

in a discussion on India to be separated, to follow in
another vehicle, while we four—Maharajah, Miss Bright,
Ronald and I—went on in the first. The two young men
were in high spirits, making a fearful noise. Something
went wrong with the harness, and the coachman got
down to put it right, leaving the reins loose on the box.
The voices, or something else, startled the horses, and
they bolted, leaving the coachman behind on the road!
We were only saved by Ronald Melville's extraordinary
agility, promptness, and coolness. He clambered over
the box, and almost on the backs of the horses, and,
seizing the reins, pulled the animals up, just in time.

At Cannes we found expecting us, my niece, Annie
Campbell (my brother Charles'* daughter), and the
Duchess of Gordon,† who had brought her up since her
mother's death, and was very anxious to have a chance
of a talk with me over the girl's future. Here also were
Sir David Brewster and his daughter-in-law, and the
Anstruther-Thomsons. These all were fellow-guests
at a dinner to which we were invited, and which proved
unintentionally amusing.

A certain Mr. Woolfield was then the principal
British resident. He seemed to have done, or got done,
everything wanted for the place, and the foreign colony
—built the church, paid the chaplain, and become owner
of most of the houses. He and his wife most hospitably
invited all our party to dine; but the Maharajah
turned crusty, "had a cold," and declined to go, to their
great chagrin, and the outspoken disappointment of
their little niece and adopted daughter, who, when
brought in to dessert, surveyed the guests generally
with evident disfavour, and demanded in penetrating

* General Charles Campbell of Kinloch.
† Widow of the last Duke of Gordon—title extinct.

accents : " Where is the ' blackamoor ' ? You promised me a ' blackamoor ' ! " she insisted, to the consternation of her uncle and aunt, at first almost too petrified with horror to cope with the situation. They made matters worse by scolding her for using such a " vulgar expression ! Who ever could she have heard speak of *the Prince* in that manner ? " They were intensely relieved to find that I could actually laugh at such a *faux pas.* The child now directed her questions at me—" *Is* he a blackamoor ? " and " What is a blackamoor ? "—and knowing how Duleep Singh would enjoy the joke, I invited her to come next day and see for herself ! His enchantment was complete when on arrival next morning, the young lady marched up to him, regarded him with attention, and finding him no darker than the Provençal peasants she was accustomed to, immediately announced, " Why, you're not a blackamoor at all ! " evidently considering that she had been most shamefully hoaxed !

At Nice we found Lord and Lady Ely, and went to a large party at their house. The Elys were great friends with the Empress of Russia, and several of her suite were there. As a rule, however, the English society there was very indignant at the airs the Russians gave themselves. (You see, it was just after the Crimean war !) When the Czarina first came, she used to go out in great state, with outriders preceding her, armed with long whips which they cracked loudly, ordering every carriage to draw up to the side till Her Majesty passed ! The English complained to the authorities, who, in dread of their wholesale withdrawal from the place, induced Her Majesty to adopt a less overbearing ceremonial on foreign soil, and to drive about in a more unassuming manner. We met her and the Grand-

Duchess Helen, with their court ladies, driving home from a church function. All were in *full* evening dress, though the Empress appeared very ill and fragile.

At dinner Lord Ely loved making jokes—not always the most refined—but it was impossible to refrain from laughing at them and *him*, his facial expressions were so exceedingly comic! Lady Ely introduced me to Lady Dufferin, and her son, then Lord in Waiting to the Queen.* He was very amusing, and I could not quite make out whether his pretty lisp was real or affected.

We expected to find John Bright at Mentone, but he had not yet arrived. However, he turned up at Genoa, and the daily political discussions commenced between him and my husband, to be continued at Rome in the intervals of the Carnival, which Mr. Bright *thoroughly* enjoyed, entering wholeheartedly into the spirit of frolic, insisting on my accompanying him and his daughter in a carriage, up and down the Corso, where we ran the gauntlet, pelting strangers, the gallant Quaker *handing* bouquets to the ladies who took his fancy! Two days later he took up his position on our balcony at the Hôtel de Londres, and exchanged shots with Lady Knatchbull at a window opposite, putting her finally out of action by a terrific shot with a sugared almond! As they were total strangers, I had to introduce him to her, to offer his apologies for his too accurate marksmanship, at the *masked ball* in the evening! It was John Bright who himself proposed to my husband that we should go and hear Dr. Manning preach in the Church of San Carlo Borromeo. " I don't suppose," he wrote, " that he will overthrow your Presbyterianism, any more than the faith I hold with the Society of

* Afterwards Viceroy of India, when he arrested Duleep Singh !

Friends." The subject of the sermon was "The Immaculate Conception of the Blessed Virgin." To me his arguments appeared very unconvincing, but there could be no doubt of his sincerity in his belief himself, and he looked worn out with penance and fasting. His voice was painfully weak, quite lost in that great church.

We had a very merry dinner one night when Mr. Bright came with his pretty daughter to our hotel— Colonel Caldwell giving us histories of what was done in India in Lord Wellesley's, and Lord W. Bentinck's time, while Mr. Bright waxed eloquent on the *wrongs* of the unhappy natives under British domination, greatly to the diversion of the Maharajah Duleep Singh.*

Ideas of " infection " were in those days still rather hazy, for at Florence I remember going to call on my cousin, Maria Phipps,† whose husband was an attaché there, and after we had been sitting talking some time, she informed me that Caroline Norton‡ was very ill of *small-pox in the house!!* I felt very uneasy, but had not the courage to hurry off at once, and almost wished she had not told me, once we were inside !

At a party at Mr. Forbes', the American clergyman, in Rome, I was introduced to Mrs. Beecher-Stowe, and had a long conversation with her. I found her a

---

* Mr. Bright was always inclined to take a severe view of the principles guiding a British, or British-Indian government. In writing to Sir John Login in December, 1861, he remarked : " The English Government knows nothing of forbearance and magnanimity when its opponent is weak or in trouble, or General Peel could not have said with truth, as he did the other day, ' England is hated and detested by every nation in Europe.' The forbearance and moderation of the American Government during its time of trouble may preserve us from war, but . . . since 1853-54, when the Russian War commenced, I have had no faith in the morality or justice of our Government."

† Sister-in-law of Sir Charles Phipps.

‡ The Hon. Mrs. R. Norton, the poetess.

most agreeable and amusing woman, altogether a younger and more pleasing person than I had expected. Of course you young ones have all heard the conundrum, very popular at that period : " How do we know positively that ' Uncle Tom's Cabin ' was the work of no mortal hand ? " and the answer, " Because it was written by Mrs. Beecher-Stowe " (Beecher's toe !). Luckily I had not yet heard it when I met her !

Rome always was a place with a pet story going the rounds, and the two staple ones when we visited it were the following.

A certain old lady, on her first visit to the Eternal City, wrote home to her family " that after all she had heard about it, she was greatly disappointed with the place itself. It was in such a ruinous condition that she wondered the Pope was not ashamed, and did not have it either repaired or the rubbish carted away ! "

The other referred to the well-known absence of mind of Lord Macaulay, the historian (at that time simple " Mr." Macaulay), who was spending the winter amid the scenes of his " Ancient Lays." We had known him already slightly in India, but his relations, the Trevelyans, were intimate friends. The anecdote was going the round of the English colony when we reached Rome, and one of the attachés at the Embassy at once passed it on to us. Like all strangers, he went by moonlight to see the Coliseum, and, as was proper in a historian and a poet, that the spirit of the centuries might have full sway within his soul, he went alone ! As he stood, rapt and gazing, in the shadow of the arches, a man jostled him, brushing rudely by. Instinctively Mr. Macaulay felt for his watch. It was gone—The thief was still in view ! Promptly the historian gave chase, and, taking the law into his own hands, as might one of his own heroes of yore, he, without further ado, knocked down the miscreant, and repossessed himself of his property ! Feeling a little anxious, after this adventure, lest other criminals might be about, he thought it wiser to return at once to his hotel, where the first thing that greeted him, ticking comfortably on his dressing-table, was his own gold watch ! His hand went to his waistcoat pocket, and drew out a strange gold watch and chain ! ! Horrified at this successful *début* as a footpad, he hurried to the *bureau de police* to give up his booty, to find himself confronted by an enraged foreigner, excitedly describing the outrage of which he had been the victim, and its perpetrator !

On Ash-Wednesday we were specially privileged to attend the ceremony in the Sixtine Chapel when the Pope sprinkles the ashes on the heads of the Cardinals, and of any royalties then in Rome. The Maharajah refused to go, as the hour was so early, and the last Carnival ball had worn him out !' Sir John was in full political uniform, and the chamberlains tried hard to make him take his seat in the ambassadors' pew. Fortunately he refused, as all the foreign representatives present proceeded after the ceremony to kiss 'the Pontiff's toe ! I was, however, shown into the tribune for the wives of ambassadors, and was its sole occupant Presumably they were mostly bachelors, for my presence seemed to arouse the liveliest amazement and curiosity amongst them !

After the ·Cardinals had received their sprinkling, and kissed the Holy Father's *hand*, the King of Bavaria (Ludwig I.) advanced and went through the same ceremony—save that he, and all who followed him, had to kiss the right *toe* instead. Then came the husband of Queen Christina of Spain, and I must say I was

rather shocked—considering the sacred associations of
the whole service—to see how, on the Duke's return to
his pew, the whole royal party, including the Queen
of Spain and her daughters, at once set to work—
amid much smothered laughter—to blow at his hair,
and dust off his clothes all traces of the ashes, using
for the purpose not only their handkerchiefs, but also
a clothes-brush, with which they had come ready provided! This occupation, and the merriment it caused,
lasted them throughout the remainder of the function,
which, commencing at nine in the morning, did not
conclude till nearly everybody in the church, including
the soldiers on duty, had been sprinkled, and so lasted
until one o'clock! The Pope chanted the service most
beautifully. He had a splendid, clear voice.

These same royalties, and in addition, "Henri
Cinq," the Comte de Chambord, had been at a big ball
a few nights before, at the Doria Palace, which we had
attended, and where we were all presented to the
Princess Doria, one of the Shrewsbury family. The
King of Bavaria, and Queen Christina, were the two
crowned heads in Rome on that occasion, and our only
rencontre with the former was that, when out following
the Campagna fox-hounds in our carriage (they met
on the Appian Way, near the tomb of Cecilia Metella),
we found ourselves just in front of His Majesty's
equipage, whose servants called out to ours to let
him pass. Nothing would induce our coachman to do
this, although we ordered him to give way, and whipping
up his horses, he kept the "lead" throughout the chase!
Though not recognised as so mad as his son, I believe
this monarch was decidedly eccentric, and this sort
of treatment was scarcely calculated to conciliate a
sovereign of uncertain temper!

Rome seemed in those days a sort of health-resort for crowned heads who suffered from the weight of their dignities, for on our next visit, King Frederic William IV. of Prussia was the visitor round whom circled all the gossip of that most gossiping capital.

The favourite *on dit* then going the rounds—I cannot vouch for its truth ; but one of the foreign diplomats is my authority—was, that it was during his sojourn at the Eternal City that his own Court circle became convinced his brain had really given way. And the following was the occasion on which the malady first manifested itself without question.

One evening, at dinner with the gentlemen of his household—there was a foreign guest also of some importance present—the menu commenced with *potage clair à l'italienne*, in which floated a very bountiful supply of *very* long strands of vermicelli. When placed before His Majesty, he regarded it solemnly for some moments, with an air of slight astonishment, then slowly raised the bowl in his two hands, and with the utmost gravity, poured the contents in a sort of libation on the crown of his head, slowly turning his eyes round the company, as if to watch the effect upon them ! Knowing that their careers, if not their lives almost, depended on it, they managed to preserve a rigid self-control in the King's presence, though it required a superhuman effort to resist the inclination to mirth at the extraordinary spectacle he afforded, blinking solemn eyes at them, like a ruminating owl, while the vermicelli decorated his hair and whiskers and hung like long icicles over his forehead and eyebrows ! His suite, I was told, were hysterical for days afterwards, and I really thought the Maharajah would have a fit, from his convulsions of laughter when he heard the story. He, and Ronald Melville, were continually making feints of trying the experiment, from that day forward, whenever we happened to have a guest at meals who bored them overmuch with his conversation !

Baron von Orlich, the traveller, whom my husband had known in India, was another old acquaintance we met again in Rome, and he kindly made out for us our route on to Naples, along the Appian Way, so that we might not miss any points of interest. He and his wife kept up a correspondence with us for many years afterwards.

At Naples we made the acquaintance of the Marchese Bugnano and his wife and mother (the latter an Irish lady), and other Neapolitan nobles ; but our stay here was cut short by the rampant political propaganda of our courier Triboux, a violent Republican and Garibaldian, who was discovered haranguing the populace, and inciting them to rebellion against the Bourbon King ! On my husband ordering him to behave himself while in our service, he became incoherent with indignation, exclaiming that he was a " free-born Swiss," and daring him, or anybody, to "touch his *sacred pairs-son!!*" I am afraid Sir John made short work of his " sacred person," and he was bundled off in a hurry, as we did not wish to be embroiled in any political disputes !

We were at Venice for Easter-Day, and went to see the Pontifical Mass at S. Mark's, when the Archduke Maximilian (afterwards Emperor of Mexico), brother of the Austrian Emperor, and Viceroy of Italy, went in procession to the Duomo. He was a fair-haired, simple-looking youth, and appeared nervous till the ceremony was safely over without any anti-Austrian demonstration.

The Brights again joined us here, having been detained

in Rome owing to Miss Bright getting measles. Unfortunately, both the Maharajah and Ronald Melville were
very ill at Venice from malarial fever, and as soon as
possible we got them away to Padua, leaving Mr.
Cawood, the secretary, to bring on our linen, which had
been away at the laundry, as well as some heavy luggage,
unaware that, according to Austrian railway regulations,
it was forbidden for a man to be in possession of female
attire. Unable to explain matters himself in Italian,
they undid the boxes, shook my nice frilled petticoats
in his face, inquiring sarcastically if these were usual
portions of his attire ? and finally arrested him as a
thief in possession of stolen property ! It was some days
before we could get him released.

CHAPTER XIV

THE MAHARANEE JINDA KOÜR

MAI CHUNDA—the Maharanee Jinda Koür, as she was called—Duleep Singh's mother, had been for many years in Nepal, where she was held practically a prisoner by Jung Bahadour, who grudged her every penny of the pension he *said* he allowed her, and with whom she quarrelled incessantly. They were really rather " birds of a feather," but that did not make them agree any the better ! Both were unscrupulous, and it would be hard to say which was the craftier intriguer.

Colonel Ramsey, then Resident at Khatmandoo, wrote Login in 1860 that he considered " that a more unprincipled scoundrel " (than Jung Bahadour) " did not tread the earth. He would have taken part against us at the time of the Mutiny, if it had not been for that providential visit of his to England, and the experience he gained there ; and for this we have to thank your poor brother,* who exerted such a wise influence over him, and persuaded him to the step. Jung has often told me so himself. . . . The sister of Princess Gouramma of Coorg, who married Jung Bahadour some years ago, is now a very fine-looking young woman, and seems happy enough. The other sister, whom he also brought with him from Benares in 1853, was sadly duped, and wanted to go back to her brothers. She is said to be very unhappy."

A private letter, from Sir John Kaye at the India

* Dr. James Dryburgh Login. See *ante*, pp. 64, 87, 88.

House, informed Login in November 1856, that the Viceroy had received a letter intercepted by Jung Bahadour, from the Maharajah to his mother, suggesting that she should come to England! Fortunately, it was easy to produce proof that the letter was an impudent forgery. Up to that time, Duleep Singh had shown not the faintest desire to have communication with his mother, but curiously enough, just about this same time, he had commissioned the Pundit Nehemiah Goreh to make the journey to Khatmandoo on his behalf, and find out, at first hand, how she really was living and conducting herself.

Unfortunately, the Pundit bungled matters, and instead of going himself—the season being unhealthy for crossing the Terai—sent the Maharanee a letter through a native banker visiting Nepal on business. Of course this came to the Viceroy's knowledge, and the Pundit was forbidden to open communications with her, except through the British Resident.

Then the idea occurred to Duleep Singh of combining pleasure with filial duty, and of going out for a cold-weather tiger-shoot to India, at the same time meeting his mother. Just at the same period he was in treaty for the purchase of an estate in England, and my husband had to send him a letter about another property in Scotland, to which he had taken a great fancy, and this is the characteristic reply he sent from Calcutta :

" SPENCE'S HOTEL, CALCUTTA,
" *February*, 1861.

" Oh ! it is too cruel of you to write to me, so soon after coming out here, about an estate in Scotland ; for now I cannot make up my mind to stay a day longer than is necessary to see my mother ! Your letter has almost driven me wild ; so you may expect to see me back sooner than I thought of when I left. I have got the Shahzadah here on a visit. . . .

" Now I must tell you that India is a beastly place ! I heartily repent having come out, for I cannot get a moment's peace, with people following me, and all my old servants bother the life out of me with questions. The heat is something dreadful, and what will it be in another month ? I hate the natives ; they are such liars, flatterers, and extremely deceitful ! I would give anything to be back in dear England, among my friends. I cannot think or write about anything else but this property ! Oh, buy it for me, if possible ! My mother is to be at Rani Gunj in ten or twelve days. I wish her to await me there, as it is quieter than Calcutta. I have heard (not officially) that she is to have from two to three thousand a year, but will know for certain when the Governor-General returns here.

" I have not yet settled whether I remain over the hot weather here, going up to the hills and then return-ing to England. I am to have elephants from Govern-ment for tiger shooting. It is already very hot. Shah-zadah is very anxious to come with me to England, but does not expect to manage it.

" Yours affectionately and sincerely,
" DULEEP SINGH.

" P.S.—My mother has decided she will not separate from me any more, and as she is refused permission to go to the hills, I must give up that intention, and, I suppose, we shall return to England as soon as I can get passage."

In that last sentence we recognised the first tokens of the extraordinary influence which from the moment of the resumption of personal contact, the Maharanee exercised over the son, who in his childhood both feared and despised her, and in his growing manhood had tried to forget her existence.

There was, however, an additional reason for this sudden determination to return to England, and it illustrated Duleep Singh's sincere desire to prove his loyalty to the British Government.

The Chinese War had just ended when he landed at Calcutta, and many of the Sikh regiments were returning home. The word passed round the troopships, as they entered the Hooghly, that their deposed Sovereign, Runjeet's son, was actually in the city! · The men flocked about his hotel in thousands, and were so demonstrative in their joy and greetings, that the officials became much alarmed, and Lord Canning requested Duleep Singh, as a favour to the Government, not in any way as a *command*, to relinquish the sporting trip up-country which he had originally planned, and in preparation for which he had gone to great expense, and to return to England with his mother, by the next home-going steamer. It was indeed a great sacrifice to ask, but the young Sikh Sovereign accepted it chivalrously and without a murmur.

He wrote to us on the passage, begging Sir John to secure a house for his mother in London, close to where we were then living, at Lancaster Gate, so that the Maharanee might have somewhere to go to at once on arrival, as it would take some time to get all her baggage and valuables landed, and passed through the customs. And a truly formidable collection it proved to be when it turned up! We were fortunate in finding a large house; next door but one to our own—" No. 1, round-the-corner," as it was called at that time, though now, I imagine, numbered something like 23. For the houses on each side of Christ Church were the only ones then finished, and it was not until many years had passed, that the row of large mansions facing Kensington

Gardens was embarked upon. Into it Sir John put such
few articles of furniture as they did not actually bring
with them, and he had cooking-places arranged for the
natives in the areas, which were a source of perpetual
attraction to the street urchins, who clung in hordes
to the railings, looking down upon a scene which they
regarded as superior in interest to any bear-pit in
Regent's Park.

I went to pay my first visit of ceremony as soon as
I understood that the Maharanee was sufficiently rested
after the voyage to receive me. I believe, as a matter
of fact though, that it was her son, and not she, who had
suffered any discomforts from *mal de mer* !

It was with some natural curiosity, not unmingled
with awe and trepidation, that I looked forward to my
first interview with the woman who at one time had
wielded such power in India. The stories told in those
days of her beauty and fascination, as well as her talent
for diplomacy and strength of will, were almost as
universal as those related in these later years of the great
Dowager-Empress of China, between whose history and
character, and that of Mai Chunda, there were many
points of resemblance. And I especially had heard
much of her at first hand, not so much from her son,
who rarely mentioned her, as from others who had
known her in the days of her magnificence : the Ranee
Duknoo and her relations, Duleep Singh's own attendants and ministers, as well as the Lawrence brothers,
and other British officers and civilians, who, with their
wives, had seen her in Lahore. It was therefore with a
sense of disillusionment and compassion that, when,
accompanied by my three youngest children, after
being received with all honour and deference by her
attendants, her women ushering me ceremoniously into

the large, heavily-curtained room, I found myself in
semi-darkness, confronting an aged, half-blind woman,
sitting huddled on a heap of cushions on the floor !
With health broken and eyesight dimmed, her beauty
vanished, and an air of lassitude, it was hard to believe
in her former charms of person and of conversation !
Yet the moment she grew interested and excited in a
subject, unexpected gleams and glimpses, through the
haze of indifference, and the torpor of advancing
years, revealed the shrewd and plotting brain, of her
who had once been known as "the Messalina of the
Punjab ! "

Of her love of authority, and imperious character, I
was to have an example. She inquired the age of my
youngest boy, Harry, whom I presented to her at her
request ? The little girls she took no interest in. When
I said, " Eight years ! " she immediately rejoined, " And
where is his wife ? " On my replying with as much
gravity as I could command at the suggestion, " He is
rather young to think of that yet," she suddenly
roused herself, and read me a regular lecture on my
duties as a mother ! It was my part, she told me, to
think of that important question as soon as my son was
able to run about by himself, and it was really scarcely
decent that the child of a " Bahadur " of his father's
rank, should not yet have a marriage arranged for him !
I must lose no further time, she pronounced, with a very
commanding mien ! Her women tried to interpose,
and smooth matters, evidently fearful lest I should be
offended by her very dogmatic expression of opinion.
In reality I was so choked with laughter, that I hardly
knew how to frame a proper apology for my misappre-
hension of the maternal *rôle !* I verily believe she had
it in her mind to undertake to remedy my negligence

herself, or at the very least warn my husband of my incompetence in carrying out this essential part of my *métier!*

Sir John, I believe, made a most favourable impression upon her—this, as you may have gathered, was not unusual with him when in contact with natives of high rank—but the Maharanee Jinda Koür expressed herself with the utmost frankness on the subject. He had of course been able to be of a good deal of assistance to her on arrival, and had expedited the passage of her jewels through the Custom House so efficiently, that she was able to wear the majority of them, when doing me the extreme honour of returning my visit in person within a few days. For this service alone she was extremely grateful to him, as she had not had her jewels (which were decidedly valuable) in her own possession since the day of her flight from Chunar Fort—the Indian Government having retained them all the years she was in Nepal.

Evidently she had gathered quite a different impression of the personality of her son's guardian from the reports of native "informers," for, after she had seen him only once or twice, she told him quite naïvely, that "had she only known what he was *really like*, and how extremely useful and kind he would prove to her, she *never would have arranged to have him poisoned*, as she had at one time contemplated!" Even *her* candour was slightly abashed when he made it (diplomatically) plain to her, that he had been all along aware of her kind project, a hint having reached him at Futtehghur!

It was indeed a very great condescension, and no small effort of exertion on the old Maharanee's part, to think of coming in person to return my visit. Though the distance from house to house was not great, there

had to be precautions to screen her from public view—
a sign of deference to their rank and sex that the elder
native ladies much appreciate—our men-servants were
banished from view, and only the maids allowed to
" assist " at the reception.

My drawing-room, of course, was on the first floor,
and I shall never forget the sight, as I viewed it from
the landing, of the Maharanee being *hoisted by main
force* up the long flight of stairs by several servants !
In her case this piece of Oriental etiquette was perhaps
not unnecessary, not only on account of her infirmities,
but because, in addition to being a heavy woman, she
had wished to pay me a special compliment by appearing
in European dress ; and as she could not entirely abandon her native garments for English underclothing,
she had donned an enormous bonnet with feather,
mantle, and wide skirt over immense crinoline, on the
top of all her Indian costume ! And this on a warm
day in June, in the stuffy London atmosphere !   No
wonder she was utterly unable to move hand or foot, and
found it impossible to take a seat, encumbered with the
crinoline, till two of her servants lifted her bodily up on
to a settee, where she could sit comfortably cross-legged,
her crinoline spreading all round her like a cheese !

We had been kept waiting for her appearance for
some considerable time after the hour named, and
now appeared the cause of the delay ! Not only had
the enduing of these unaccustomed habiliments
taken long, but her jewels had at the moment arrived
from the Custom House, and so delighted was she at
the sight, that she forthwith decorated herself, and her
attendants, with an assortment of the most wonderful
necklaces and earrings, strings of lovely pearls and
emeralds being arranged, in graceful concession to

English fashion, as a sort of fringe or frilling inside the brim of the bonnet, in the place where the custom then was to wear a semblance of a "cap!" The extraordinary figures which the poor Maharanee and her favourite women cut, in this attire, can be better imagined than described!

She had brought with her, as a companion and confidential attendant, a young slave-woman named Soortoo, who had been born in the zenana, and as a child had been Duleep Singh's playmate, being about the same age. There was something particularly engaging about Soortoo. She was pretty, and of graceful manners and address, and had a frank, open countenance, and a simple disposition. She seemed brimming over with happiness at seeing England, and genuinely attached to her mistress and her son. She had been given in marriage, at an early age, by the Maharanee, to a man of rather low caste in Benares, but had been ordered to accompany her imperious mistress to England, with very little regard to the fact that her small baby, and other children, had been left behind!

Duleep Singh took his mother down to Mulgrave Castle, which he then had on a lease from Lord Normanby; and there she remained with him, resisting all efforts of his friends to make her arrange a separate establishment in another house on the estate, until June, 1862, when the Maharajah took a house for her in London, and placed her under the charge of an English lady.

There was no doubt that the Maharanee's presence had a bad influence upon Duleep Singh, undoing much of the benefit of his English upbringing and Christian surroundings, and tempting him to lapse into negligent,

idle, native habits. She herself expressed no objection
to his change of religion, and allowed him to form hopes
of her own conversion, but she was not one to care much
for these things, nor one to seem likely to prove a
creditable result of missionary effort !

For some years Login had been exerting all his
energy, and devoting his time, to the endeavour to
induce the Indian Government to fulfil their obligations
to his late charge, and when they seemed unwilling
to do so, to arouse interest in Parliament, and in influential circles, on his behalf. When his efforts seemed
on the point of exerting successful pressure, and it was
found that his opinions had weight in quarters not anticipated, the Indian authorities used all means at their
disposal to sever connection between him and his late
ward, and destroy the complete confidence that existed
between them. All this I have so fully entered upon in
another place * that it is unnecessary to more than allude
to it here. The India House so much resented the fact of
the correspondence he had had with Sir Charles Phipps
on Indian Government schemes (though it was not of
his own seeking, and they were aware of it only by
his own act as soon as it commenced) † that in February,
1858, they informed him that his guardianship was at
an end, and his salary must now cease ! He was able to
point out that, in addition to the office of Guardian,
he had been made Superintendent and "Agent to the
Governor-General with the Maharajah," and that these
functions would not necessarily cease when His Highness
was regarded of age. They then graciously allowed him
three months *on half-pay*, for the audit of his accounts.

* " Sir John Login and Duleep Singh," by Lady Login, published in 1890
by W. H. Allen & Co., Waterloo Place.
   † See *ante*, Chapter X.

However, when the first Secretary of State for India, the Earl of Derby (then Lord Stanley), took up his post, he, " fully appreciating the very conscientious and efficient manner in which Sir John Login had discharged his duties," ordered that full salary should be paid him up to December 1st, 1858, and Sir James Melvill, on behalf of the late Court of Directors, taking his cue, wrote :—" That the Court could not allow the connection which had existed for so many years between you and the Maharajah to cease, without expressing their entire approbation of the manner in which you have performed the duties of your important office, as evinced by the good results of the careful training for which the young Prince is indebted to you."   My husband, on his part, could not refrain in his reply from remarking that " it was a source of much gratification to himself that he had been able . . . to establish and confirm a feeling of goodwill, loyalty, *and respect*, towards the British Government, *on the part of one from whom such sentiments could scarcely have been expected*."

Nevertheless, the Court were resolved, in some measure, to visit on their subordinate the fact, that his efforts to see justice done by the Government to his ward were *almost* crowned by success, by refusing to sanction the Maharajah's wish to make some provision for his late guardian, or his family, to compensate him, and them, for the pecuniary losses involved by his guardianship, and thus he felt compelled to resign his commission in the East India Company's service, after holding it for twenty-six years !

He was not the first, and by no means the last, of the servants of the Indian Government to set his own private interests lower than his sense of justice and the honour of the British name.

Though no longer holding an official position as a Government agent in respect of the Maharajah, he was able to work still more effectively in a private and business capacity for him.   The Government now insisted on regarding Duleep Singh as of full age, when they wanted his signature without his late guardian's concurrence, and as a minor whenever they objected to his giving Sir John a power-of-attorney to transact his affairs for him; and in this undignified quibbling and shirking they persisted for the next few years !

But these intrigues and resentments of the India House officials had no influence on the opinion held in higher quarters.   As I have shown, Her Majesty's request that I should undertake the charge of Princess Gouramma was subsequent to all this, which took place in the early part of 1858.   The rule of the Company was already doomed more than six months before that, and it came to an end in August of that year.   In September, 1858, Sir C. Phipps asked Login's opinion of the Queen's proclamation on taking over the Government of India, and Her Majesty herself, as we have seen, in writing Lord Derby, mentions this fact.   He was also asked, in July, 1858, by the Duke of Marlborough, then in the Ministry, to come and coach him in Indian matters.   And, in the same way when, three years later, the authorities, and his well-wishers, perceived how undesirable was his mother's close association with the young Indian prince, my husband was appealed to, on all sides, to use his influence to put an end to it.

There had already been correspondence on the subject from Her Majesty, through Sir Charles Phipps, when there fell on Sovereign and people the overwhelming blow of the unexpected death of the revered and noble Prince Consort. The news was brought to me straight from Windsor by my husband, who had gone there direct to inquire, having been rendered anxious by the bulletins and information given him at Buckingham Palace, and the notes from Sir Charles Phipps. He did not, of course, ask to see Sir Charles that day, but was much touched and gratified to receive from him, at such a time, the following short letter, dated " Windsor Castle, Dec. 16, 1861 " :

" MY DEAR LOGIN,
   " You will have known the reason why I was unable to see you on Saturday. I was overwhelmed with anxiety, alas ! too well founded, and with persons pouring in upon me with inquiries from every side.
   " Thank you, however, *very much* for coming down to inquire. I have written to the Maharajah, who will, I know, be deeply grieved.
   " The Queen keeps very calm between the paroxysms of her grief.
                              " Sincerely yours,
                                 " C. B. PHIPPS."

There is something especially pathetic and moving in that little allusion, that half-raising of the veil of silence which, at the time, so completely shrouded the figure of the Sovereign in her personal sorrow.
   Even at that time of deep affliction, the Maharajah's welfare was an object of concern to Queen Victoria, and by her direction Sir Charles Phipps wrote (January 4th, 1862) to urge Login *not* to give up any position or influence he could have over him. " I should have written sooner," he says ; " but you may conceive what this house is at present, for the very air we

breathe is an atmosphere of sorrow, and that is a bad medium in which to transact business."

Duleep Singh's religious feelings were at this time in an unsettled and emotional condition; at one moment filled with a sudden impulse of missionary ardour, for which by temperament and lack of study he was entirely unsuited, but which was none the less perfectly genuine; at another attracted by the most extravagant and ignorant forms of sectarianism, so that one never knew from day to day what fresh idea he might not be pursuing.

The sudden death of his secretary, Mr. Cawood, was to him a great shock, and, on the spur of the moment, he wrote in August, 1861, from Auchlyne, to ask my husband at once to request permission from the Indian authorities for his return to that country, with his mother, giving up all his pension and emoluments, and taking only a *jagheer* in the Dehra Dun, where he intended henceforth to devote his life to the welfare of the native Christians! "God has touched my heart," he wrote, "and has brought me back to follow that path that leads to everlasting bliss! . . . I have spent too much of my time in worldliness, and am anxious now to do what is my duty towards God. May the Lord long continue to make this the sole desire of my heart!"

Sir John was away at Vichy, when this letter was forwarded to me at Llandulas in Wales, whither I had gone with the children for the summer. Fortunately I opened it, and wrote at once to Duleep Singh, begging him to take time and thought before embarking on such a serious step, or even speaking of it openly; and it seems that Colonel Oliphant, who was now living with him as a sort of equerry, gave him the same advice.

It was impossible, even with all his faults, to fail to hold in very affectionate regard such an impulsive, boyish nature. When in London, he still made the practice of joining us on Sunday mornings to go with the whole party to church, and return to the children's midday dinner, and felt himself quite defrauded if we omitted from the *menu* the regulation joint of roast beef! The people at the hotel—Claridge's—he declared never could be induced to believe that he preferred it to anything else !

There was one Sunday, however, when he did not turn up, much to our surprise, as he had never failed ; and on our return from church we found Mrs. Claridge, the hotel proprietor's wife, who had known us many years, waiting to see Sir John in private. In great distress, she, after much hesitation, informed him that she felt it her duty to beg him to prevent the Maharajah, . for whom she somehow felt responsible, from being led astray to do things in her house she could not allow. It then turned out that a young friend of the Prince's, who had lately joined the sect of " Plymouth Brethren," had prevailed on him to believe that attendance at Divine services, and the institution of clergy, were quite unnecessary ordinances ; *he* could preach and pray with him just as well, and even administer to him the Sacrament in his hotel sitting-room ! To the scandalised horror of the waiters, this young man attempted to do so, and the outraged landlady, after refusing sanction, fled to my husband for support.

When it appeared that Duleep Singh was in danger of dropping back into native ways, and of yielding, through indolence, to *any* arrangement of his own affairs that would give him the handling of a lump sum of money, Sir John thought it best and most dignified to hand back to the-Maharajah all documents connected with his case, and withdraw from the charge of his affairs.

This seemed to bring his former ward to a better perception of what should be his course, and decided him to ask permission for his mother's return to India. Sir Charles Phipps wrote at once to Sir Charles Wood at the India Office, strongly urging that no obstacle might be placed in the way of granting his desire. The Government point of view was very neatly put by Sir John Lawrence to Login at this juncture—Lawrence had just been made member of the new Indian Council at home :—

" There can be no doubt whatever that the Maharanee is better out of India than in it ! There, she is sure to do mischief—here, I admit, she will be equally the evil genius of the Maharajah ! It is for the Secretary of State for India to decide *which interest is of paramount importance ! !* "

It was in the middle of a letter written to Sir John at this period, and referring to his mother's affairs, that Duleep Singh suddenly interpolated the remark : " You will be glad to hear that my mother has *given me leave* " (mark how the man of twenty-two had resumed the shackles of native custom !) " to marry an English lady, and I think I have found one who will make me a good wife ! *Pray don't* TELL *this to anyone !* " Heartily rejoiced at the idea, as he rightly conceived, we made haste to write and congratulate him and ask a few more particulars. To our amusement, the following reply was received :

" I am afraid I must have expressed myself in a curious manner in my last . . . to make you think I

am engaged to be married. But I wished you to understand that if you should hear of it soon—*be not surprised!!* I would willingly tell you her name, but I
cannot muster up courage to propose! although I feel
sure I shall be accepted!'"

And then no more came of it!!! Some time after,
I got him in a corner by himself, determined to get
to the bottom of this curtailed novelette, and the
dénoûment struck me as so unutterably funny, that
I fear I did not at all conform to the *rôle* of the
sympathetic confidante, but positively shrieked with
laughter; and the Maharajah himself, who had commenced his tale with a woe-begone air, so manifestly
enjoyed the recital, that he quite forgot to be miserable
over it in the end!

Apparently he had reason for being sure of the fair
one's willingness, only unfortunately (like others before
him!) he made too certain, and forgot that delay
is sometimes fatal! When at length he " screwed his
courage to the sticking-point," he found that he was
just a day too late, and the lady had accepted another
suitor! Nevertheless, it seemed, she allowed him the
satisfaction of knowing that it was his procrastination
alone that lost the day, and that she regretted as much
as he did the result of his want of resolution! As far
as I could gather, they mingled their tears in a sad
farewell, and he consoled himself by shooting over her
husband's moors, once the marriage was an accomplished fact!

In December, 1862, my husband took a short trip to
India, being asked by the Board of Indian Tramway
Company—now the South Indian Railway—to go out
to Bombay as their representative, to confer on their
behalf with the Governor, Sir Bartle Frere. He returned

to England in April, 1863, having thoroughly inspected
the various lines proposed throughout the Bombay
Presidency, but was prevented, through the advance
of the hot weather, from. carrying out his intention
of travelling over Bengal in the same manner.   Many
letters reached him from his old native friends and
servants in Oude, begging him to let them see him also.

He had never known what it meant to be obliged
to take precautions on account of his health, and on
his return made no difference in his previous habits,
though so lately transported from the heat of Bombay
to the treacherous weather of an English spring.   Crossing Hyde Park one morning in May, in a bitter east
wind, without an overcoat, he contracted his *very first*
severe illness, and was ordered to the seaside afterwards
to recuperate.   This was the occasion of our going first
to Felixstowe, on the Suffolk coast, then a small village
with one-hotel and a few lodging-houses.   .It became our
home for fifteen years from that date.

We had been there only a short time when, on
August 1st, a frantic telegram arrived, despatched
by mounted messenger from Ipswich, twelve miles off,
then the nearest telegraph office, in which the
Maharajah implored my husband's presence *at once* in
London, as his mother, the Maharanee Jinda, had died
that morning !   The Maharajah had himself been
hastily summoned from Loch Kennard Lodge, in Perthshire, only two days before, and had written to Sir John
that very day, to say that his mother seemed better
since his arrival.

Poor Jinda Koür, who had been living in Abingdon
House, Kensington, for the past year, waiting the
Indian Government's decision as to her further destina-
tion, had thus departed on her final journey, leaving her

household in a wild turmoil of grief and contternation, which Sir John was wanted to allay. Though really unfit for the effort, he, who had always been at the beck and call of all who needed him, refused to delay a moment, and responded forthwith to the summons of his former ward.

All arrangements had been left till his arrival. He it was who had to console and pacify the lamenting son and servants, and arrange for the temporary housing of the remains, in an unconsecrated vault in Kensal Green Cemetery, until such time as measures could be taken for their transference to India, to receive the Hindoo funeral rites. A very simple ceremony marked the conveyance of the body to Kensal Green ; but as a mark of respect, and to the gratification of the Maharajah, a good number of Indian notabilities attended this. Those who knew the Maharajah's natural nervousness, and the effort which it cost him to speak at all in public, were very much touched and impressed, by his conquering his shyness, on this occasion, so far as to address a few well-chosen words to his mother's native servants, comparing the Hindoo religion with the Christian's hope, and giving the reasons " for the faith that was in him." All who witnessed it spoke of it as a very impressive incident in a strange scene.

CHAPTER XV

ON the evening of St. Luke's Day, October 18th, 1863, my dear husband, John Spencer Login, was called away—suddenly, quietly and peacefully, sitting in his chair, alone in his room, with not a soul to see the passing—to the presence of that Friend and Master Whom he had served faithfully and constantly through the fifty-three years of his life. Not a sound, not a struggle, had disturbed the calm in which we found him, lying back in the long rest which his marvellous energy had never suffered him to indulge in of his own act. Well had he earned repose! He had never spared himself. Flesh and blood could no more, and his heart had worked unceasingly until it stopped, and the end came! The end indeed, as far as this world lay; but could those who knew him doubt, that " in the heavenly mansions there was a place prepared " for a larger, fuller exercise, of the qualities of heart and mind, the powers of sympathy, faith and patience, which had made him such a counsellor and support to those in need of help and guidance?

It was a Sunday. He had seemed in his usual health, and attended church. In the evening, as was their custom, the family and household joined in singing their favourite hymns, and the last one sung, " Jesu, lover of my soul! " he had been heard singing under his breath as he went upstairs to his dressing-room. This was the last seen of him alive! Though barely four months had elapsed since he first came to Felixstowe, as everywhere, the time had proved long enough for him to make an extraordinary impression on the people of the place, his own early training, and sea-faring instincts, causing him to take a special interest in the lives of the fishermen and coastguards, and he loved to question and exchange ideas with them during his daily rides along the beach. The memories of his amphibious boyhood revived with the smell of the sea-weed and the salt water, for he was an Orcadian, and a sailor by instinct, and had narrowly escaped volunteering for Sir John Franklin's last fatal expedition.

So the coastguardsmen of the station begged to be permitted to pay their last respects to him, in full uniform, at the funeral ; and, learning how he had served the flag in many times of war, in various ways, insisted on themselves bearing the coffin shoulder-high to the grave in Felixstowe churchyard, a mile away. My last view of it was thus, as it went away from the door, with Lieut. Hart, R.N., in charge, the hearse and mourning coaches following empty behind, most of the mourners walking in the procession, headed by the Maharajah Duleep Singh, who shared with my two boys the post of chief mourners.

It was really marvellous how so many of his old friends and former associates, in addition to our own relatives, had made a point of being present, at great inconvenience in many cases to themselves, specially Lord Lawrence (then Sir John), who was shortly going out to India to take up his position as Viceroy ; Sir Frederick Currie ; General Sir James Alexander, K.C.B., Mr. John Marshman, the historian, and the Rev. William Jay, formerly Chaplain at Futtehghur, who read the burial service. The first-named wrote at once to

SIR JOHN SPENCER LOGIN.

my eldest boy and girl, offering all assistance in his power, on the death of his " dear old friend," and Lady Lawrence was equally kind. To a mutual friend, at the funeral, Lord Lawrence made the remark: " I never met another man who so perfectly combined the most straightforward truthfulness, with a complete courtesy of manner." Indeed, letters and offers of help poured in from every side, from those who had learnt to know and respect him, and amongst the very kindest, and most sympathetic, were those received from a quarter whence words of commendation are naturally held of high value. The first was addressed to my eldest daughter, who had written to announce the death on my behalf, in the first hours of my bereavement.

" St. James's Palace,
" *Oct.* 24*th* (5 *p.m.*), 1863.
" My dear Miss Login,

" I can hardly attempt to express to you how shocked I was to see yesterday, when arriving at Edinburgh, the account of the sudden death of my dear friend, your father. I had hoped that he had entirely recovered from his illness, and that we might hope for a long-continued life of usefulness. Lady Login knows how strong was my regard and friendship for him. I find it quite impossible to say how much I regret the loss of so excellent and valued a friend. There were, how-ever, dear Miss Login, few people so well prepared for a sudden call to his Maker, for few people had such strong feelings upon religion, or acted so uniformly upon Christian rules. If I dared to intrude on your dear mother's sacred grief, I would beg to be allowed to assure her of my sympathy in her loss, founded on the deep regard and respect I feel for the truly good man whose loss we mourn. . . . For you, also, I feel deeply. What must have been your love for such a father ! . . . I have only just arrived in London

Q 2

(5 p.m.), or I should have asked to be permitted to join to-day in the last sad tokens of respect. It would be very kind if you would write again soon, to tell me of Lady Login,

"Believe me, very sincerely yours,

"C. B. Phipps."

"Windsor Castle,
"*Oct. 27th*, 1863.

"My dear Lady Login,

"The Queen has this morning commanded me to write to you in Her name, to express to you the *deep* and *very sincere sympathy* with which She has heard of the overwhelming affliction which has fallen upon you! Few, indeed, can so well enter into the grief under which you must now be suffering! You are well aware of the high opinion which the Queen entertained of your excellent husband, my valued friend. Her Majesty had frequently shown this, not only in the honour bestowed upon him, but in the confidence so often reposed in him, and never disappointed. He was a thoroughly *good, conscientious* man. What higher praise can be earned on earth? What better passport can there be to Heaven?   :

"I hardly know anybody who could be better prepared for a calm, though sudden and entirely painless, end. I did not intend, when I began this letter by the Queen's command, to enter into my own feelings; but I had a very *great* and *real* friendship for your most excellent husband, and to me these thoughts are very soothing. I only carry out the Queen's repeated instructions, in assuring you that sympathy for you is most sincerely combined with true regard and respect for him that is gone.

"Believe me always, dear Lady Login,

"Sincerely yours,

"C. B. Phipps."

"WINDSOR CASTLE,
"*Oct. 28th,* 1863.

"MY DEAR LADY LOGIN,

"I had written, but not sent, the accompanying letter by the Queen's command, when I received yours this morning. I feel very strongly the kind exertion you made in writing to me, and I pray God may strengthen and support you! You cannot overrate the regard I had for my dear friend, your husband, and my admiration of his character. I am very glad to hear that the Maharajah has shown so much feeling of the debt of gratitude which he owed to his kind and gentle, but always honest, mentor; it will, indeed, be a terrible loss to him, for Sir John always told him the truth, and gave him the sincerest advice.

"The Queen read your letter with the greatest interest. If there is anything kind from Her Majesty that I could say, and have not said, I have so far gone within Her commands!

"The Queen has been very sorry to read the account you gave of Princess Gouramma's health; She wishes to know whether you think that it would be injurious to her health to come down here to see Her Majesty?

"The Queen does not forget the kind manner in which you and Sir John undertook the care of this poor child, at great personal inconvenience. If it is too much for you to write and answer this yourself, pray ask your daughter to do so.

"Always sincerely yours,
"C. B. PHIPPS."

I have already told how at this time I was summoned to London on account of anxiety about Princess Gouramma's health.

Duleep Singh's grief at my husband's death was indeed most sincere and unaffected, and many at the graveside spoke afterwards of the touching eloquence of his sudden outburst there, when he gave vent to the words,

"Oh, I have lost my father! for he was indeed that—
and more—to me!" And I remember the sort of tense
expression on his face when, on his arrival, having
come immediately he got the sad news, he asseverated
solemnly : "If *that* man is not in heaven, then there's
not one word of truth in the Bible!" His wish was
in all things to act the part of a son to him who was
now taken from him, both in the funeral obsequies,
and to those left bereaved by his death.

He had just purchased Elveden, the place he lived in
for many years in Suffolk, and it was a great grief that
his late guardian had not been able to inspect it; but
he was very firmly resolved, all the same, that he should
be buried there, in a new mausoleum which he purposed to build as a family burial-place, and that the
interment at Felixstowe should be only temporary.
I had, however, the arrangements made from the first
so that they might be permanent, and later the
Maharajah was persuaded to erect, in the Felixstowe
churchyard,* a very beautiful monument of red, and
grey granite, and white marble, surmounted by a cross,
which, standing out as it does on the highest ground in
the neighbourhood, is visible for many miles at sea,
and served for years as a " leading-mark " for mariners
—a use to which to put his resting-place, he would
have, of all others, desired!

The Maharanee Jinda having so recently died, it was
now necessary for Duleep Singh to carry out his intention of conveying the body to India for the funeral rites,
during the cold weather; and with many regrets for
having to trouble me at such a time, he had to write
to me on December 13th, while I was still suffering from

* Now (1916) surrounded by entrenchments and wire-entanglements, and
strongly guarded as a very vulnerable point on the coast.

the shock of seven weeks earlier, to beg me to search amongst Sir John's papers for the arrangements made at Kensal Green, when he himself had been too prostrated with grief to know what was being done.

A few days later he wrote about my own pension and money matters, and was anxious that I should know that he would do all on his part, to make me feel at ease about my own and the children's future, before he left England. All the designs for the monument were selected and sent to the Queen, by Her wish, for approval before he sailed; and Mr. Jackson, the sculptor, came down to take drawings and do part of the work for the bust of my husband, in my house, so that the Maharajah might see some of the progress when he came to stay with me (or rather, at the Hotel close by), as he did for one or two weeks in February before his actual departure.

His kindness and consideration for me were beyond words, and he was really like a son in the way he thought of, and for, me and my children. He had fully meant to have a good time wild-duck shooting up the Deben River, and brought a punt and duck-gun for the purpose, but it was characteristic of him, that, as he confided to me, he found he could not endure the officious attentions of the hotel-keeper, who " Royal 'Ighness "-ed him at every sentence, and would never leave him alone a moment, trotting at his heels assiduously like a faithful spaniel (a thing Maharajah could never support!) every time he came to and from the hotel to our house. One of the children's chief amusements was to watch, with the aid of a big telescope, from our tower-room, the procession approaching along the beach, and " chaff " Maharajah over the failure of his efforts to shake off his encumbrance! It really *was* rather comic

to see Duleep Singh—not fond, at any time, of unneces-
'sary pedestrian exercise, except when under training
for shooting—making devious and extended *detours*
across heavy shingle, weed-grown and slippery rocks,
and obstructive groynes (locally known as "shies,"
because walkers generally "shy" at them, I suppose!)
in the vain hope of tiring out his attendant, who, short-
legged, stout, and dumpy, as he was, stuck pertinaciously
to his self-imposed *rôle*, and turned up infallibly, panting and smiling, at the finish!

Disappointed as he was at that juncture in his hopes
of the English marriage he had fixed on, Duleep Singh
was as firmly determined to seek a wife without further
loss of time—his manner of compassing his object
appearing somewhat quaint and crude according to
our ideas. He was honestly anxious about his own
future, in his desire to live up to the standard of
conduct which his late guardian had inculcated, and was
very fearful lest, if he married a woman-of-society only,
such as he might meet with in an ordinary way, he
would be too weak to resist the temptations of a life
of mere idleness. He had a fixed idea that the proper
sort of wife for him was a very young girl, whom he
could train and educate to be "an help-meet"—an
experiment that generally risks turning out a dangerous
failure!

Nothing that I could say, though I reasoned much with
him, would turn him from the intention he expressed, of
paying a visit on his way out, to the American Missionary
School in Cairo, which had greatly interested him when he
saw it with us, very many years before, and requesting the
missionaries to provide him—if they had such an article
on hand—with what he called "a good, Christian wife!"
To others it sounds a most extraordinary and impossible

suggestion, and I cannot but think that, in his case, such apparent gambling with his own future happiness, was marvellously over-ruled and ordered by the Divine will.

I received, at that time, a letter from Sir Charles Phipps, which refers both to the monument to be erected to my beloved husband by the Maharajah, and the inscription to be placed on it, and also to this strange project of matrimony that Duleep Singh had confided to me.

" OSBORNE,

" *Feb.* 17*th*, 1864.

" MY DEAR LADY LOGIN,

" The Queen was very much grieved at the account you gave of the poor little princess in your letter, and directed me to telegraph at once to inquire for her, in Her name.

" It is very sad to see one so young cut off, but I think you have long thought that her lungs were in a very unsatisfactory state.

" I shall be greatly interested to see the sketch of the monument which you and the Maharajah have approved, and when I go to London shall certainly go to see the model. There has rarely lived a man with a more extended and pure benevolence, and I have certainly learned more of India, and Indian affairs, from him, than from any other man.

" I fear, from what you say, that Princess Gouramma is in a very dangerous state. . . . The dear Maharajah is not always very wise in his decisions, and I fear there is nobody *now* who has much influence over him. He must miss his faithful Thornton, too. I suppose there is no doubt about his going to India, as you say he intends doing ?

" Very sincerely yours,

" C. B. PHIPPS."

Again—

"*February 20th*, 1864.

"The design for the monument is very much liked; it is both quiet, handsome, and in good taste. What do you think of the enclosed inscription? It is simple and short, which I think you wished, but it can easily be added to if wished.* The Queen will *Herself* select a text.

"Ever yours sincerely,
"C. B. PHIPPS."

To show that he was serious in the proposal he announced, the Maharajah insisted on making out, signing, and handing to me the following curious memorandum, which, although afterwards known to one or two persons, I have never before made general allusion to.

"*November 15th*, 1863.

"I promise to pay Lady Login £50 (fifty pounds) if I am not married by 1st of June, 1864, provided my health keeps good.

"DULEEP SINGH."

It is written on a half-sheet of notepaper, and on the back is added:

"N.B.—That is, if I am [not?] confined three months to my house, or ordered by my Doctor (of course showing a 'Doc' certificate) to go abroad.

"DULEEP SINGH."

.   .   .   .   .   .

This time of my sore trouble is one that I would fain hasten over, but there is one letter, of all the hundreds I received then, that I cannot forbear quoting, not only on account of the writer's high place in his country-

* This inscription was somewhat amplified by the Maharajah before being cut on the monument; the text is the one chosen by H.M.

men's respect and esteem, but because my husband specially venerated his strong sense of truth and justice, and valued his personal friendship above that of almost any of his contemporaries then living.

> "LLANDUDNO, N. WALES,
> "*Oct. 26th,* 1863.

"DEAR LADY LOGIN,

"I have just heard from the newspaper, the great affliction that has befallen you. I cannot forbear to write, to tell you how much I grieve for you and your children. I know no particulars, but this I know, that you and they have suffered a loss which can never be repaired.

"There was so much true goodness, honour, and kindness in Sir John Login, that he did much to make happy all around him ; and these qualities, so apparent to his friends, were even more conspicuous in the bosom of his family. I remember his many kindnesses to me when I met him abroad seven years ago, when I was out of health. I shall always think of him as one whom it was a privilege and an honour to know! I can say nothing that will lessen the blow which has been permitted to fall upon you, he whom you mourn knew well the Source of highest consolation, from that Source alone you can derive help to sustain you in this time of your fearful trial. My daughter Helen is in Edinburgh, so I can send no message from her, but I know she will be full of deep sympathy with you. Excuse this note, which does but poorly express what I wish to say, for you know that my regard and esteem for your husband was deep and sincere.

"Believe me always, dear Lady Login,
> "Your sincere friend,
> "JOHN BRIGHT."

I was privileged, in after years, to have many more letters from the same hand ; but none, you may be

sure, that pleased me more. Mr. Bright was so good as
to come and see me sometimes when in London, in the
midst of all his press of parliamentary work; and in
his outspoken, cordial way, told his opinions and his
views on diverse subjects. I immensely enjoyed these
talks, though, as my own convictions and ideas were
generally diametrically opposed to his, he never minded
my presenting them in very blunt terms, and we used to
argue and *almost quarrel*, in the vehemence of his
statements, yet never lost the feeling of unanimity in
all that was fundamentally essential. I think there
were few statesmen of his calibre, who would have
taken the pains he did, to convince a lone widow,
with no vote or political interest, of the urgency
of his reforms? Almost as if it was of paramount
importance that she should be brought to a right way
of viewing each subject on which his heart was set!

CHAPTER XVI

THE MAHARAJAH'S MARRIAGE AND CONTROVERSY WITH
THE INDIAN GOVERNMENT

THE Maharanee's Jinda Koür's body was landed at
Bombay, and, under the superintendence of her native
servants, underwent the ceremonial burning, the ashes
being conveyed to, and scattered on, the sacred waters
of the Nerbuddah.

At the same time, the Maharajah wrote to his great
friend, Mr. Ronald Leslie-Melville, to inform him that,
on his way through Egypt, he had met a young lady
of semi-Oriental birth at the Mission School he had
mentioned before, and that he was so satisfied that she
would prove all he wished for as a wife, that they were
to be married at Alexandria on his return journey,
after he had carried out the purpose for which he had
proceeded to India. Truly the acmé of incongruous
associations, to go in search of a wife, and carry out a
courtship, in the middle of a funeral voyage ! return
to complete the proceedings, tie the nuptial knot, and
bring back a bride in place of a coffin !

I only once heard of a parallel instance, and that was
in the case of the first Earl of Gainsborough who, having
married four times, might be excused a certain familiarity with the sensation ! On the occasion of his fourth
honeymoon, he utilized the opportunity to bring down
at the same time, the coffins of his three previous wives,
to be interred in the same family fault in the little village
church of Teston, close to his residence at Barham Court.

Being a busy man, he might not otherwise have had such a good chance to superintend the operation!

A bare announcement of the Maharajah's intention was also sent to Colonel Oliphant, his equerry and superintendent of the household ; and, of course, the fact had at once to be communicated to the Queen, who immediately sent Sir Charles Phipps to see me, in Lancaster Gate, to try and find out more particulars, as Her Majesty was naturally greatly disturbed over the intelligence. Sir Charles came up from Windsor on purpose, and his advent was heralded by a mounted groom in the royal livery, who brought a note to make the appointment, all which was intended as a special recognition of my recent widowhood, and consideration for my deep mourning.

Little more was known, except that the bride was only fifteen years of age, until the marriage had taken place, and the newly-wedded pair were on their way to England. Of course, there was an immense amount of talk everywhere about the marriage, and considerable consternation in many quarters. I was inundated with questions and inquiries.

You may imagine that I was considerably relieved by a letter which I received from my friend Lady Leven, who was the first person actually to see the new Maharanee, for it was some time before I was able to accept Maharajah's invitation to go and stay with them at Elveden, and judge for myself of the choice he had finally made. My own health began to give a good deal of trouble, and the result of the shock, and time of anxiety, was telling on me. I had not been strong for a good many years, and was subject to attacks of asthma, so much so that, in the autumn of 1865, I was ordered by the doctors to the south of France, and obliged to stay there through two winters and springs.

Lady Leven wrote me from Roehampton, on July 29th, 1864, and told me how much she liked what she had seen of the young Maharanee, though, of course, it was difficult to judge until she spoke English, as, for the present, she was only acquainted with Arabic, of which, by the way, the Maharajah knew only a few words !

" She is not," she wrote, " the wonderful beauty that Edwy (my son) supposed ; but she is remarkably nice-looking, with very fine eyes, and a sweet expression. In that respect she is better-looking than Gouramma, and a size larger. She looked simple and quiet, and rather dignified.

" I asked the M.R. if her head was turned by her marriage ? and he said that she knew nothing of her position, and did not care for her jewels when he showed them to her. . . . I fancy she is entirely occupied with him. She is most submissive, and if asked if she would like to do anything, answers : ' Maharajah wish—I wish ! ' They are going immediately to the Highlands, and he is very anxious that Lord L. and Ronald and I should visit them there, and I have persuaded Lord L. to agree. The rest of our party would go either to N. Berwick for sea-bathing, or stay at the Inn at Aberfeldy.

" I should like to see more of this girl. He says her name is ' Bamba,' which means ' pink,' and that she was pink till six weeks ago, when she had jaundice !

" He says that, *as* she is not strong, *he is doctoring her !* and the day he brought her here begged she might have nothing but cold water, because of some dose he had given her ! I must remonstrate about this, or he will certainly kill her ! . . .

" She looks as if she had a perfect temper, and

seems a simple-minded girl, above marrying for rank; and her ready submission, if it does not last too long, will make them happy together."

Lady Leven then gave a most lively description of her difficulties about the Maharanee's clothes. The Maharajah *would* interfere in everything concerning his wife's attire, and had the most absurd notions on the matter. The large crinolines then in vogue were not at all suitable for her, and Lady Leven tried to convince him that it would be far better not to dress her in European fashion, but in a modification of the Egyptian costume she had been accustomed to, which was infinitely more becoming.

"You can fancy how it is now," she remarked, "with two dressmakers in the house, and he finding fault if she does not look like other people, and yet insisting on her dresses being cut short, and no trimming of any kind, and choosing colours irrespective of the becoming! It is all from intense anxiety that she should look well, but I mean to try and persuade him to give up dress and medicine to professionals, and devote himself to her mind instead!

"Mme. Goldschmidt* saw her here, and thought her very nice-looking, and all our girls were charmed with her. Colonel Hogg † also met her. . . . I hope she will make as good an impression on others as she did on us. I scarcely know why, but I feel as if I cared almost as much about his wife as I should about R.'s.

"Ever yours,
"S. LEVEN."

Although I was not able to see the Maharanee then, Duleep Singh came to me himself not very long after

---

* Jenny Lind, the famous *cantatrice*, a neighbour of the Countess of Leven at Roehampton.

† Afterwards Lord Magheramorne.

this, when I was up in town in lodgings in Prince's Street, Hanover Square. It was in the dusk of the late afternoon of a foggy day, and the remembrance often comes back to me of him, sitting there by the fire with the daylight slowly fading, while he told the tale of his wooing and marriage of this shy young child—for she was little more—who had no desire for the position he could offer her, and in her heart wished to be left to devote herself to the life of a missionary, for which she was being educated. He thoroughly enjoyed telling his story, and was in the highest of spirits, and triumphant over having just managed to " win his bet " with me by speeding up the legal formalities and his own movements, to and from India, within the specified date !

To all my remonstrances as to the indecent haste with which he cut short his mother's " cremation," so as to permit of his return quickly to Egypt, and to his having allowed pressure to be put on a young girl to consent to such a hurried marriage, he responded only with peals of laughter, treating the whole matter as a joke. I can see his eyes rolling now, the gleam of his flashing teeth in the dark shadows, and his hilarious shrieks of mirth when I questioned him as to how he could possibly have conducted a conversation with his *fiancée*, if she knew no language he spoke, and he nothing of hers ?

" Oh, that was quite simple ! I had a dragoman to interpret ! " " Interpret, Maharajah ? What do you mean ? You never had a dragoman there when you were talking to her ? What could he say ? " " Oh, quite easy, quite easy, I assure you ! All I had to say was, ' I love you ! Will you be my wife ? ' to him, and he turned it into Arabic, and then her answer he translated to me ! "

All this farrago was narrated with a succession of

L.L.R.   R

shrugs and expressive gestures, contortions of merriment and droll faces, as to make it extremely doubtful
how much was jest, and how much earnest; but the
bare idea of the situation, in the way he told it, was so
irresistibly comic that I could do nothing but laugh
with him, and had to abandon the attempt to show him
how he had outraged the sense of propriety of the
powers that be!

.   .   .   .   .   .

In the years that followed I saw Maharajah, and his
wife and family—there were six children—only from
time to time, as, after my husband's death, I lived
chiefly in retirement, at Felixstowe. I stayed with
him once or twice at Elveden after my return from
abroad, taking my two remaining daughters, and I met
him occasionally in London, and saw his wife and
daughters there also; but I think only about fourteen
letters or so had passed between us in the course of as
many years—a contrast to the constant correspondence
of the times now past. No one could help appreciating
the gentleness and lovable qualities of the Maharanee
Bamba, she was a really good woman, and a consistent
Christian, and tried in every way to fulfil the duties of
a very difficult position, not at all of her own seeking,
and which was doubly hard for her, in that she had had
no sort of preparation or up-bringing to equip her for
it. No one who came in contact with her could fail to
feel for her both respect and affection, and she has
transmitted to her children qualities which were often
lacking in their father's conduct.

For some long time after the marriage, the Maharajah
kept his wife down in the country, with a governess
to instruct her in English and in general knowledge

December 28th, 1865, Lady Leven wrote to tell me that the Maharanee had a new governess, in place of the one, Miss Hart, who had been with her since her first coming to England. She and the Maharajah had been to " dine and sleep" at Windsor. She wore the native costume which had been designed for her, and in which she was photographed—the Maharajah presenting me and his god-daughter with several copies. It became her very well, and in it she looked far better-looking than in European dress. It had a full skirt, and Turkish jacket with wide sleeves ; on her head was a jaunty cap, like a fez, made of fine large pearls, worn on one side with a long tassel of pearls hanging almost to her shoulder. Her hair was plaited into several long, tight plaits, hanging straight down all round. This had rather a curious effect. She wore this only on state occasions. Ordinarily, her hair was coiled on her head in an immense plait. Of course, she was loaded with jewels besides.

Her Majesty and the Princesses were exceedingly kind and immensely interested in her, *and her toilette !* and Lady Leven told how the Princess of Prussia (Princess Royal, then over on a visit) and Princess Helena (Princess Christian) *would* stay in the Maharanee's room to see her hair plaited ! The Queen kissed her, as an acknowledgment of her rank, and pleased the Maharajah very much by her complimentary speeches ; and the two Princesses made her sit between them all the evening, cross-questioning her about Egypt and her life there.

Many years afterwards, when I had occasion to write to Lady Leven, to ask her if she could chaperone my youngest daughter (who was also her god-daughter, as well as Duleep Singh's) to the Caledonian Ball, as she had been good enough to look after her at one of the

R 2

State Balls at Buckingham Palace, I heard from her that the Maharajah was entirely taken up writing an Opera,* and that Ronald Melville had seen him in London, "living alone with two pianos," and thinking of nothing else! At that time (June, 1882), he was already engaged in a violent quarrel with the India Office, but I knew nothing from himself of the pitch of exasperation to which he had been reduced, or of his money difficulties, until the summer of 1883, when he wrote that he was coming to pay me a "farewell visit" before he finally left England for good, and had done with its deceitful bureaucrats!

I was then living at St. Vincents, near West Malling, in Kent, and he came down to spend a long day with us, very full of his grievances and the injustice with which he had been treated by the British Government— and unfortunately he had much reason in his complaints. I have already gone elsewhere in such detail into his case† that I do not wish to go over old ground here, except in so far as it refers to the then position of the dispute. He told me he had taken passage to India for himself and his whole family—who, mind you, had been all, save the Maharenee, born and brought up in England, and were practically English in tastes, language and education!—and intended to resume native life, and be "done with England and her hypocrisies for ever!" He said that the Government made such deductions from the pension they had agreed to settle on him, by way of life-insurance for his family, and interest charged on advances for the purchase of Elveden (which latter money he had understood was *given* in satisfaction of a claim he had against them), that he had no longer the

---

* He sent me the libretto.
† " Sir John Login and Duleep Singh."

means to support the rank which Her Majesty, and her Ministers, had given him when he first came to England. That the Government informed him that, at his death, his landed property would be sold, and that there would be only a provision of £3,000 for his eldest son, which amount he considered insulting. This was undoubtedly the point that roused his bitterest animosity. He had told me before, and repeated it again, that had they only let him have a stake in the country, allowed him a property which he might.consider his own, to leave to his sons, and given him an English title to pass on to his descendants, he would have been perfectly contented. It was the instinct to found a family, to feel that his sons had something to look to, which is so firmly rooted in all men, but in the Oriental is almost a religious tenet, that they set themselves deliberately to uproot ; and, in consequence, turned in the end an easy-going, contented, and loyal subject, into a rebel, maddened by a sense of injustice.

Part of the surplus revenue of the Punjab—£200,000 a year—had been ear-marked by the Treaty of Bhyrowal for the support of the descendants of Maharajah Runjeet Singh. The accumulations of this fund in thirty-five years amounted to an enormous sum, and each successive Governor-General clung to it, rather than allow it to be reduced by a lump sum of, say £200,000, which, settled definitely on Duleep Singh, not *as a loan*, would, as I understand him, have amply sufficed to satisfy his wishes.

Instead of this, he found himself saddled with an expensive property to keep up, in which he had only a life interest, with about £4,000 clear after various deductions, to do it on. Was it wonderful if he resolved to cut the painter ? Possibly a disaffected and rebellious prince of first-grade rank, might be found a more ruinous item in the political expenses of the Indian Government ?

Yet, in the midst of all his invective against her Ministers, at the mention of his widowed Sovereign his eyes filled with tears, and he fairly broke down in alluding to her unfailing kindness and affection towards him. I saw then that any hope of his reconciliation with the terms of the Government, could only be effected through her intervention, and it seemed laid upon me, as the sole person who could revive the memory of old hopes and associations, connected with him, that I should at least try to arouse her interest in his situation.

It was twenty years since my husband's death, and the Maharajah had no longer the position, and close intercourse, he had held at Court. The officials about Her Majesty were a new generation, who knew nothing of the footing he had formerly been on. Sir Charles Phipps had long been dead, but I still held communication with the Queen through her present private secretaries, for a reason which I shall mention shortly ; so I resolved to make a personal appeal to Her Majesty, through Sir Henry Ponsonby, and did my best to induce the Maharajah to refrain from rash and precipitate action, until I could receive a reply from Osborne to my letter.

I could not help observing how, when he first met us all again that time, his manner had a certain formality foreign to our old intercourse, but bit by bit, as the day wore on, it seemed to drop from him, and his old cordiality reasserted itself, almost without his being aware of it.

One of my elder sisters, Mrs. White, was then staying with us, and though a very old woman, she still retained the peculiar knack of playing Highland reels on the piano, in imitation of the bag-pipes. Remembering Maharajah's delight in these tunes, she was asked to give an exhibition of her skill, and, once she was started, continued to reel one off after another. Immediately, as if bewitched by the music, the Maharajah began dancing the steps, on the gravel sweep outside the drawing-room where she sat playing. The faster she played, the higher he skipped, all with the set and drawn face of one in agony, for walking was to him at this period torture, and he was a perfect martyr to tender feet ! He kept imploring her to stop, for, as he assured us, the effect upon him was like that of the music of the " Pied Piper of Hamelin ! " and he *must* dance on as long as she continued ! Unfortunately, she was very deaf, and the more he called to her, the faster she played ; and we—I am afraid—thinking he was only joking, for a long time were too convulsed with laughter to come to his assistance !

No sooner had Duleep Singh left the house than, perceiving that no time must be lost, I sat down to write to Sir Henry Ponsonby. As it happened, I had to write to him on another subject, connected with a son of mine in the Navy, and therefore took the opportunity of informing Her Majesty of the Maharajah's " farewell visit," and of the frame of mind in which he was setting out for India. To me he appeared a sadly changed and embittered man, but I wished Her Majesty to know that he had shown emotion when speaking of her constant personal kindness to him. To this Sir Henry Ponsonby replied on July 25th, 1883 :

" . . . I gave your letter to the Queen, who read it through, as she is much occupied by the Maharajah's movements, and agrees with you in what you have written. Lord Kimberley says the Indian Government feel no anxiety as to his visit to India ; but the Queen does not take this sanguine view, and fortified by what you say, I am again to communicate with the India Office on the subject."

Altogether, about thirty-eight letters, some of them documents of many sheets, passed between me and Sir Henry Ponsonby on this subject, and about seven on the same matter with Lord Cross, his private secretary, Mr. Clinton Dawkins, and Sir Owen Burne, at the India Office ; also several from Sir Fleetwood Edwards, Sir Henry Ponsonby's successor as Private Secretary. It would make too long a story to give you more than a few extracts from all this flood of correspondence.

A few days later, on August 5th, Sir Henry informed me that the Maharajah had himself sent a letter to the Queen, of the contents of which Sir Henry sent me a summary, it having been written without my knowledge, though I afterwards was shown a copy of it. In it he stated his case with great moderation and respect, in language very different from the intemperate and hysterical style he used in the latter years of his life, which latter, being the only effusions that ever attained public notoriety, have had the effect of prejudicing the British people against his cause, and of making them the more convinced that he was merely making impudent and preposterous claims against the Government of India.

His private landed estates in the Punjab, he said, yielded £50,000 per annum ; his moveable property was estimated at more than £100,000. Neither had been restored to him, except a portion of his jewels in 1849. In 1858 he came of age, and was allowed £25,000 a year. He then became a naturalised British subject.

In 1862 the sum of £105,000 was allowed him out of the accumulations of the Four-lakh Fund, for the purchase of Hatherop Castle in Gloucestershire, which was acquired and settled upon him for his life, and his eldest son, or eldest male descendant, after his death. This was done under the advice of the Government. The Gloucestershire estate was not a success, and was afterwards sold. The Government advanced him altogether £198,000 for the purchase of the Elveden estate, and the re-building of the mansion and other matters, but held a mortgage on the Suffolk estates for the amount, and made him pay them every year a sum of £5,654 for interest. Other heavy deductions, such as insurance on his life, and pensions for the widows of Sir John Login and Colonel Oliphant, reduced his income so much that he could not keep up Elveden, which Government had arranged to sell at his death. His disappointment at the loss of his position in Suffolk was great, and he thought his treatment undeserved by any act on his part. He had been led, therefore, to consider the advisability of removing to India, where, on his present means, he believed he and his children 'would enjoy greater advantages than in England.

"I should, however," he avers, "very unwillingly leave England, where I have lived happily for so many years, and especially where I have experienced such great kindness from Her Majesty, now my gracious Sovereign, towards whom I entertain deep feelings of devotion and loyalty . . . I am convinced that I have never had my just rights under the Treaty of 1849, for the following reasons :

"1. I believe a provision of at least £40,000 per annum was intended to be a permanent charge on the vast revenues of the State of Lahore, for the benefit of myself and my successors.

" 2. I feel convinced that I am justly entitled to the accumulations saved out of the Four-lakh Fund,* and that I ought to have received those accumulations as my right, instead of being placed in the position of a borrower from the Government, and paying interest on its advances.

" 3. I believe that I am rightfully entitled to the restoration of my private estates in the Punjab, and to restitution of my moveable property taken in 1849— or an equivalent.

" 4. Whatever may have been the intention of Lord Dalhousie and his advisers in 1849, the interpretation which has been put upon the treaty by the India Office is very different from the expectations with which I was brought up. The India Office, however, declines to consider these claims. . . . The India Office may not have meant to wrong me ; but it has certainly decided in its own favour, and against me, every question in which I am interested ; and I cannot, with my present information, accept those decisions as just or satisfactory to myself.

" . . . If my original rights under the arrangement of 1849 were submitted to impartial and competent judges, who would hear and sift the evidence, and if they were to decide against me, I should at least hold Her Majesty's Government acquitted of arbitrary action. But if, because of my peculiar position and circumstances, or because of my unavoidable acquiescence hitherto in the decisions of the India Board, I am denied that justice and redress which, in ordinary cases, would be open to all others of H.M.'s subjects—I must submit to my fate ! and in that case the sense of injustice done me will alone lessen the regret with which I should leave the home of my adoption ! "

With reference to the Maharajah's remark as to " the interpretation now put on the Treaty of 1849 by the

* A lakh of rupees then represented £10,000. Consequently, four lakhs= £40,000.

India Office being very different from the expectations in which he was brought up," Sir Henry wrote to me :

" I do not know that there is anyone who could tell us what those expectations were, unless you can throw any light on the subject ? The India Office deny that he ever had any private estates in the Punjab."

To this I was able to reply (August 9th, 1883) :

" I have no intention of being led into a discussion of the legal aspect of H.H.'s grievances.   All I have to say is to repeat what was my husband's opinion of the view that ought to be taken of the Lahore Treaty, because it was the view held by Sir H. Lawrence, and the native chiefs who signed it on the part of the M.R., I suppose it is in these views that the M.R. means that he was brought up, by his allusion in his memo. to the Queen ?

" I fear my husband's views were more comprehensive and exalted than those of the M.R.

" The latter thought more of getting a large sum for *himself* ; whereas Sir John Login wished him not to sell his birthright as Head of his family, but to claim the Headship he was entitled to, and see that *all* were looked after as well as himself.   His whole education of the M.R. was aimed at this—to render him wholly satisfied to accept . . . when of age, the provisions of the Treaty of Lahore, as understood by those *who signed for him*, and by Sir H. Lawrence and his brother,* in whom the Sikhs had full confidence. . . .   If I can help to throw any further light on the matter, pray command me . . ."

Sir Henry replied to this, on August 12th :

" I have to thank you for the valuable information in your letter, which I have given to the Queen.   I

* The first Lord Lawrence.

think your letter and enclosed papers (which I return
with thanks), fully explain the broad and liberal views
of Sir John Login, and that there does not appear to
have been any special promise held out to the M.R. in
his youth which has been disregarded, as he implies.
The Queen has asked him to pause before he makes up
his mind to go to India.

" You can tell him that She feels for him as a friend,
and is anxious that what is done should be for his benefit,
and that though She calls on Her Ministers to inquire
most fully into his case, She has no power to alter any
decision they may arrive at on the financial aspects
of the question. . . ."

I was able, on the 20th August, to report in return :

" I gave the Queen's gracious message to the Maharajah
when he came here a few days ago with his legal adviser,*
and he expressed himself as deeply grateful for all She
had done, and was doing, for him, and was very earnest
that I should say to the Queen from him, that he would
gladly abide by the decision of three English Statesmen
whom She should name, to consider his claims, if they
were unconnected with the India Office, and if one of the
three understood law. . . . Before leaving, the lawyer
said to H.H. in my presence, that he had read enough
of Sir John's papers to convince him, that H.H. has for
the last twenty years been simply putting fetters on
himself, and that he ought to implore the Queen to
express Her wish that all transactions between him and
the India Office since he ceased to act by Sir John's
advice, should be wiped out, and a fresh departure
taken, because it was evident that he had eagerly
accepted, in his difficulties, all baits of money offered,
instead of insisting that the terms of the treaty should
be carried out. To this H.H. cordially assented, and
asked me to beg this favour for him at the Queen's
hands ? . . . H.H. informed me that ' he has assured

* Mr. P. H. Lawrence.

Her Majesty that he will not now go to India without her consent and approval.' . . ."

On August 29th, Sir Henry wrote me from Balmoral :

" Dear Lady Login,
    " The Queen thanks you for allowing Her to see the enclosed papers " (letters from Sir Charles Phipps, etc. . . .) " which cause Her to remember with regret the length of time these claims have been under consideration.
    " Her Majesty has made known to Lord Kimberley the Maharajah's wish that a new departure should take place in his communications with the India Office. . . .
    " The Queen is glad to learn that the Maharajah will not go to India without her approval, and She thinks that a visit to that country would be painful and unpleasant to His Highness, in the present state of affairs, as the Government of India have telegraphed home that they will object to his going to any place north of Allahabad, or to his visiting any native state.
    ." Perhaps you would let the Maharajah know this ? . . . ."

I was greatly relieved to find that the Queen had been pleased to have her memory refreshed by the sight of those old letters of Sir Charles Phipps ; for after sending them I recollected that they might unwittingly have caused pain by the revival of sad recollections, seeing so many of them were written during the last few weeks of the Prince Consort's life.

When I gave Her Majesty's message to Duleep Singh, he immediately remarked : " The Viceroy forgets that I hold an official withdrawal of all restrictions as to my place of residence in India, as well as in England !

but as I am not going out to India at present, it does not matter ! "

The Maharajah's lawyer at that period, a man of standing, accustomed to English procedure, and recommended to the Prince by Mr. Mitchell Henry, M.P., was new to the methods of business at that time prevalent at the India Office. Writing to me at this juncture, he said :

" . . . The India Office do not seem to be very communicative, and in private they are only abusive —I may say, vulgarly abusive ! The more I look into the matter, the less I am satisfied with the words and actions of the India Office towards the Maharajah. They can be shown to be in the wrong; but to attain redress is another question."

I was very desirous to make clear to Sir Henry Ponsonby that I did not agree with some of Duleep Singh's advisers in expecting the Queen to upset a treaty ; and had pointed out to him that I was resolved not to lend my aid to any attempt to get up a legal cast for lawyers or grievance-mongers, to enable them to abuse Government.

" The poor Maharajah," I said, " has been in bad hands, and I tell him he must suffer for having allowed such a book as that of Major Evans Bell to be published in his name. . . . He is sensible enough to see that I can only have his interests at heart, and that those who urge him to agitate in Parliament and in the papers do not really care for his good, but only to glorify themselves. . . .

" It was against my advice that the Maharajah and his advisers sent lately a telegram for two natives of the Punjab to come to him in England. . . . I think he wishes now that he had listened to me ! "

I had continual difficulties with the contradictory advice given by interested advisers to the Maharajah; and was extremely indignant to find that, after empowering me to write to Her Majesty, to implore that his case might be submitted to the arbitration of three impartial statesmen, the Maharajah had been persuaded to write himself to the Queen, to *withdraw* that proposition ! His lawyer wished also to give me to understand that H.H., under *his* directions, had been in communication with Her Majesty on the subject of his claims *before* I made my appeal ! and I was compelled to specifically deny the right of H.H.'s legal advisers to dictate to me what should, and what should not, be placed before the Queen ! All this I had to explain to Sir Henry, for I felt " that the M.R.'s true interest is to be perfectly open . . . and to conceal nothing."

On September 26th, 1883, Sir Henry replied that all I said was " most important," and that " he had read the enclosures with much interest, and thanked me for sending them."

CHAPTER XVII

LATER YEARS AND DEATH OF THE MAHARAJAH DULEEP
SINGH

YET, in spite of these representations, the India
Office refused to make any alteration in their treatment
of the Maharajah, and as the time passed, while he still
waited on in England for two years longer, hoping
vainly for some prospect of settlement, or for more
sympathetic consideration, I had the inexpressible
pain of witnessing the slow attrition of the work of
my husband's energies and devotion, as month by month
I detected fresh evidence of mental and moral deterio-
ration ; for his mind, from brooding ever on a sense of
unjust usage, gradually lost its balance, and he became
an easy prey to mischief-mongers, eager to seize an
opening to embarrass the English Government.

On August 23rd, 1884, he announced his departure
for India, as he could not otherwise undergo all the rites
of re-initiation as a Sikh ! The letter was that of one
quite " off his head," and he concluded by bestowing
on me his blessing, as " eleventh future Gooroo ! " *

He had somewhat prepared me for this a fortnight
previous, when he informed me that " a great storm
was gathering in India, and he trusted to render such
services as would compel the British nation to recognise
his claims ! His mother had told him of a prophecy
that he was to return to India to teach the Sikhs. This
country (England) was going to the dogs ! It was sad

* There were ten " Gooroos "—or Sikh Prophets.

to contemplate such a great empire going to pieces ! "
It was difficult to discern whether he had grounds for
his assertion at this date, that "the advance of Russia
is beheld with intense joy in the secret hearts of the
Princes of India," and that it was a matter of only a few
years (say thirty !) before the British Raj would be in the
throes of dissolution ! " But you will see," he exclaims,
" what I, the loyal subject of my Sovereign—though
most unjustly treated !—will do when the time comes !
But I won't sound my own trumpet too loud. I have to
express regret at the bad opinion I had formed of your
late husband. I see now that Sir John could not have
acted otherwise. Lord Dalhousie would not permit
him to do what he otherwise would have done."

It was in this spirit of determination to exhibit his
loyalty to his Sovereign that the Maharajah set forth
with all his family. It was only when all his arrangements were made, and the P. & O. liner on the point of
sailing from Southampton, that he received on board
(as he stated in the public press at the time, and the
statement has never been contradicted) a visit from
Colonel Sir Owen Burne, on behalf of the Secretary of
State for India, and was offered a bribe of £50,000 if he
would remain in England ! And this was the man who,
the moment he arrived within the jurisdiction of the
Viceroy of India, was arrested at Aden, before all the
passengers, and, with his family, landed and refused
permission to proceed further !

Knowing the disposition of the person on whom such
an indignity was placed, and the soreness of feeling
under which he was labouring at the time, from a fixed
conviction of injustice in his treatment, is the sequel
matter for surprise ? For his renunciation of Christianity, for his repudiation of his allegiance, for his

bitter invectives against the nation and Government
that had thus rewarded his years of loyalty, I offer no
excuse ! But to anyone who knows the Oriental mind,
its both childlike, and childish, resentment of any form
of injury and insult, its dependence on the " justness "
of the British " Raj," and the disorganisation of its
mental and moral faculties, that at once ensues when
these fundamentals are disturbed, the extraordinarily
clumsy and arbitrary methods of policy followed can
only excite stupefied amazement !

Outraged in his tenderest point, and furious at the
insult put on him, the Maharajah threw in the face of
the Government the pension he had hitherto drawn,
left his wife and family in their hands to support,
abjured his allegiance, and announced his intention of
offering his sword and his services to the Emperor of
Russia !

From that moment the European journals were filled
with bombastic proclamations on his part, and accounts
of interviews he vouchsafed to numerous reporters,
each fresh manifesto only doing his cause still greater
harm in the eyes of the British public. For some time
I had no direct communication with him, and only
heard of him through his sons, whose own affairs did
not appear to be managed by the India Office with any
more sympathy and tact than had been those of the
father. But in 1887 the Maharanee Bamba died, and
the Queen expressed some desire that I should take an
interest in, and charge of, the three daughters of Duleep
Singh. It was decided, however, by the India Office,
that they, together with the youngest boy, Prince
Edward, should be placed in charge of Mr. Arthur
Oliphant, at Folkestone, whose father had acted as
Equerry and Comptroller to the Maharajah at Elveden.

By Her Majesty's wish I invited the three young Princesses to pay me a visit at Gracedieu, Watering-bury. I wrote to Sir Henry Ponsonby at the time, all was arranged, and the date fixed; their brother was to escort them, and a room was secured for him in the hotel, just as I used to do for his father when my accommodation was limited. I was then informed by Mr. Oliphant that, in addition to their brother, it would be his duty to accompany them if they came to me on a visit; and, as both I and their brother recognised, this was tantamount to putting a stop to the idea, for if he came as Equerry in charge, he must be accommodated in the same house, and I had not the room to do so! It seemed to me that to keep up such state, unless accompanied by adequate allowances, was rather a detriment to the young Princesses, as it would debar them from many invitations they would otherwise receive. I could not help expressing to Sir Henry Ponsonby, that after the trust reposed in me by Her Majesty, I felt keenly this marked slight put upon me by the India Office, all the more that it was in such contrast with the courtesy shown me by the Marquess of Hartington, when Secretary of State for India.* It really seemed as if the India Office, at this date, was not above administering petty pinpricks, as they refused to repay me the cost of purchasing a full-length portrait of Duleep Singh, sold by auction at the death of the widow of John Partridge, the painter, and which I had secured at a few hours' notice, as the Maharajah's children had no means at the moment at their disposal.

* He caused it to be placed on record that I had rendered such services to the Government of India, both in a charge I had undertaken latterly under their jurisdiction, and also in tracing a missing document relating to the Coorg revenues, that I was entitled to ask for any special favour I desired, and I was accordingly granted an Indian cadetship for one of my husband's nephews.

The answer I received finally, after many months, was that the *revenues of India* could not be applied to such a purpose ! I had thought that possibly they might spare the amount out of the Maharajah's stipend, which they were not then paying him !

I could not help representing to Sir Henry Ponsonby about this time (November, 1888), that "it seemed a pity to perpetuate in the children the error committed with the Maharajah, in not definitely settling with him when he came of age." Prince Frederick, the second son, would be twenty-one in a month, and did not know what allowance he was to have, nor what profession he could follow !

I had a good deal of correspondence also at this time with the eldest son, Prince Victor; and though he spoke most affectionately of his father, who, on his part, was devoted to his children, he plainly intimated his conviction that on the one subject of his grievances the Maharajah was mentally upset, and that he (Prince Victor) considered that "his assumed hatred of England, etc., . . . has now become a permanent fixture in his mind. On all other subjects he is as sensible as he always was ; but he seems quite unhinged on the only question of importance both to himself and us. . . . How painful all this is to me you may imagine ! I am going to fight for the Queen, and I must of course thus be placed in everything against my father. . . . It is quite impossible for me to correspond with him at present, and when I joined Her Majesty's service, I felt and resolved, that I must consider myself fatherless. I wonder if it has struck you that the India Office are treating me in almost the same way as they treated him, by never settling anything definitely once and for all ? . . . The great complaint I have is that all we get

is not from *capital* settled on us, but merely an allowance . . . subject to the whims of the India Office. . . .
The feeling of unsettledness caused by this . . . makes
all our interest in life very half-hearted."

I brought these views of the young Prince to the
knowledge of Her Majesty, but I am afraid at a rather
unfortunate moment, when it happened that some debts
he had incurred were about to be paid off by the India
Office, which, apparently, preferred to expend lump sums
of money in this fashion, rather than give definite
capital. He was given at the same time the post of
extra A.D.C. to Sir J. Ross, then commanding in
Halifax, Nova Scotia, which proved an enjoyable, but
scarcely an economical billet ! I could not help thinking
that this was the plan he had fallen on to " spoil the
Egyptians," as they declined to make for him any
settled future ! As he himself expressed it :

I never now hope for any good future either for my
father or myself in England. . . . I have a very double
rôle to play in life, not of my own making or will, but
forced on me by my father's actions, and his treatment
by the India Office."

I was greatly disturbed all this time, as I wrote to
Sir Henry Ponsonby, about the Maharajah's state of
mind. I had written to him to urge his returning
quietly to England, trusting to the Queen's gracious
clemency and never-failing kindness to overlook his
past conduct, though I assured him that I had no
authority from anyone to write in this strain, but was .
prompted solely by my husband's affection for him.
For, although his conduct of late had been utterly
indefensible, I could not but feel that there was *some*
excuse for his absurd and ever-increasing demands,
since no final settlement had ever been made with him,

in the terms of the Treaty, when he came of age. He was then quite prepared, and ready, to have the capital tied up, so that no extravagance on his part could touch it.

From June 10th, 1888, onwards I occasionally received letters from Duleep Singh, first from Boyark, Kieff, and afterwards from Paris, and I kept Her Majesty informed of the purport of them, and any fresh developments; for her interest and sympathy in his case never slackened.

They were undoubtedly extraordinary effusions! some of them madder than others, occasionally absurd in their recriminations and suggestions, but all of them bearing evidence of an unhinged mind, and in some cases written with the caligraphy and spelling of a small schoolboy! They were signed " DULEEP SINGH, Sovereign of the Sikh nation, and proud, implacable foe of England ! " In the same sentence he would speak of " dying as a patriot in compassing the overthrow of British rule in India," and the prospects of the opening of the pheasant-shooting season in the course of a month in Russia ! At the same time he expressed himself as most obliged to me, and other friends, for our kind endeavours on his part ; but assured us that they were, and would be always, in vain, and begged to be left alone to go his own way, as he was quite contented !

I had ventured, on November 9th, 1888, in writing to Sir Henry Ponsonby, to ask if it was " quite hopeless " to think of any amicable arrangement with the Maharajah ? Why should his offer of submitting to arbitration be quite impossible, as he would accept an *adverse* interpretation of the Treaty from arbitrators when he would reject it, as interested, from the India

Office authorities ? He had been always told by those who signed for him (a minor) that they had understood it in one particular sense, the same that was taken by Sir Henry Lawrence, Lord Lawrence, Sir Frederick Currie (members of the Punjab Commission) and Sir Herbert Edwardes. He had never been given to doubt this was the absolute meaning it bore, until Lord Dalhousie, shortly before the Maharajah came of age, wrote to Sir John Login that it was not intended to give the Maharajah the balances, and that he was to disabuse the Maharajah's mind of that impression! I had often been present at Futtehghur, when the Sikh chiefs in the Maharajah's suite, discussed the clauses of the Treaty with the boy, in the company sometimes of our own high officials, and they all agreed in the balances belonging of right to the Maharajah. I remarked also, that recent researches into the Sikh annals had led me to believe, that there might be more reason for his claim on account of private estates belonging to his father, than I had up to this time had occasion to think.

To this I received the following reply :

" BALMORAL CASTLE,
" *Nov.* 13*th*, 1888.

" DEAR LADY LOGIN,
" The Queen commands me to thank you for your letter and to return the enclosed, which she has seen. There are so many points of importance in your suggestion, that she must consult the Secretary of State upon the subject.
" Yours sincerely,
" HENRY F. PONSONBY."

But before any steps had been taken to carry out this fresh effort, I had to write Sir Henry that I had since received a letter from Duleep Singh, conceived in such a spirit of hostility, disloyalty, and bitterness, that nothing was possible to be done with him so long as he exhibited a like temper! It was evident that he most bitterly resented any reference to his former loyalty and devotion to Her Majesty, and to her kindness to him, and, like a naughty child, took a kind of impish glee in putting all his own actions and motives in the worst light, wounding my feelings in their tenderest point, and trying hard to make out to me— who knew the facts—that from his boyhood he had been a perfect little monster of duplicity, and set himself to deceive all the good folk concerned in his up-bringing! The one ray of light in the darkness of the ruin of all our hopes for him was, that the fact of being *reminded* of his former strivings after a higher ideal of life, was evidently scourging his conscience, and possibly in a measure responsible for the present ebullition of bravado.

It had always been my own conviction, that the very unwise efforts of certain good people, to make the Maharajah—though totally unfitted for it in character, or in learning—take a prominent part in religious meetings, Bible-classes, and addresses, would only lead to disaster. And the sequel, unfortunately, only proved me right in my augury, as he used his acquaintance with the Scriptures, even at this juncture, in a mere profuse quotation of texts, torn from their context, and with an utter irrelevance to their meaning, which produced an effect of horrible profanity.

He had already warned me to " think no more of the Duleep Singh you once knew, for he is dead, and another liveth in his place ! " Now he remarked :

" . . . It would be mockery on my part to address you as ' My dear Lady Login,' and sign myself ' Your affectionate,' simply because I would shoot down on the battlefield any of your relations without the slightest hesitation, as I would do any other Englishman! No, my Lady, I cannot sacrifice my honour for the sake of acquiring money . . . and cannot subject myself to be placed between two stools ; therefore from this day forth close all correspondence with your Ladyship. Once more good bye! I remain, your most obliged, DULEEP SINGH."

This I thought seemed final! But two months later, evidently quite forgetting his definite farewell, he wrote again, enclosing (open) a letter to his former playmate and companion, Colonel F. Boileau, which commenced, "My brave Colonel," and in which he remarks as a pleasant piece of " small-talk " :

" I wonder if you and I will one day meet on the battlefield, for generally the unexpected happens ? Poor Sir John Login ! Had he come to life now, I think he would be in his grave that next instant again ! . . . Oh, for a general European War ! . . . Would you believe it that I am endeavouring to land in India at the head of a small European volunteer army of my own ? Does it not seem ridiculous on my part ? . . . With my kind regards, that is, if a proud rebel be permitted to send them, yours always, DULEEP SINGH, Sovereign of the, etc. . . ."

He still continued to send me letters, all much in the same strain, up to October, 1889. In spite of his denials, he was interested in the book that I had been asked to write by some of his friends, and for which Colonel Malleson, the Indian historian, wrote an introductory chapter. With reference to it, the Maharajah remarked :

" My Lady, the British will not believe that you wrote the book from disinterested motives. For they will say that I desired you to do so, as you still receive an allowance from my former stipend. At any rate, the India Office will put this forward. Please do not talk much to my son about this matter, for it will lead to disappointment. . . . As I do not desire to be connected with the publication of the book your Ladyship is about to bring out, I cannot give the information you ask me for. . . ."

In December, 1887, I had already written to Sir Henry Ponsonby about the proposed publication. I had told him that, before taking any steps, I would like to know, if possible, if my adopting the course suggested would have the Queen's approval, for I thought the India Office would supply certain *data*, since they themselves could do nothing to make the truth public, and might be glad to have it known unofficially ? In this supposition I found afterwards that I was mistaken. The answer to this from Sir Henry was, that " The Queen commanded him to say that she has no objection at all to the publication of the letters relating to the Maharajah Duleep Singh." Some objection was, however, made subsequently, by the India Office, to the publication of the letters that passed between Sir John Login and Sir Charles Phipps on Indian affairs, though they contained nothing that could do harm, being only Sir John's private opinions and suggestions, given at Colonel Phipps's request. But the correspondence had always been a sore subject with the India Office, and they had, soon after, shown their annoyance by declining to place him on the Indian Council, which had been foreshadowed in it, when this was formed. This, at least, was the opinion of Lord Lawrence, and also of Mr. John Bright.

The India Office now endeavoured to dissuade me

from publishing my husband's views on these matters, and from stating the Maharajah's case as it appeared to me, and although I had· received Her Majesty's sanction to my publishing extracts from Sir Charles Phipps's letters (so long as they conveyed no personal views of the Queen or Prince Consort), they took the extreme step of trying to induce Her Majesty to put pressure on me not to use them, though not quite successful in the attempt, as the message was passed on in the following terms :

"OSBORNE,
"*July 27th*, 1888.

"DEAR LADY LOGIN,

"It has been suggested to the Queen to ask whether you do not think that in the present state of affairs, the publication of these letters will scarcely do the good you hope for, but may more probably excite Prince Victor, who has promised to be less extravagant in future?

"Yours sincerely,
"HENRY F. PONSONBY."

By the same post Sir Henry wrote that "he did not imagine there would be any objection to my publishing extracts from Sir Charles Phipps's letters relating to Sir John Login ; but if these conveyed any opinions of the Queen or Prince, it would be desirable to submit such correspondence . . . to Her Majesty before publication." Of course I replied to this that I had had no intention to .do anything different to this, but saw no reason for refraining from the publication of my book itself, in deference to the India Office, as I had already made an agreement with my publishers, and had my husband's memory and good name to think of.

On January 12th, 1889, the Queen replied most kindly

to my request to be allowed to dedicate my book to
herself :

"Her Majesty would, in ordinary circumstances,
have willingly complied with your request ; but She
fears that, in the present unfortunate state of affairs,
Her acceptance of the dedication of a book which
will contain so much about the Maharajah would
be misunderstood, and therefore Her Majesty regrets
that She is unable to accede to your wish."

She, however, graciously consented to accept a copy
of the work, and expressed her thanks for what she
called " this interesting volume." I fear her appreciation of it was greater than that of its subject, the
Maharajah Duleep Singh, who complained that in it
" the late unmitigated scoundrel, the Marquess of
Dalhousie," was made out to be " the embodiment of
justice and truth ! " etc., etc., . . . though he con-
ceded that perhaps if I had stated his (the Maharajah's)
present opinion of the aforesaid statesman, it might have
interfered with the sale of the book ! After a lengthy
tirade in the same strain, he wrote again a fortnight
afterwards that, though his determination remained the
same as before, still " a moral victory in the House of
English Parliament would be very soothing to his
pride ! " So he withdrew his objection to my book,
and thanked me for my efforts, for he knew they were
kindly meant ! Though he had refused to help me in
compiling it, it was not " from any spirit of unfriendli-
ness, but merely because I was still going on the lines
of the Treaty of Annexation," whereas he was now
demanding the restitution of his kingdom ! Although
his present income was only four hundred pounds, he
was quite happy in his own way, as a free man !

Eight months later, I suddenly and unexpectedly

received the following, in the handwriting of his son, Prince Victor, but signed by himself:

> "GRAND HOTEL, PARIS,
> "19th *July*, 1890.
>
> "DEAR LADY LOGIN,
>
> "I have been struck down by the hand of God! I am lying ill here with a stroke of paralysis, and as the sickness may be unto death, I pray you to forgive me all I might have said against you.
>
> "I have written to ask pardon from the Queen, and should I get better, my son is determined to drag me to England, where I shall hope to see you once more, and shake hands, and let bye-gones be bye-gones.
>
> "Your affectionate,
> "DULEEP SINGH."

I at once communicated with Sir Henry Ponsonby, who informed me (July 24th, 1890):

> "The Queen has duly received the Maharajah's letter. But of course the whole question is one of such grave political importance, that Her Majesty could express no opinion upon it without consulting Her Ministers.
>
> "She therefore lost no time in forwarding the appeal to Lord Cross, and he necessarily must discuss the matter with his colleagues, so that no immediate decision can yet be made known.
>
> "Yours sincerely,
> "HENRY F. PONSONBY."

In the meantime I heard from the two sons that their father "thanked me very much for all my messages, and sent his love;" that he was slowly recovering, and they hoped soon to move him to Folkestone; that the Queen's reply had been friendly, and that they had also received the official pardon.

I heard also to the same effect from the Earl of Leven,

who had gone at once to Paris on hearing of his illness.
He told me that the letter to the Queen was written
before his arrival, and quite spontaneously. "He did
not talk," he wrote, " of the Sikh religion. I quietly
assumed that that was all nonsense, and he did not
gainsay me."

I personally never saw Duleep Singh again. He continued to live mainly in Paris. He had married again,
an Englishwoman by birth, and had two daughters
by the second wife.

In April, 1893, he paid a short visit to Folkestone ;
his youngest son, Prince Edward, being then very ill
(the poor little boy died a few days afterwards, and was
laid beside his mother, the Maharanee Bamba, in
Elveden churchyard). Five months later, I received
from Prince Frederick Duleep Singh a letter informing
me of the very sudden death of his father, in Paris.
Neither of his sons was present. Later, a telegram
informed me of the date and place of the funeral.

Thus, after his wayward and troubled life, he passed
to face the great reality in a foreign land ; but was laid
to rest in the churchyard at Elveden, where he had
hoped to make the home of his descendants, and found
a family typical of the spreading ramifications of the
British Empire.

With his two sons as mourners on that sad day, was
joined my sole surviving son, then a captain in the
Royal Navy, as representing the guardian who had
loved and watched over him in his early years, so full
of promise.

I cannot refrain from inserting here, as a fit close
to my recollections of one who, in spite of many dis-
appointing faults and failings, had endeared himself
in many ways, and as a proof of the sincere friendship

and affection of which the real Duleep Singh was capable, two letters received by me from him in later years, after his own marriage. They were written respectively in 1866 and 1876, after hearing of the deaths of my eldest daughter in France, and of my eldest son in India, both of them playmates of his in his boyhood.

1.

"ELVEDEN HALL, THETFORD,
"*Monday, Feb.* 26, 1866.

"MY DEAR LADY LOGIN,

"It is with the deepest sorrow I write in reply to your sad letter, and heartily sympathise with you in the affliction it has pleased God so soon again* to send you. It is needless for us to mourn for those who sleep in Jesus, though nature of course is weak, but the Lord will not do anything to us unless it is for our good.

"Poor Edwy! † it will be a sad blow to him, and I earnestly hope it will be the means of bringing him out to serve the Lord with his whole heart.

"You have now great interest in Heaven, having there your Dear late husband, and the first-born daughter.

"I pray God that as He has been pleased to send you this trial, that He will grant you strength to bear it, and to make it to work for your and yours good.

"Believe me, with much love, to be ever affectionately,
"DULEEP SINGH."

2.

"CARLTON CLUB,
"*Dec.* 29*th*, 1876.

"MY DEAR LADY LOGIN,

"I cannot find words sufficiently to express my very deep sorrow at your great loss. It must indeed

---

* I had lost my youngest child only two months previously, and my husband two and a half years before.

† My eldest son, whose death is alluded to in the next letter, had only just sailed for India.

be very heartrending to lose one after another one's children, and it has pleased God to send you sorrow after sorrow. But who knows His ways or dares to rebel against His commands? It is needless for me to point out to you where only you can find comfort, and may God give you strength to bear the heavy rod He has laid upon you!

" I shall be very grateful for a line containing full particulars of poor Edwy's death, when you have received them, if not giving too much trouble?

" Please convey to both your daughters my deepest sympathies in this their very great loss.

" Yours most sincerely,

" DULEEP SINGH.

" P.S.—Your letter only reached me here this moment, or I should have replied sooner."

Though there may appear traces of a certain form of conventional " cant," rife at that period amongst many pious people, in the first letter, it did not really argue want of genuine regret and sympathy on the part of Duleep Singh, but arose from an over-scrupulous desire to express himself as his then religious guides inculcated. It was very different to the style he used when under the care of his old guardian.

CHAPTER XVIII

I HAD indeed had my own share of sorrow during the years that followed my husband's death. My health, after the shock of that sad event, gave a good deal of anxiety, and I was told by the doctors that it was absolutely necessary for me to avoid the English winter and spring. As I did not wish to separate from my children, and the transport of such a large party was a matter of expense, I arranged to take up my residence for a couple of years in the neighbourhood of Pau, with my daughters (there were four of them), their governess, and the nurse, and also a niece of my husband's, whose mother was in India, and very anxious that her girl, at school, should have this opportunity of a time on the Continent.

My eldest son was then in an office in London, preparatory to going out to India under the *ægis* of Lord Lawrence, the Viceroy; and the youngest boy, " Harry," was at Wellington College, until he joined the *Britannia* as a naval cadet. Dr. Edward Benson, afterwards Bishop of Truro and Archbishop of Canterbury, was then headmaster, and gave the boy a large portion of his personal attention, as, being in perpetual scrapes, and· very idle at his lessons, he appeared to require caning on an average once a week! Nevertheless, Dr. Benson took a very warm interest in his troublesome pupil, and many were the letters he wrote me about him. Nor did he cease to do so in later life; long years afterwards they met accidentally on the platform at Paddington Station, and the Bishop (as he then was) made him travel in the same carriage as far as Exeter, and showed by his conversation that he had followed his career through all his various ships in the Navy. On the other hand, the schoolboy retained the highest respect for his headmaster, and made a special pilgrimage to Canterbury to see him enthroned as Primate.

We spent two winters at Pau and Biarritz, the first in an " apartment " in Maison Nulibos, whence we had a fine view of the procession of ox-carts with produce, and of the sea of multi-coloured umbrellas on market-day; the second winter we were at Maison Couture, 19 Rue Montpensier, where there was a pleasant garden and a balcony, of which the young people took full advantage. It is now a Convent of the Sœurs d'Espérance, or Blue Sisters.

The summer was passed in the Pyrenees and by the sea, and we also made one or two expeditions into Spain, driving across the frontier in our private carriage, and once penetrating by rail as far as San Sebastian and Tolosa. My uncles and my youngest brother having fought in the Peninsular and Carlist Wars, I was anxious to see something of the country; but having no knowledge of Spanish, and the Spaniards of those days stoutly resisting any efforts to address them in French, we could not manage to get to Pampeluna as we had purposed. Thus my impressions of Spanish hostelries remained a compound of dirt, flies, fleas, and the crowing of cocks! This was accounted for, at Tolosa, when we-discovered that, in order to ensure our having *poulet* for the next day's *déjeuner*, the landlady locked up overnight in the attic next our bedroom, the rooster that she destined to fill that *rôle!*

But the beauty and colouring of the scenery, and the picturesque appearance of the people and architecture, filled with delight my eldest daughter, who at her early age showed great talent as an amateur artist.

The old Château de Vieuzac at Argelès, was our home for some months, and we also were two seasons at Luz, and at St. Sauveur, for the baths. We got to be much attached to our French servants, especially " Pierre," and " Jean-Baptiste," the *cochers*, and " Marcel," our manservant. I fear that the antics of some of the juveniles rather scandalised the good people of Argelès ; but they were already well broken in to the eccentricities of " les Anglais," by the proprietress of Château Vieuzac, Madame Lassalle, herself an old Scotswoman, an heiress of considerable means, who had married many years previously a well-known *avocat* of Pau, and had only one son, the apple of her eye, then Captain in a native Indian regiment, in the Queen's service.

Madame Lassalle had lived so long in France, and amongst the peasantry, that she had almost entirely forgotten her native language and had never learnt to speak French properly. Her attire looked as if it had been picked out of the rag-bag, and she generally went about with a shawl over her head. She had been for many years a widow, and her chief idea was to save, and amass money, for this beloved son. With this object in view, she used to let the château furnished for the summer, and herself retire to a sort of lean-to shed *in the· garden*, which reminded me much of the accommodation of the Trappist or Carmelite nuns I had seen at Biarritz. Here she lived on the frugalest of fare, scraping together every penny to send to the soldier in the East, who was really earning good pay, as he was in the Civil Commission in addition. But I think she preferred this style of abode to any other, chiefly from the convenience of being on the spot to harry the gardener, who was a peasant of very low intelligence, and animated by a determination to do as little work as was compatible with retaining his situation! At all hours of the day, but especially the very early morning ones, the figure of old Madame Lassalle—sometimes in the sketchiest of *déshabillée*,—might be descried, chasing her henchman round the fruit-trees, and the rows of haricot-beans, while her voice, in strident tones, demanded fiercely, in the most appalling of accents : "Marcellin! Marcellin! ou es tu? Ho! cet *animal!*"

The tower of Château Vieuzac, a fine old fortilace built by Edward the Black Prince, in the days when the Angevin Kings held this portion of the Pyrenees, stands a few yards away from the modern house, and here one of my daughters, my niece and the German governess, had their quarters, and instituted nightly raids on the special breed of gigantic spiders which infested the building. Carrying each their candle, they solemnly perambulated in procession the different storeys of the tower, the governess bringing up the rear, armed with the kitchen tongs, in which the intruder was firmly secured. Obeying old Scottish tradition, they refrained from capital punishment, and when the cortège, with its flambeaux, issued forth to the outer air at the summit, the pincers came apart, and the delinquent dropped over the parapet into space, whence, doubtless, after a temporary oblivion, he returned to his old quarters, and thus provided a subject for "alarums and excursions" each succeeding night!

This recurrent nocturnal ceremony so impressed the good people of Argelès, that one of their number was deputed to inquire of our servants what particular religious function was being enacted, since plainly some Britannic form of exorcism was in question ?

Those were happy days for our young people, though, as it proved, all too brief ! When at Pau, they spent their time making excursions amongst the lovely *côteaux* of the Pyrenees, sometimes sketching, sometimes in huge riding-parties with their friends—I have known often one-and-twenty of them thus join forces, under the escort of one elderly gentleman of dignity and resource, whom we mothers could trust to bring the cavalcade home in good time for the six o'clock *table d'hôte* at his hotel, especially when any favourite *plat* of his was on the *menu !*—sometimes taking part in the Carnival sports, or in the simple gaieties of the British colony.

Charades and practical jokes were rather a favourite form of diversion, and I can remember on one occasion at Biarritz, after a fortnight of deluging tropical rain, such as is hardly ever experienced in the British Isles, when the children had been compelled to keep indoors, and it was impossible to keep them out of mischief, two *soi-disant* "ladies of the Empress Eugénie's suite" appeared in our *pension*, and terrified the poor English governess in charge of Lord and Lady Bantry's children (the parents were at Vichy), by announcing that the Emperor had given explicit orders to clear out the visitors from certain hotels, to make room for the extra members of the court, for whom there was not room at the "Villa," and that they themselves must have her "appartement !" Never had they dreamt, the wicked ones ! that her mystification would prove so easy, as they preened themselves in their clothes borrowed from Madame Antoine, the landlady, aired their best French with an exaggerated Parisian accent, and proceeded to apportion the rooms before her face, till she tore downstairs to ask me what she was to do ? Such an excitement, and huge delight, it created in the hotel staff—who were all in the secret, and lined the stairs and corridors, headed by the *chef* and his satellites, to receive the distinguished visitors—who had been careful to send up their cards, beautifully written in copper-plate style by the German governess—ring-leader of the mischief—as " Madame la Comtesse de Fouldye " and " Madame No-aller ! " Their enchantment knew no bounds when it was discovered that their escapade had started the rumour in the town, that their Imperial Majesties had unexpectedly arrived at the Villa, late in the evening, but did not wish it known !

.   .   .   .   .   .

But three short months later all this came to a sudden end. My dearest and youngest little one, " Mabel," in years but seven, but with a mind far beyond her age, whose sayings struck many outside her own family, passed rapidly away on December 12th, after an illness of only a few days. In her unconscious-ness, just before her death, she kept repeating the French words, " Jésus Christ vient pour moi ! "

Scarcely had this blow fallen, and I had in the interval parted from my eldest son, who came to us on his way to India, when my eldest daughter, Lena, whose health from a child had given us great anxiety, though her sweet disposition, and bright intellect, made her an universal favourite, fell into a sudden and rapid decline, from which she never rallied, and a few weeks after her twenty-first birthday she also went from us, on the 20th of February, 1866, and was buried in the same grave with her little sister, in the cemetery at Pau.

After this terrible double bereavement, we moved for a few weeks' change and bracing air, to the Hotel d'Angleterre at Biarritz, and it was there that I made the acquaintance of Sir Charles and Lady Tennant, (then Mr. and Mrs. Tennant) of The Glen, Peeblesshire, whose eldest daughter of seventeen* was dying slowly of consumption, and whose case and disposition, in many ways, bore resemblance to that of my own dear child. A link was thus formed between us two mothers, and a very close friendship formed between their next child, " Posie " (Pauline) and my little daughter, which lasted for many years, and gave rise to a constant correspondence. On our return to Scotland that summer, Mr. and Mrs. Tennant kindly invited our whole party to stay at The Glen, and I then first saw the present Mrs. Asquith, as a fascinating baby of three, even then showing signs of a marked personality, though I could never believe in her exceeding the extraordinary charm and magnetism of her sister " Posie," afterwards Mrs. Gordon-Duff.

I have told before† how, when dying, the poor little Princess Gouramma had begged me to act a mother's part to her infant child, to whom I was sole godmother. My brother, Colonel John Campbell, applied, after his wife's death, to the India Office, for some portion of the mother's income to be extended to the child, for her education, as he himself had little means beyond his retired pay. Sir Charles Phipps unfortunately proved a true prophet, when he wrote to me that he feared the Secretary of State would consider the child as John's, and that they had done all that they could in giving the allowance for the poor Princess's life. When the

* Named " Janet."
† Chapter XII., p. 193.

India Office refused his request, John came to me in great distress, and begged me to try and get Her Majesty interested on his behalf to procure some small allowance. I was to represent that by his wish, as well as her mother's, I was to take the child into my own care, and, if desired, the money paid to me, as it was solely for the child's benefit he wanted it. He knew that this was the Queen's wish, expressed directly she heard of the mother's death, when she sent a message to me to " hope that at some time or other I might be able to show the poor child to Her." And, as Sir Charles wrote a few days later : " One other wish H.M. has expressed, which is that *Her* presents to the Princess may go to the orphan child." I was very unwilling, at first, to apply to the Queen as John wished, but consented to do so, and Her Majesty, with the above understanding, made her wishes known to the India Council, and a pension of £250 was granted to my niece.

I was unable to take charge of the little girl at once, and my brother begged to be allowed to keep her with him for a time, since I was ordered to go abroad for my health. On my return, I told him I was now ready to have her, but he said some friends of his, who had had her with them for some time, were exceedingly attached to her, and anxious to adopt her as their heiress. As I was still in bad health, and not yet settled in a house, I weakly allowed the matter to " slide," though aware that both the Queen, and the India Office, were under the impression that I had the child under my care.

. On August 4th, 1867, my brother John called to see me in Lancaster Gate, and discussed various family and business matters. It so happened that my two elder brothers had for the past year been much engaged, as supporters of a law-suit on behalf of a sister's son,

Charles William Campbell (in Borland),* being, in fact, his claim to the earldom of Breadalbane. The case was favourably considered by the Court of Session in Scotland ; but on being brought up on appeal to the House of Lords, was given against my nephew. Naturally, my brothers, already pretty well-known men in society, were for a time familiar names to the general public.

It was not till some time afterwards that I heard that my brother had suddenly disappeared, and no one knew what had become of him ! In fact, I had been one of the last people who had seen him. For he had left his lodgings on the 7th August, carrying only a small hand-bag, with no luggage, as if going out for the day, refused the offer of his landlord to call a cab, saying he would find one in the street, and, from that moment to this, no further trace has ever been found of him ! He had left a note that day at his club for his eldest son,† then home on leave from India, making an appointment for a few days later, which he never kept. But so averse were the son and brother—General Charles Campbell—from making any talk or stir in the matter, which might cause his annoyance were he to return suddenly, that they left it for *three months*, till the 1st November, before calling in the aid of Scotland Yard ! Of course, by that time it was too late, and all trace had evaporated !

There was this much excuse for them, that in the summer of that year a family in the West-country had become a general laughing-stock, by raising a hue-and-cry in all the papers, to obtain tidings of one of their members who had incontinently vanished, and whom

---

* Afterwards Major-General.
† Then Captain in Q. O. Corps of Guides, afterwards Major-General R. B. P. Campbell, C.B. Died in 1897.

they declared must be wandering as a lunatic, or suffering from loss of memory. The individual in question was a clergyman,* and to the mortification of his relatives, he was unearthed by a zealous country constable, in the disguise of a *carter* in Wiltshire, which he had adopted to escape from the too close surveillance of his friends ! Terrified of exciting the same ridicule, which of all things he dreaded—he himself being an inveterate jester !—my brother Charles restrained his nephew from taking any decisive measures to ascertain his father's fate, until actually on the eve of his own departure, to rejoin his regiment in India.

The mystery of John's fate has never been elucidated. That he met with foul play, and that very shortly after he left his lodgings in Jermyn Street, the police had no doubt. There were, they acknowledged then, very many more of these total disappearances in the course of a year, in London, than the general public had any idea of, and as he was known to attend many racing meetings, and to be a judge of horseflesh—he had been at one time Superintendent of the Government breeding-establishment in India—it was possible that he might occasionally find himself in very doubtful company. In his last note to his son, he mentioned that he had to " go on business about a lump of money," but both the son, and his landlord, were given to understand that it was a mere matter of a few hours, or perhaps a day or so.

Many were the tales evolved, and circulated, with regard to this " mystery," at the time, especially in view of the romantic interest attached to his marriage with an Indian Princess. The one that had most vogue, perhaps, was to the effect that he was kidnapped and

* He was, I believe, a brother of Captain Speke, discoverer of the sources of the Nile.

murdered by natives of India, lurking in concealment in London, either out of revenge, or to recover jewellery belonging to his wife, which he was carrying in that little black bag in his hand. Such an idea had little credence in the family—poor Princess Gouramma's Oriental jewels were not of great value, though it is true that none of them were found amongst his possessions. Her relatives,* on the other hand, had never shown any sort of resentment at her marriage with a " sahib."

It was a strange thing that there was a previous instance, in our family, of the second son of the laird of Kinloch being lost to the knowledge of his kin, our uncle Gregorio having disappeared in the same way.† In his case, it was rumoured, intelligence of his death finally transpired, but my father, for one, to the end stoutly refused to accept it as authentic. But of my poor brother no further tidings ever reached us, though false scents were started in all directions, all of which my youngest brother, Major Colin Campbell, religiously followed up, only to be confronted with disappointment.‡

But, for my part, I could not follow indefinitely the policy of waiting, as urged by some, while ignorant of the well-being of the child I had made myself responsible for. In deference to the wish of my eldest brother, I did delay for some considerable time before writing to Sir James Hogg at the India Office, as one of her

* See Chapter XII.
† Note p. 7.
‡ My uncle John's memory is (in my mind) kept green by a presentation made by my brother, Rear-Admiral S. H. M. Login, to the Officer's Mess at the Royal Naval Barracks, Portsmouth, on Trafalgar Day, 1905. The very handsome cup he then gave his messmates, surmounted by a figure of Nelson, was in reality the Calcutta Derby Cup won by my uncle's horse, which he presented to my father as the thing he himself valued most highly. It was inscribed " in token of gratitude to his brother-in-law," my father having procured two commissions in the Indian Army for two of his sons. (E. D. L.)

trustees—he had filled the same position to her mother also. Only that very day had he and the Indian Council been informed of John's disappearance, and that the child was in the charge of a Mr. and Mrs. Bartlett, at Rock Ferry, near Birkenhead, who wanted to be made her legal guardians. The council, and the Queen also, had been, up to that moment, under the impression that she was in my care, and were not a little annoyed with me to find that this was not the case, so that it was well that I had lost no further time in acknowledging my supineness in the matter.

Then began a somewhat trying period of " alarums and excursions," in order to obtain the custody of the child, which was not without its comic side.   For months I had a most amusing correspondence, weekly and sometimes daily, with Sir James Weir Hogg, who had a keen sense of humour, and Mr. Lawford, the legal adviser to the India Office, on the subject.   Mr. Bartlett, who was an attorney, exhibited all the legal quibbles and subterfuges imaginable, combined with a melodramatic melancholy worthy of Mr. Mantalini himself !   Sir James, and the other officials, were deter-mined that the child must not be left to his upbringing, and resolved to make her a ward of court.   As I had expressed no desire to be appointed guardian under the Lord Chancellor, they asked me whom I would advise to be named to undertake the office ?   I suggested my brother Charles.   However, without awaiting my reply, they and the Lord Chancellor insisted that I was the only right person, and when I consented and had been duly appointed, I was instructed to remove her from the Bartlett's custody, though allowed to do so with as little injury to their feelings as I wished.

Three times appointments were made to meet me for

this purpose, and not kept! Then it was urged that I must take into my service the maid she was accustomed to; but I had already got a nurse! Then, "Mrs. Bartlett's health would not stand the shock," and there must be delay. Again, it was settled that a confidential servant of mine was to go and receive her, accompanied by the lawyer's clerk, when it was discovered the house was shut up, and the quarry flown to the Continent! As this was "removing a ward from jurisdiction of the Court," a severe example had to be made of the gentleman. Even then his expedients were not exhausted, and when all was settled for my governess to go and receive her—"Here's another dodge!" wrote Sir James to me, "Mr. Bartlett has been here, and declares the child has scarlatina!!!" By this time the residents of Rock Ferry were all absorbed in the game; Mr. Bartlett was not regarded with favour, and many neighbours volunteered their services to get the child away from him—the Vicar had "seen the child that day, and she was quite well!" So, with full instructions to take lodgings and see the little girl well nursed, if she was really sickening, the governess started bravely, armed with all authority, and with the clergyman's assistance, actually succeeded finally, in spite of a few more attempted evasions on the part of Mr. Bartlett, for the wife appeared more sensible, and really fond of the child for its own sake. Poor woman! I was sorry for her, for she did not long survive the parting. Her money proved to be only an annuity which died with her, so there could have been no truth in the idea of her adopting and making an heiress of little Victoria. In spite of the attorney's asseverations, that the child would never part from them without the most heartrending paroxysms of grief, the poor little thing seemed more dazed and bewildered than anything else, and in a few days was not only reconciled, but evidently relieved to be allowed to exhibit natural feelings of childish interest, and pleasure, in the novelty of her surroundings and the society of younger friends than she had been accustomed to. Though between seven-and-eight years of age, she was entirely without education, did not even know her letters, and had been allowed no playmates save a page-boy.

What a funny little old-fashioned oddity she appeared, clothed in a style most unsuited to her age, very proud of a frock made out of a piece of Indian silk, striped purple and crimson, and of her " best " hat, a hard, round, flat-topped felt, shaped after the cut of a stage-coachman's, but adorned with apparently the entire plumage of a bird of paradise, and two sizes too large for her childish head, which it " bonnetted " completely ! All this was soon remedied, and the child, who for the past three years had answered to the name of " Gip," or " Gipsey," knowing of no other, found herself, under her proper one of " Victoria Gouramma," a very different creature, and quite a personable one.

I delayed as long as I dared taking her for her first interview with the Queen, who had expressed a desire to see her, until a little of her awkwardness, and what we Scots call " dourness," had rubbed off. It was with some trepidation that I ventured on the experiment of introducing her into Her Majesty's presence, without telling her exactly who it was that she was about to see ; but I had had some experience of Queen Victoria's dislike of children who were in any way " primed " with proper speeches, and drilled into rules of behaviour for their audiences, and I took the opportunity, on entering the audience-room, to advance alone first, and explain the child's complete ignorance of the Queen's identity. Her Majesty was most gracious, and highly interested and amused at what I had done, promising to overlook any mistakes that arose in consequence. But I could see that she doubted my assertion that the child was *completely* unaware of who she was !

She soon had full proof, however, of the fact. The two Princesses, Princess Louise (Duchess of Argyll), and Princess Beatrice (Princess Henry of Battenberg), came in afterwards, and were witnesses of the following amusing dialogue—Her Majesty running towards them, on their approach, to warn them, " She has no idea who we are ! " Both greeted me most kindly, though it was seven years since I had last seen them, and they were then but children themselves.

" Come here, Victoria ! " said Her Majesty, " Tell me, do you know who I am ? "

" No ! " rather stolidly. Then, after a little pressure. " I suppose you are an old friend of my aunt's ! " adding somewhat indifferently, " I have seen such a lot of them ! " An idea seemed to strike her, and she confided to the very kind lady who now had her on her knee, " There was one *very* nice old lady she took me to see, who gave me a lovely box of sweeties ! " .

The hint was unmistakable, and I was on thorns as to what might come next ; but the Queen, convulsed with laughter, made me a sign to say nothing, and the rest of the royal party thoroughly enjoyed the joke ! What made it the more pointed was, that all the time Her Majesty had been holding a small case in her hand, on which the child's eyes were fixed, evidently expecting a present of some sort. This the Queen now handed to her, with a laughing apology for having forgotten the fact that sweetmeats might be more to her liking, and pressing the spring, showed a beautiful crystal locket adorned with the royal monogram.

"This will perhaps serve to remind you of this 'old friend of your aunt's,'" said she, very graciously. "Those are my initials. My name is 'Victoria' too; the same as yours."

"Oh, no, that can't be, I know!" said the small Victoria, with more animation, and shaking her head very wisely. "There is only one other Victoria, for my aunt told me so!"—this most reprovingly—" and she's the one we pray for in Church!"

I do not think that my niece ever "bettered" her first interview with her mother's godmother, nor did the two succeeding ones tickle the Queen's sense of humour to the same extent, though on the last occasion, which was her presentation at Court, I saw a smile spread over the royal countenance when the young girl, in her perturbation, forgot the instructions she had received in correct procedure, and, observing that, as I preceded her into the presence, Her Majesty greeted me, as she did those known to her of old, not suffering the act of homage, but giving the firm hand-clasp of a friend— on the Queen graciously extending to her, as *débutante*, her hand for the customary kiss, seized and shook it warmly to the visible amusement of the members of the grand circle!

For thirteen years, until her marriage in October, 1882, after she came of age,* Victoria Campbell lived with us as a member of my family; and all the time Her Majesty took a very sincere interest in her, and frequently mentioned her in the correspondence that still went on, as I have shown, on several other subjects. But, though letters passed with the Queen's private

* She married Captain H. E. Yardley.

GROUP OF THE ROYAL FAMILY AT OSBORNE (WITH THE EXCEPTION OF THE PRINCE OF WALES).

secretaries, Sir Thomas Biddulph and Sir Henry Ponsonby, it was a period of less personal intercourse with the Court than it had been before, my own widowhood, and Her Majesty's seclusion after the Prince Consort's death, making this a natural result. Indeed, I had not seen the Queen herself, as a widow, until I took the child that time by appointment to Buckingham Palace, and the change in her struck me much.

But she never forgot my claims to remembrance on occasions of State functions, and tickets for seats were sent for the Thanksgiving Service at St. Paul's in 1872, the Jubilee Celebrations in Westminster Abbey, and even an invitation to the semi-private wedding of Princess Louise to the then Marquis of Lorne, to which only a very few with special rights were admitted ; " in consideration," as Sir H. Ponsonby wrote, " of your name of Campbell."

Two little instances I may give here, as proof of the Queen's marvellous memory for personal details relating to those with whom she came in contact.

She had been discussing with me the pre-occupations inevitable to the mother of a large family, and I, always rather hazy about figures, remarked in corroboration, " Indeed, yes, Ma'am ! when, like me, one ,has *five* children to think of." Whereupon she corrected me at once, greatly diverted. " Five ? You mean *six*, Lady Login ! " And she was quite right too ! It was *I* who had miscounted my flock !

Then, when I took Victoria Campbell to see her after she had been some years in my charge, Her Majesty rather embarrassed me by suddenly observing : " Lady Login, haven't you another daughter, named Edith ? How is it she has not yet been presented at Court ? " It was a little difficult to explain, that it really had been

a sense of economy, in my altered circumstances, that
had made it seem unnecessary—and of course I had to
rectify the oversight, as she plainly gave me to understand I was to !

When, in December, 1876, tidings reached me, through
what seemed a doubtful channel, of the sudden death,
in an unexpected locality, of my eldest son, the blow
was hard to credit, and doubly hard to bear.

My boy Edward had been in India since January,
1866, having only one short leave of absence for three
months (which meant barely six weeks in England) in the
summer of 1873. Mercifully, for part of that brief
period, my sailor son was also in England, though he
sailed before it elapsed, in H.M.S. *Active*, Captain Sir
William Hewett, V.C., for the Ashantee War. This one
month, and a week or ten days that they had been
together in Bombay, a year previously, when Harry,
the younger one, was a midshipman in the *Volage*
(Captain Sir Michael Culme Seymour), one of the Flying
Squadron, on a cruise round the world, was actually
the only time the two brothers saw each other from the
time that they parted after the death of their little
sister at Pau in 1865, when the sailor-boy was fourteen.
For Harry sailed in 1866, in H.M.S. *Zealous*, for Esqui-
mault, round Cape Horn, and for five years, just after
losing my two daughters in France, I had both my sons
absent at the two extremities of the globe. For six
months of that time I knew absolutely nothing of what
had become of the younger one, though I made all
inquiries possible of the Admiralty, where my first-
cousin, Admiral Frederick Campbell, was First Lord's
Secretary. My only consolation was in the steadfast
sympathy and concern of the elder son, as soon as he
learnt of my anxiety. His was an intensely affectionate

and unselfish nature, and he possessed the same sweetness of disposition as had characterised his sister Lena
(the one who died), whom he resembled in other ways,
so that, like her, he gained friends wherever he went,
and was held in esteem by all who met him.

It is only to show the changed conditions of the
world from those times that I speak of these things here.
Those were indeed the days of long waiting in silence
for news of the absent, and would seem impossible now.

My son's appointment was in the Finance Department
at Bombay where he was in charge of the Home Money
Order Branch, a new experiment, of which he was the
originator, and for which he had received the thanks and
commendations of the Viceroy and Council. In the last
letter received from him, he spoke of spending Christmas
with an aunt* and cousin at Nagpore. On December
19th, I was horrified and bewildered to learn, from an
unexpected quarter, that a telegram, from a member of
a strange commercial firm in India, announced the bald
fact—" Login died Galle 16th, tell his mother."

The thing was impossible ! A cruel mistake ! An
appalling blunder ! This was my first, my most natural
idea. What should take my son to Galle, in Ceylon,
of all places ? What take him outside the Indian presi-
dencies for a voyage like that ?—he, who was saving
all his money for a trip home, hoping to get married ?
There was evidently some mistake in the name ; the
message was not for me ! and I resolved that my other
children, anyhow, should not have the joy of their
Christmas shattered by false tidings of evil. How I did
it, I hardly know ; but, keeping my own counsel, with
a heart nigh breaking with the sickening stroke, I wrote
and telegraphed to my friends and the Indian authorities

* My sister " Maggie," Mrs. Meiklejohn.

and said no word of all that darkened the world to me, to my two daughters and my niece, till St. Stephen's Day. Then I broke to them, as gently as I could, what had been told me, adding that so far neither confirmation nor denial of the report had yet reached me. Hoping and fearing, a weary *month* went by, till letters came to prove it all too true! And week by week, with every mail, *his* letters came, through all that time of waiting —he never had missed writing through all the years since he first left home, and he never did up to the end. Gay, cheerful, heartening letters, with never a word of the fever and dysentery that was sapping his life away! talking of a holiday, and change to the Central Provinces in a week or two, and never telling how he had been ordered a short sea-voyage by the doctor, on the bare *chance* of its restoring his strength. He was *carried* on board the P. & O. steamer *Geelong*, and died half an hour after the ship cast anchor at Pointe de Galle. There, in the cemetery, he lies buried, my eldest boy, laid to rest by strangers, with no one near who knew him before, save his faithful Goanese " boy ! "

The sailor son was now the only one left to me, and all my hopes centred on him. There was much in him to remind me of his father; he had inherited from him both his love of the sea, and his gifts of organisation. Edwy showed another side of his father's character, took more interest in public matters, finance and diplomacy, was a fair shot, and a fine horseman. He had also the Scotsman's passion for golf, and he it was who, in 1873, first suggested the feasibility of making links at Felixstowe, to his old Colonel in the London Scottish, then Lord Elcho.

Harry, the younger one, had not been the steady home-writer that his brother ever was, and when he first went to sea at fifteen, he actually changed his ship, being drafted from the Flag-ship on the Pacific Station to H.M.S. *Pylades*, stationed on the S.E. coast of America, without sending a line ; so that I had absolutely to get one of the attachés to the Ministry at Rio de Janeiro to find out if he really was on board that ship, and make him write !

He had been five years away from home when he first came back, and it was in the saloon of the troopship *Orontes*, in which he had been given passage, that I saw him first after all that interval. They had dropped anchor at Spithead only an hour before, and my impatience not suffering me to wait till the ship came into port next day, I chartered a sailing-boat from Portsmouth Hard, and went out to her, meeting on the way the Captain of the *Orontes*, who gave my boy twenty-four hours' leave and congratulated me on my enterprise. The first lieutenant, who received us, sent for him and took me below. As we entered the long saloon, a man in naval uniform, nearly six foot high and very broad in the chest, came in from the other end. "There's your son," said my conductor. I was much aggrieved at the tall stranger, who still advanced, shutting out with his bulky form all sight of the boy I was searching for eagerly. The intruder came to a dead stop, and stared blankly at me and my companions, while I attempted vainly to peer over his shoulder by standing on tip-toe! Suddenly he recognised, and greeted by name the Vicar of Southsea (Canon J. S. Blake), who had accompanied me, while at the same moment, the lieutenant, grasping the situation, exclaimed : "But *this* is your son, Lady Login ! Did you not know him ? " Was it wonderful that I had failed to do so ? He had left me a boy, and had returned a man ! A

second glance revealed him as the living image of
his father, but of superior height, and younger in
years than I had ever known the latter, for he was
only twenty after all.   Not many mothers, I think,
have had to be re-introduced to their son by a total
'stranger !   .

That was in 1871, and in that same year he was off
again round the world in the Flying Squadron.   In 1873
he went off in the *Active* to the First Ashantee War,
and his brother, who was in England for that one brief
visit, had the pride and pleasure of hearing Commodore
Sir William Hewett, his commanding-officer, at a
dinner-party at Ryde, inform the assembled guests—
not knowing that anyone was present who would know
of whom he spoke—" Well, I have got hold of a perfect
wonder as a 'mate of the upper-deck' !   I have never
seen anyone to come up to him for work, and the more
you give him to do, the happier the beggar seems !
He just grins with delight, and puts it through, working
like a navvy ! "

Six months before this, in April, 1873, I had ventured
first, for I was very chary of using any private influence
I might possess, to the detriment of officers of perhaps
greater claims—to commend my son Harry to the
Queen's favour, should she be disposed to include him
amongst the officers of the Royal Yacht.   Sir Thomas
Biddulph, after referring to other business, said " that
it would give him great pleasure to see my son appointed
to the Royal Yacht," and if I could get the Admiralty
to submit his name amongst others to the Queen,
" I will take care," said he, " that Her Majesty knows
who it is, and your anxiety in the matter."

But when my son was ordered to the West Coast of
Africa in the Flagship, for the Ashantee War, and com-

mended there for his good work, his superiors advised me not to ask for the appointment just then, as he was pretty sure to get his promotion for war services (which indeed proved true !) ; but to wait until he was qualified, with two years sea-time as Lieutenant, and then get his name put on the list.

Accordingly, when he had been for some time First Lieutenant of the *Plover*, I once more moved in the matter, and wrote to Sir Thomas Biddulph on October 23rd, 1877, to say that if he could give me hope that his name would be favourably looked at by the Queen, if sent up by My Lords for the 1878 appointment, he could get very high recommendations from the captains and admirals he had served under. Sir Thomas very kindly gave me a hint that he was aware that great pressure had been put upon the then First Lord, Mr. W. H. Smith, "*in very high quarters*," for a recommendation to the Queen for a special lieutenant ; but that, as the Admiralty seemed to be very just in selecting officers, for professional services rather than private interest, he thought, if my son's claims were so good, he would advise me to put him forward, backed by all the certificates at his command. I urged that my health had suffered from my anxiety on behalf of this my only remaining son, for he had been invalided from Prahsu with Ashantee fever, and was now serving on the rather unhealthy West Indian station, and referred to the fact that, on relinquishing the charge of the Princess Gouramma, Her Majesty had bade me ask " any favour I liked ; " but I had wanted nothing then.

Sir Thomas then assured me that " he had drawn Her Majesty's attention to my son's claims . . . and was quite sure they will be fairly considered if the Admiralty proposes his name. . . . These appointments are matters of great difficulty ; first to obtain the recommendation from the Admiralty, and then the pressure from various quarters . . . is considerable. Independently *of your own claim*, I must say your son's are, in my opinion, very good. The time will be about next June in all probability, and I wish you *may succeed.*"

Sir Thomas Biddulph's successor as Private Secretary to Her Majesty, Sir Henry Ponsonby, interested himself also in my son's behalf, from August, 1881, to 1890, and from him I heard each time the Admiralty list was sent up. In 1883 this procedure was interrupted, through Her Majesty making a special request for the appointment to be given to Prince Louis of Battenberg, who was, up to that time, my son's junior, though they had been associated together a good deal. In spite of this, Admiral Sir Cooper Key urged me to try and get my son's name sent in to Her Majesty, as unless soon promoted to Commander, he would otherwise have little hope of ever rising to the rank of Admiral.*

He was at length made Commander in 1889, and appointed to the *Anson*, in her first commission as flagship in the Channel Fleet, and the first mastless battleship ; and on their memorable summer cruise up the Baltic, had nineteen royalties photographed on the quarter-deck one afternoon at Elsinore, when, to the knowledge of the Captain (now Admiral Sir Bouverie F. Clark, K.C.B.) and himself alone, on the fore-bridge, the ship had struck an obstruction in the channel two hours previously, and was making water ! They subsequently ascertained by sending down divers when they reached Kiel, that one of the bottom-plates was damaged, and she would need docking on her return to England.

* Had not the promotions been accelerated by compulsory retirements in 1904, he would not have attained this rank.

They were a very merry and unconventional party of Sovereigns, Princes and Princesses, who spent two solid hours on board, though they came only for half an hour, and romped and roamed over the great ship like a pack of school-boys, insisting on seeing and testing everything. I fear that, much as the two responsible officers appreciated the honour, and the pleasure the length of their stay conveyed, there was some relief, in their anxiety about the good ship's seaworthiness, when they were seen off safely in the King of Denmark's barge! A photograph then taken is an unique record of such a gathering, and the few copies allowed to be struck off greatly cherished as a historical record by those who possess one. It came about from a simple request from one of the officers, that the Princess of Wales (Queen Alexandra) would allow herself to be photographed for the men of the ship's company to stick up on the mess-deck. " Certainly, with pleasure ! " she responded graciously. " Why, there are nineteen of us ; let us all be done together ! We may not have such another chance. Emperor ! Emperor ! Come up here ! " she called down the companion-way to the Tsar of all the Russias, who had vanished into the wardroom ; and the Autocrat, who seldom allowed any portrait to be taken, was summoned, much against his will, and the group arranged by herself, she standing in the centre, still in the glory of her beauty.

These are the names of those included :

The Emperor Alexander III. of Russia ; the Empress Marie Feodorovna (Dagmar) ; the Czarevitch (Emperor Nicholas II.) ; the Prince of Wales (King Edward VII.) ; the Princess of Wales (Queen Alexandra) ; King Christian IX. of Denmark ; Queen Louise of Denmark ; the Crown Prince of Denmark (King Frederick VII.) ;

the Crown Princess of Denmark (Queen Christine); their eldest son (King Christian X.), and second son (Prince Axel); the Duke of Clarence; Prince George of England (King George V.); the Duchess of Fife; Princess Victoria; Princess Maud (Queen of Norway); Prince Charles of Denmark (King Haakon of Norway); Princess Waldemar of Denmark (*née* Princess Marie of Orleans), and Prince John of Glücksburg, brother of Queen Louise of Denmark. Vice-Admiral Baird commanding the Channel Squadron was the only, nonroyalty admitted to the picture.

The barbettes of the *Anson's* 13-inch guns—considered marvels in those days !—had dark corridors running round the outside of the double-armour-clad, revolving, inner turrets, lit at intervals by electric bulbs. My son, in the semi-obscurity, had been for some twenty minutes acting *cicerone* to two ladies, who showed extraordinary interest in, and familiarity with, the construction of the various warlike implements, and scientific paraphernalia, of a modern ship-of-war. Their English was perfect, and they were so simply natural and friendly in their conversation with him, and he so absorbed in his demonstrations, that he thought no more of their identity, but that they were particularly unaffected and pleasant members of the royal suite. In passing one of the lights, his eye was attracted by the curious brooch that one of them was wearing, and he had another look at it when the next electric ray fell on it. To his consternation, he recognised the royal arms of Russia in brilliants and enamel, and a glance at the wearer's face showed him, by her resemblance to the Princess of Wales, that he had for the past twenty minutes been in close converse, all unknowingly, with the Empress of Russia herself !

He had many tales to tell of the Kaiser, who was at Kiel to receive the Fleet ; though, as I have mentioned, this was not his first inspection of the *Anson*.*

He, however, gave her a very thorough overhauling this time, penetrating into every corner, and seemed specially taken with the fittings in my son's cabin on the barbette deck ; the flat sponge-bath strapped tight to the roof, in the fashion that top-hats are (or were) fixed in railway-carriages, particularly took his fancy. " Splendid idea for stowing a tub ! I must make my fellows take note ! "

He had been exceedingly exercised over a saluting ceremony that took place on arrival at Kiel. " Why did you run up the White Ensign at the main, and salute it with twenty-one guns before entering the harbour ? " he asked the flag-lieutenant, the moment he boarded the *Northumberland*. " Not the White Ensign, your Majesty ! That was your own flag, Sire ; *your* flag as Admiral of the Fleet ! " " Well, would you believe it ? " —much relieved—" None of my fellows could tell me that ! "

After that incident, it was a source of much amuse-ment to hear that he lost no opportunity of flying this special flag on his private barge, on every possible occasion, even in foreign waters, tearing about at the Piræus, for instance, with it fluttering at the stern, to the bewilderment of the uninitiated, who took it for some special compliment to the British nation, the plain St. George's flag at a distance being difficult to distinguish from the White Ensign.

His rank of Honorary Admiral of the Fleet in the British Navy was a source of immense gratification to him, and bore witness to his grandmother's astuteness

* See *ante*, Chapter, XI. (pp. 166, 167).

in so honouring him. When the date arrived on which
the Fleet was due to leave Kiel, he asked Admiral
Baird if they could not stay one day longer, for some
special reason ? but was told their programme was given
them by the Admiralty, and without orders from home
they must not upset it, as the King of Sweden was
expecting them at Karlskrona.

"I'll telegraph to my grandmother," said Kaiser
Wilhelm, and accordingly did so.

The reply from the one who understood his character
best of all, filled him to over-brimming with pride and
self-complacency. "You are Admiral-of-the-Fleet—
give your orders ! "—which he promptly did.

CHAPTER XIX

UNTIL the summer of 1878, I continued to live mostly at the house at Felixstowe where my husband died, and we all grew to identify ourselves much with the place and people. The former was in those days much smaller, and more primitive, than it has since become, especially after the Kaiser and Kaiserin, with their children, have so frequently " honoured " with their presence the house on the cliff, which in our time went by the nickname of " Ely Cathedral," being the residence of the late Mr. Charles Eley of sporting-powder fame. Doubtless their visits were not without their purpose, which was even then suspected by many !

The old church at Felixstowe, dedicated to S. Felix, the apostle of East Anglia (who landed there to begin his evangelisation of the Saxons, and is said to be buried in the porch), had fallen into great disrepair, and was not large enough to seat the regular congregation, let alone the enormous crowd of visitors to the little watering-place who then attended it in summer-time. The parish, a large one, had been allowed to be held by its last two incumbents in conjunction with the adjoining one of Walton, at that time a much more populous place, and both advowsons had been acquired by purchase, by a vicar of very extreme evangelical views, and of exceedingly quaint personality. The diocese of Norwich was so vast that in any case the systematic " overseership " of the present day would have been impossible to one Bishop, and the occupant of the see, though an earnest and hard-working prelate, saw no necessity for the division of responsibility by the appointment of "gig-bishops," as they were then irreverently termed.

The Vicar of Walton-cum-Felixstowe felt no qualms at reducing the ministrations in his cure of souls, which embraced a district covering nine square miles, to the lowest compatible with legal requirements. He had four churches to serve, including a mission-chapel at Bawdsey Ferry, and the chapel for the garrison at Landguard Fort, for the performance of which duty he drew pay as chaplain from the War Office, and thus was enabled to keep a second curate, at seventy pounds a year !

This multiplicity of places of worship was the occasion of endless complications, for the good man had an inveterate objection to making definite arrangements and plans of any kind. His assistants were never allowed to know till the last moment—often not until the Sunday morning itself, for such a thing as a service held before eleven o'clock in the day was beyond his conception—whether the sermon prepared would be preached to soldiers, fishermen and coastguards, farmers and farm-labourers, or a congregation of London visitors ! Details of the kind never troubled him in the least ; why should they ? He had a certain number of sermons, composed probably in his university days (for he was an M.A. of Oxford, had taken a good degree, and was said to have been a distinguished Hebrew scholar), as they bore undoubted marks of his own authorship ; and these he used strictly in rotation, so that they became as familiar to his hearers as they were to himself ; and when in the fading dusk of a gloomy November afternoon (evening services were impossible, as there were no facilities for lighting the church), eyesight and memory failed him, one had an irresistible impulse to prompt him with the next sentence. Short and pithy texts were his strong point, and he had a curious twitch of the nostrils when he wished to be impressive, which gave him the appearance of an old buck-rabbit, and imparted to his speech the identical sanctimonious snuffle which is somehow always associated in one's mind with the traditional Puritan preacher, the resemblance being enhanced by the fact that, in the pulpit, he invariably wore the black gown and Geneva bands of the Nonconformist pastor. It is an impossible accent to reproduce, but sounded irresistibly comic when, with an air of awe-inspiring solemnity, he would stand up in the lofty " three-decker," and after an impressive pause, enunciate slowly, with nasal vehemence : " M-harcus, mhy son ! " or " On-ly Lhuke was with me ! "

On one occasion he surpassed himself. It was a hot Sunday in summer, and after a toilsome, dusty walk of, in most cases, two miles shadeless pilgrimage, an over-flowing congregation sat packed into the high loose-boxes which formed the pews of the church, and which in many cases concealed fine old poppy-head stalls of black, worm-eaten oak, corresponding with the solid oaken beams two and three feet square, that stretched from wall to wall of the nave, and, though blocking the view, gave the fabric strength. The school-children, ranged on forms, filled the aisle, admonished by a sort of nondescript verger or beadle, who paced up and down to keep order, armed with a seven-foot rod of office, tapering like a billiard cue, with which he attempted to correct the unruly ; but being somewhat uncertain in vision, and in hearing, not infrequently missed his aim,

and injured the head-gear, or poked in the eye, some
unoffending female in the congregation ! In the gallery
at the west end, sat one or two singers *and* the organ,
of which the parish was immensely proud, it being a
comparatively new acquisition, and, of its kind, a fine
specimen—a barrel organ with about fourteen hymn-
tunes and two or three voluntaries ; but with several
pegs missing, so that when a hiatus occurred, the black-
smith, who officiated at the handle, put his head round
the corner of the instrument, and supplied the missing
note in a deep bass bellow !

The bell continued long after all were assembled, and
the organ played slowly all its tunes, and began its
répertoire all over again, and still no clergyman appeared!
The congregation waited, but as there was still no sign of
him, began to disperse. On this the Vicar was descried
in the distance in his ramshackle pony-carriage, lashing
the unfortunate white pony into a feeble resemblance of
a gallop ; he arrived, tore into the vestry, and reappear-
ing, breathlessly hurried through the morning service.
When it came to the sermon, he made his customary
little pause—his congregation, I fear, regarding him the
while with an amount of frigid resentment, when, blandly
smiling round on them, with an air of apology, he
mildly remarked : " Fear not, little flock ! " repeating
the words a second time, in a still more encouraging
tone, to give additional emphasis ! As if anxious yet
further to try our gravity, he made a deprecating
pause, and in a hesitating manner remarked : " Before
commencing the consideration of these words, I would
like to offer some apology for inconvenience caused . . .
er . . . er . . . delay in arriving . . . er . . . er . . .
quite a misunderstanding . . . thought had arranged
. . . to be elsewhere . . . unfortunate mistake . . .

er . . . er . . ." Continuing in the same breath, and with no change of voice : " *These beautiful words will be found written in the twelfth chapter of St. Luke's Gospel and the thirty-second verse.*" He looked mildly surprised, after this announcement, to discover that, though none were asleep, all his congregation suddenly disappeared from view, and were simultaneously suffering from violent coughs and colds ! As a matter of fact, owing to contradictory instructions delivered the previous day, both his curates and himself had all three turned up to take the duty at Landguard Fort, quite five miles off !

The Vicar also had a wonderful faculty for scenting out any stray cleric on a holiday among the visitors, and pressing them into his service to assist in some capacity. In this way, of course, his congregation frequently benefited by the ministrations of able men and fine preachers. But there was another side to the question, and having endured the vagaries of a strange clergyman of a melodramatic turn of mind, who *acted* the scene of the temptation of Eve, and *imitated the voices* respectively of Adam, Eve and the Serpent (the latter a sort of hissing squeak !) in the pulpit, and in the lectern read the eleventh chapter of second Corinthians, with the refrain recurring "so am I," as a kind of Punch-and-Judy show, in which the big Bible played a part—at the close of the service I asked my governess if she would ascertain from the clerk the gentleman's name, in order that I might avoid hearing him again. Conceive the dismay of the unfortunate young woman when, as she asked the question, the vestry door opened alongside, and the individual himself responded, in a very loud voice, laying a warning stress on the concluding words : " The Rev. David Ap Thomas, at your service, and I live at Notting Hill *with my wife !* "

The old church being in such a parlous state, and needing restoration, and enlargement, to fit it for the requirements of a growing population, I, and other friends there, moved heaven and earth to raise a sum for the purpose. In this we were partially successful, two transepts and a new chancel and organ-chamber, with new organ, were added. Having induced Mr. John Bright to plead my cause with Lord Cardwell, I got from the War Office a grant of the materials used in the construction of a condemned coast-battery, and a Scottish architect devised a method of employing these old Government bricks—hard as stone—in a diagonal fashion, which gave rather the appearance of Kentish "rag." I then tried to work the Admiralty, in view of the fact that it was the only high building on the coast, and on high ground, to re-erect the old tower, which had been partly burnt down many years ago, and never rebuilt, as a signal-station for coastguard ;* but although the idea was very favourably regarded by the local naval authorities, it came to nothing.

It was greatly against the Vicar's wish that all these improvements were made ; he had seen no occasion for them ; indeed, he had tried to restrict the services to alternate morning and afternoon on a Sunday, and four celebrations of Holy Communion per annum, whereof one was to be on Good Friday ! But I was able to invoke the Bishop's authority on this point, as it was illegal so to treat a parish church.

However, with the help of our good friend the 9th

* My father's monument in the churchyard was already used as a " leading-mark " by the fishermen. And now (1915) the Church is within the military prohibited area, and surrounded by barbed wire entanglements. Possibly signals are made from its roof ?

Baron Kinnaird, a very strong churchman, and others, we got the new chancel and one transept finished, and it was arranged by the Bishop of Norwich (John Thomas Pelham), that as he was coming to preach at Felixstowe, on a certain Sunday, he would dedicate the new chancel by celebrating in it for the first time, even although the interior fittings were not complete, and there was to be a formal opening ceremony a Sunday or two later.

All this was communicated to Mr. M——, who had made up his mind that no one, not even his diocesan, should interfere with his pet project of having the opening of the building performed by Dr. Ryle, then at Mildenhall, afterwards Bishop of Liverpool, for whom he had an unbounded veneration.

On the Saturday afternoon, the Bishop being expected the following forenoon, I went up to the church, where, with the assistance of the builder engaged in the work, I made all ready for the service, and left as the dusk was falling, passing on the road, the Vicar, driving the well-known pony-chaise. Satisfied that though the building was in a rough and bare condition, the Bishop would feel content that all essential was prepared, I arrived at the church on Sunday about ten minutes before the hour fixed, to find a packed congregation— for this was the Bishop's first visit in the memory of man—all gazing in blank astonishment at a very dirty canvas cloth (an old sail, in fact!), hanging over, and completely concealing the new chancel-arch and chancel, and in front of it, on the level of the nave, a very ricketty deal table, and two wooden chairs! The whole had the effect of a theatrical drop-scene, as the canvas being very worn and semi-transparent, and the new chancel lighted by four windows, one could not only distinguish its main features, but its carved choir-seats, reading-desk, different levels of pavement, even the altar, with new altar cloth and furniture, and all the preparations for the service of Holy Communion, in a kind of misty distance—the only incongruous element, the unmistakable figure of the Vicar's wife, in her best bonnet, seated in solitary state in the front row of choir-stalls, and the slouching outline of the old clerk, with the air of a conspirator, tip-toeing about in the background!

Voices raised in distinctly acrimonious tones were heard proceeding from the vestry, which was part of the new building, and the voluntary had to be repeated more than once, ere a remarkable procession was descried through the misty folds of the canvas. Then the short, stumpy figure of the clerk appeared, holding up one corner of the curtain to allow the Vicar to pass, robed in surplice and black stole, and behind him the Rural Dean. So far, old Versey could manage with an effort, and by standing on tip-toe on the uppermost step of the three under the arch of the chancel. But having allowed these two dignitaries to pass through the aperture, dropping it behind each, there loomed through the canvas the shadow of a form twice their stature, and voluminous in the full canonicals of a Bishop. With a crimson face, the luckless clerk held back the heavy folds as high as he could, but alas! the aperture was so low, that their Diocesan presented himself, for the first time, to the faithful, bent nearly double, and squirming with difficulty through a hole barely large enough for him to pass!

Sad to relate, when the service was over, and the clergy retired again in the same fashion, even though the organ was pealing its loudest in the concluding voluntary, the resonant tones of the episcopal voice were plainly audible to the loitering congregation, administering the soundest rating, I should imagine, any incumbent ever received from his " ordinary ! "

Felixstowe church was the stage of many irregular, and possibly irreverent, scenes. I have heard a strange clergyman, taking duty, apostrophise the clerk in the middle of a baptismal service with : " Hold your tongue, sirrah ! and don't tell me more lies ! " and the only manner in which I succeeded in stopping the choir-men from using the font as the general receptacle for their hats—so convenient it was, just inside the door—was, after warning them that rigorous action would be taken, by filling the bottom with water ! They had a custom of waiting outside to gossip till the last clang of the bell, and then entering the church in a violent hurry, all in a body. The first man, a young buck with a brand-new " topper," grinned at me defiantly, and tossed his headgear in as usual. What a titter went round the school-children, and how sheepish he looked, as he heard the ominous splash, and fished it out all dripping !

And there was the retired Admiralty clerk, who reported for the newspaper, and loved to air his long words, and his superior erudition. He solemnly endued a black velvet smoking-cap with a long, yellow tassel, as soon as he had settled himself in his seat, as a protest against " draughts," and shouted the word " Hades," at the top of his voice, whenever, in reciting the Creeds, there came the passage, " He descended into Hell ! " His language was as exuberant in relation to mundane matters ; he never " thought," he always " opined." In describing a choir-supper, he gave it the air of a bacchanalian feast, by relating that a nephew of mine " must have made a great hole in his aunt's cellar by his manipulation (!) of the punch-bowl." When asked what sport the harriers had had one day, he announced that there was " a great paucity of hares," and he, for one, was returning home to lunch, because " nature abhors a vacuum ! "

I think the air was productive of originals, for they seemed to abound in those parts. The biggest landowner in the district was Mr. George Tomline, who had bought up the Duke of Hamilton's property in the country, and his rights, as Lord of the Manor, in the foreshore between the Orwell and the Deben. For many years he had a permanent lawsuit with the War Office on the subject of his dues, and actually levied a toll on every ton of material landed for the building of the great fort at Landguard, because the jetty built by Government had been put up on his foreshore without his sanction asked ! His chief delight was, in every way, to annoy and harass the War Office officials, and I shall never forget seeing him attempting to drive his two pampered ponies—he usually drove a very handsome pair in a mail-phaeton—straight up the side of a grass-covered cliff, on the top of which there was an obsolete Martello tower, and which was enclosed as Government property within a wire fence, just cut by his orders, because someone had told him there *used to be* a right of way there ! He was standing up in the carriage, lashing at the animals, who had never before been expected to take a rise at an angle of forty-five degrees, a groom, pale with fright, hanging on on one side, and his terrified agent in the rumble behind ! As I passed, driving myself on the road below, he called out : " Come on, Lady Login ! Follow me, too ! We'll defy them !" But "Lady Login" declined to risk her neck, and remained convulsed with laughter, watching his progress !

The 'amusing part of his feud with the War Office was, that he was a great personal friend of H.R.H the Duke of Cambridge, then Commander-in-Chief, who was frequently his guest at Orwell Park, and to whom, in his will, he bequeathed a good deal of his personal property. I tried to get the Duchess of Teck to induce her brother to use his influence with Mr. Tomline to help with the re-building of Felixstowe Church; but though she wrote me very kindly about it, she said that the Duke hardly liked to move in the matter, as it would seem interference on his part, and she knew that I would understand the difficulty? So, though I got Mr. Tomline, who was ever most kind and obliging to me personally, to do many things for the church, and for the people of the place, he would never subscribe a fixed sum which could by any possibility be construed into an assistance to Mr. M——, the Vicar, to whom he had a violent antipathy.

On the other hand, he took a liking to the Vicar of Trimley St. Mary, the next parish, who was a great contrast to poor Mr. M——, being a bachelor, sporting in his tastes, and somewhat of a dandy. He drove about in a tilbury, sometimes tandem, handling the reins very neatly, and wearing always lavender kid gloves and a flower in his button-hole; indeed, his turn-out was recognisable at a distance on this account. I think Mr. Tomline was sorry for him, because he had the misfortune to be brother to Palmer, the poisoner, and had had the courage to keep his surname, when all the other members of the family changed it for another one.

I felt very sorry for poor Mr. Palmer on one occasion, when I was present at a meeting on business connected with the schools, and there was some talk about a quarrel on between Mr. Tomline and the Vicar, over a piece of

ground given by the former, which it was proposed
to use as a playground. Why, where there is some skele-
ton in a cupboard, not wanted to be dragged into view
by the company, does the stranger present invariably
pitch upon it, and hale it forth? When Mr. M——, in
his usual contradictory spirit, opposed the suggestion,
H.M. Inspector of Schools, presiding in an official
capacity, to the stupefaction of the company, demanded
to know the reason of his objection, and kept repeating
—" Why? Do you think he would sow it with
strychnine to poison the children?" (strychnine was
the poison employed by the notorious Palmer!), and
seeing that no one answered, he put the question
directly to the Vicar of Trimley! As the Inspector
was a personal friend of my own, I had to explain
privately afterwards, why we all hurriedly started
asking wild questions to change the subject!

Mr. Palmer, as the sporting parson, seldom was seen
in clerical attire, and almost the only time on which I
saw him in a surplice, it was a very short one, worn
without any cassock over hunting-coat, breeches, and
a pair of top-boots, with spurs! As the occasion was the
dedication of a new piece of churchyard, when the
Archdeacon and all the neighbouring clergy perambulated the enclosure, headed by a choir, the figure he
cut, striding over the graves, and hopping across rough
hummocks of ground, with his nether appendages
very much in evidence, was anything but decorous!

A state of permanent war also existed between Mr.
Tomline and another large owner of land at Felixstowe,
Mr. John Chevalier Cobbold, conducted by the latter
with due deference to the courtesies of the *salle
d'escrime*. It took the form frequently of a diverting
rivalry in the development of the place as a seaside

·resort. Mr. Cobbold had been the first in the field as a
builder of houses and hotels, but Mr. Tomline owned
the greater extent of land, and had the longer purse.
He began to build enormous hotels, lay out roads and
streets of houses, erect a pier on the Orwell estuary,
and finally constructed a private railway at a cost of
a quarter of a million.

To further all these schemes, and to carry on his war
with the War Office, he suddenly conceived the idea of
entering Parliament, and partly because Mr. Cobbold
was Conservative, determined to contest the seat in
the Liberal interest. His attempts to gain popularity,
and canvass for votes, were diverting in one naturally
autocratic in temperament, who had been accustomed to
indulge in violent fits of passion when opposed, and who
was also very impatient of any sort of contradiction.

He lent his park for the annual cottagers' flower
show for the district, which in those days was regardéd
as a very important function, being still a novelty, and
attended by everyone, high and low, for miles round.

He possessed a very fine collection of modern paintings at Orwell Park, and had often promised to show
them to me. So, being at the flower show, by his
desire I accompanied him up to the house, and he
started to take me through the rooms, beginning with
the large drawing-room.

Glancing out of the window, we discovered that the
crowd of holiday-makers, who had been following
him closely all round the show, had pursued him right
up to his own door, invaded the garden, and having
run him to earth again, were darkening all the French
windows, with their noses glued to the panes, staring
in upon us as if gazing at the bears in the bear-pit at the
Zoo! And, sooth to say, Mr. Tomline's massive frame,

with the shaggy mane of grizzled locks, and his fierce, tawny eyes, bore a distinct similarity to old Ursa Major.

With the incongruous spirit of urbanity now rampant in him, he turned to me, fired by a sudden idea. " Look at those people ! Do you think they would like to come in, too, and see these things ? " and he started forward to throw open the window. " For heaven's sake, Colonel Tomline ! " I cried—he always liked to be given his yeomanry rank—" if you will take my advice, you will send first for your housekeeper before doing that ! " But no ! his impatience never allowed him to wait before doing anything on which his mind was set. Heedless of my warning, he opened the window, muttered in his gruff tones to the half-dozen standing there, " Would you like to come in ? " and turned to the fireplace to pull the bell.

Before he could cross the room it was invaded by a mob ! Absolutely he had to force his way to the bell-pull through a solid phalanx of bodies, and when his repeated peals brought a terrified footman on the scene, he had to shout his orders to him across a seething multitude, for it was impossible to approach. I shall not easily forget the white, scared face of the unfortunate housekeeper, when she appeared, and found what her master had left her to cope with ! for, after frantic efforts to reach my side, and imperative signals to me to follow him—which I found physically impossible—he had turned and bolted through a side-door near him, into an adjoining room, and I saw him no more, but only had the recollection of the expression on his face, seen across the moving mass of figures, to guess at the turmoil of wrath and stupefaction in which he was engulfed !

I was told that the vision of that human avalanche, viewed by a spectator outside the building, was one of the strangest sights imaginable. It was like a gigantic hive of bees, my informant told me, to see the people streaming from all quarters, as hard as they could tear, across the lawns and the flower-beds, and in at that one window-opening. Absolutely, the show-tents were emptied like a flash, the crowd penetrated into every room of the great building, and one old " gaffer," not by any means the cleanest in person of the community, was in the habit of boasting for years afterwards that he had been " in every chammer—a've been in the Colonel's *bed ! !* "

After my husband's death I occasionally let my house at Felixstowe in the summer, and it was in that way that I got into correspondence with Mr. Edward FitzGerald, the poet, who engaged to rent it from me for two or three months, as the doctor had ordered him sea air ; but when the date arrived he could not be persuaded to make any arrangements for taking it over ! He wrote at last, saying that he would be so much better pleased if I would continue to stay in it till he was ready to come, he paying the rent as he had arranged ! This I did for a week or two, and he drove over from Woodbridge to inspect it on a pouring wet day ! So far as I know, that was all he ever saw of it, for I could not stay on, and went abroad, and I believe it remained empty until I again took possession !

Another tenant was Samuel Warren, author of " Ten Thousand a Year." He was extremely fidgetty over all the arrangements, and the letters I had from him were innumerable, all " franked " with his signature in the bottom left-hand corner of the envelope. This, he explained to me, with engaging naïveté, in one of our numerous interviews, was because his autograph was so much sought after, that many people were glad of

extra ones to give to their friends! I hurriedly turned
the conversation, lest he might discover that his precious
envelopes mostly found their way into my waste-paper
basket!

At Kew we had known the two Hookers, father
and son, successive Curators of the Gardens. The
senior, Sir William, was most extraordinarily myopic,
and I fear was made the victim of perpetual practical
jokes in consequence. At a large luncheon party we
gave, being told that in the épergne in front of him there
were several artificial flowers introduced amongst the
real ones, as flowers were scarce, " but, of course," it
was suggested, " to the eye of a connoisseur, the decep-
tion would be at once palpable," he exclaimed with
emphasis, drawing from the bunch a pelargonium of
unusual hue, and to most observers very plainly a
counterfeit, " Well, there can be no question about this,
anyhow! No one could mistake this for artificial!"
So much for the botanical infallibility of even a world-
wide celebrity!

I remember meeting Emil Hohlub, the African
traveller, at Sir Joseph Hooker's many years later, and
being much diverted with his accounts of the " Ama-
zulus," as he called the race that afterwards proved
themselves our very formidable foes. He had the
greatest admiration for their strength of character,
and the remorselessness with which they pursued any
fixed purpose appealed to his Teutonic mind. " I have
been told they are a distinctly honourable and truthful
nation," I ventured to remark to him. " Did you find
this to be the case ? " He assumed an air of the most
terrible earnestness as he replied in his rather halting
English, solemnly wagging his head : " Alas ! they
are indeed truthful, *too* truthful ! If a Zulu say ' I will

kill you to-morrow,' you need have no doubt but that he will keep his word ! "

Amongst the original characters I came across during the fifteen years I spent in Suffolk, was my landlady, the widow, *en secondes noces*, of Sir Thomas Cullum. The house we rented was named " Vernon Villa," after the famous Admiral, having been built by his grand-niece, Lady Harland, who had erected several of the houses in the place, and made this one her own favourite residence. It was rather in the Italian style, with a tower-room, or observatory, looking out to sea, and the woodwork was very massive and beautiful, most of the doors being solid mahogany and other choice timber from Honduras and South America, possibly relics of family inheritance from her naval relative.

His portrait, in a very fine group of three figures— the artist unknown to me—hung over the mantelpiece in the dining-room, one of the others being his great adversary the Dutch Admiral De Ruyter. The third, I am uncertain about, but he was represented as host to the other two, pouring out a glass of wine for each, from a decanter of Madeira or Malmsey. Facing this picture was a portrait of Sir Robert Harland, by Romney.

Although proud of the association of the house with old Admiral Vernon's name (plans of the capture of Portobello and Chagres hung in one of the rooms), I was reluctantly compelled to use the designation simply of " The Villa " all the time I lived there, merely because, in the mouths of the Suffolk country-people, the name invariably came out as " Wermin Willa," which was anything but a pleasant idea !

The house was left in Lady Harland's will to three ladies in succession, for their lives, after which it passed to relatives of her own absolutely, and Lady Cullum

was the first inheritrix. She lived at Hardwicke, near
Bury-St.-Edmunds, and being a solitary widow without
children, had become absorbed in her three hobbies,
dogs, gardening and servants, whereof the dogs certainly
stood first in her affections. She owned several of these,
but one was always pre-eminent ; to its health, fancies,
and predilections, all things had to give way. It was
treated as if a child of her own ; had its own chair, plate,
mug and napkin at her table, was helped solemnly by
the men-servants in turn with the other guests ; had its
own stamped and crested notepaper, on which invitations,
in its name, were issued for parties to the children of the
neighbourhood ; and when, in the course of nature, it
died, it was mourned as if it had been human, and a
monument erected to its memory in the grounds.   I
have a recollection of an imposing column in the midst
of the lovely gardens at Hardwicke, on which was inscribed the one word " Dot," as a lasting record of the
most celebrated of all.   " Dot of Hardwicke," in his
mistress's eyes, apparently rivalled very nearly the
reputation of the historical " Bess " of that ilk !

The next house to ours at Eelixstowe, called Harland
House, was, in the first years of our stay, the summer
residence of Lord Alfred Paget and his family, and the
young people and mine made great friends. His eldest
son, now General Sir Arthur Paget, and my boy Harry,
were close companions, and were in a continual state of
borrowing and wearing each other's clothes, and
frequently sharing rooms. I remember once a nephew
of mine who was often with us—then a cadet at Sand-
hurst—playing a practical joke on Arthur Paget
when the boy was staying in our house. There was a
very old four-poster, canopied bed, in the boys' room,
which Arthur Paget occupied. Colin Campbell dis-

covered that it must have been originally some sort of
a camp bed, for on removing a bolt or piece of wood,
it could be shut up, with mattress and all inside.
Accordingly, one night the whole house was aroused
by the most awful commotion, yells and groans !
The unfortunate boy had awoke to find the bed closing
in on him, quite in the "Castle of Otranto" style !
By the exertion of terrific force, the footman rescued
him, and a tell-tale string revealed the fact that someone had waited till he was sound asleep, and then
surreptitiously jerked out the wedge on which the bed's
stability depended, causing head and heels to come
gradually together.

Both Lord and Lady Alfred were the most unconventional of people, and never happier than with their
hands employed in the roughest work, and attired in
the shabbiest of garments. She mended up and painted
the furniture of the seaside cottage they often let, and
taught her daughters to be equally useful ; and Lord
Alfred would come in to see you in the heartiest way,
straight off the yacht on which he had been "trawl-
ing" all night, clad in oilskins and his "sou-wester,"
whence the sea-water and "spume" ran in rivulets
all over your drawing-room carpet. But he was the
kindest-hearted of men, and he it was who spoke about
my son Harry to the Prince of Wales in later days,
when H.R.H. *promised* that his name should be put
down on the list for the Royal Yacht !

When my youngest son returned, for the first time,
from the sea, in 1871, it was about three years after my
eldest brother, General Charles Campbell, had sold the
old family property in Perthshire. It had been a very
bitter blow to all of us, since for many generations we had
been Campbells of Kinloch, and he is the last owner to

whom the countrypeople, to this day, ever accord the recognition of the territorial title, according to Highland usage.

The purchaser was Lord Kinnaird, a very strong Scottish Episcopalian, and he bought it for a residence for his brother, the Hon. Arthur Kinnaird, who afterwards succeeded him in the baronage, since Francis, Lord Kinnaird, had but the one child, a daughter, married to Colonel (later on Sir Reginald) Ogilvy. I had formed a very warm friendship with Lord and Lady Kinnaird, when they came to Felixstowe on account of their daughter's health, and Lord Kinnaird offered to let me the house and shootings of Kinloch for two months, in the autumn of 1871.

It was for me a mingling of pain and pleasure thus to reside once more, if even for a short time, in my old home ; but I wished my children to know the place and the people, and I was both touched, and gratified, with the warmth of the welcome we all received from my father and brother's late tenants. One or two of my sisters, and many nephews and nieces, I was able thus to invite as guests during our stay.

Our advent seemed to revive old customs and associations, and the people hailed with joy the gillies' balls we once more instituted, which had fallen into abeyance since we scattered all to our separate homes.

There was one old farmer there, a godson of my uncle José Campbell, and a principal tenant on the estate, though he habitually wore garments more befitting a " tatie-bogle " (a scarecrow, as you say in the south), and dwelt in a low, ramshackle building, more suitable in English eyes for a cow-shed than a human habitation, who asked me point-blank *why* " Kinloch " himself— so they designated my brother—did not avail himself of this opportunity to see once more his old friends, and the home of his fathers ? " Sure, it's just that he cannot summon up the courage to face us all, nae doot ! " he concluded generously. " Bid him have nae fear we'll cast it up against him ! " he asseverated with emphasis. " Let him but come and gie us a hand-shake, and bid us good-bye, as he did not do when he left us, and we'll forgie him ! What for did he want to go and part wi' the auld place like yon ! If it was the siller he was wanting, he need not mind for that. Had he but come to me and said, ' Joseph Murray, I'm hard pressed the noo for a bit cash,' why, there's twa thoosand punds o' mine in the bank, that he was just welcome to for the asking, rather than see the old name gone fra' the Strath ! "

A number of young men in the house, the shooting party, the gillies' dances, and constant visits from old acquaintances among the country-people, made it advisable to replenish our supply of whiskey, and we drove over the hills to what had used to be a well-known small " still," in the direction of Aberfeldy, which went by the name of Piteelie. Here, by the permission of an obliging " gauger," we were supplied with a small keg, and when it had been deposited with care in the bottom of the waggonette, the proprietor drew me aside to remark confidentially : " Now, ye'll just be verra careful, mem, with yonder whuskey ! Gin ye'll tak my advice, ye'll pit a good wheen watter til't, or ever ye lat the young gentlemen fill their flasks. Mind ye, noo ! it's ' fifteen abave proof,' and reel dangerous in the hills, it's that soft, and mild, and persuasive ! And if you're no taking tent, they'll be sitting on a stane out-by yonder on the moors, and the air will be sae keen, they will never guess its strength, and they'll tak a wee drappie, and then they'll tak an' sit, an' drink, an' drink, and think it's *watter !* "   I am happy to be able to testify that, in spite of his dark prognostications, every body concerned " took tent," and though excellent liquor indeed, there were no such dire consequences, and over-indulgence as he hinted at !

It was during this visit to Kinloch, that one of the elder cottars on the property, told us how his father used often to speak of having watched as a wee laddie, on a misty summer morning, from the hill at Caplea, the young men gathering on the road below, headed by the laird's son, to march over the hills to Aberfeldy, there to enlist under the banner of " bonnie Prince Charlie " in the '45.   Somehow, it spaced the 126 years that intervened to have the story only at second-hand !

CHAPTER XX

THE seats allotted to me for Queen Victoria's first Jubilee in 1887, were in a gallery over the West door of Westminster Abbey, whence we had an uninterrupted view up the nave, which was in semi-darkness, on to where a brilliant light, fixed in the entrance to the choir, flooded for a moment each figure in the Royal Procession, as it finished its slow and stately progress up the church, ere it was wrapt from our sight in the galaxy of colour and light, beyond the choir-screen, of which we caught only fleeting glimpses. From our position we had a view of the outside procession ere it reached the West door, for, when the roar of continuous cheering reached us inside, we ran out on to the outside temporary staircase by which we had gained the gallery, saw the cavalcade of Princes sweep past Westminster Hospital, and were back in our places, by the time the trumpeters of the Guards sounded the first fanfare, from the summit of the choir-screen facing us.

There are figures in that procession that will never fade from my memory! First and foremost, the Crown Prince "Fritz," as we all called him, that gallant and knightly figure in its shining cuirass, and his consort, our own dear Princess Royal. Little did we all guess, seeing him thus the embodiment of manly strength, that already the fiat had gone forth, and shortly, for how brief a space! he would wear an earthly, in preparation for a heavenly, crown.

There, too, walked the Crown Prince Rudolph, clad all in white, leading very tenderly the blind Grand Duke of Mecklenburg-Strelitz, whom I had known as a bridegroom. Then, besides the Indian native rulers, accompanied in some cases by their wives, and the Sultans of Johore and Zanzibar, for the last time a representative of the Sandwich Isles, or Hawaii, as it is more properly called, appeared at a State function, in the person of Queen Liliuo-Kalani, in her sable dress with its gold embroideries.

In the course of a long life, I had opportunities of noting the advance made in the regulation of Court and State functions, the management of large crowds by police and military, which had previously been a very weak point in our social system, and the gradual evolution of a system of organisation of traffic, and supplies, when any great national festival, or event, is in prospect. As a nation we were formerly very backward in these matters, and had a passion for a sort of happy-go-lucky, trust-to-the-inspiration-of-the-moment policy, which resulted in the awful congestion, and fiascoes, of the Coronation of King George IV. and the funeral of the Duke of Wellington, when the block of carriages, and ill-regulated crowds, brought the day to a close before the programme was completed!

I had been an invited guest in the tiny chapel of Buckingham Palace, at the very first marriage in Queen Victoria's family, that of H.R.H. the Princess Royal of England to H.R.H. Prince Frederick William of Prussia, and had places given for myself, and two daughters, at the Thanksgiving Service at St. Paul's in 1872, one of the first occasions, after her widowhood, that Her Majesty showed Herself to Her people in semi-state.

This was the first time that I had noticed any thought-out plan, on the part of the police, for the controlling of the crowd. As is well known, all idea of the kind was conspicuous by its absence, in the case of the Peace Rejoicings after the Crimean War, or the marriage of the Prince of Wales to Princess Alexandra of Denmark, when the bride's carriage was so effectually mobbed, that for long periods it was brought to a standstill, and my son Edwy, as an Eton boy, announced triumphantly, that the College charged in a body through the intervening line of police, and he rode on the step of the carriage, alongside the Princess, all the way up the Castle Hill at Windsor! London mobs were a " tough " lot in those days, and usually managed to follow their own sweet will; and we know how, in 1866, when the great Reform Meeting was held in Hyde Park, and John Bright spoke to the people—how I teased the " Quaker " about it at the time !—they showed their wrath at the gates being closed, by throwing over the high ornamental railings for a distance of several hundred yards ! I saw them, torn from their stone sockets by sheer weight of numbers, and lying flat and twisted, from the Marble Arch almost to Hyde Park Gardens, two days afterwards, as I drove from my house in Lancaster Gate.

At the Thanksgiving Service, the roadway of St. Paul's Churchyard was kept clear of traffic, for the carriages of those attending the service, by means of heavy wooden barricades, and one or two other points had barriers to relieve pressure. It so happened that, on coming out, we could find no sign of our carriage, and waited on till all had departed, throwing ourselves on the protection of the police. They conducted us to an alley, barricaded at both ends, which they had turned into a sort of guardhouse, and we thus had an opportunity of " assisting " in safety at the critical moment when,

the majority of notabilities having got away, and the
temper of the howling, and raging crowd, having reached
breaking point, an enormous Inspector, in stentorian
tones, roared the long looked-for signal : " Let loose the
mob ! " Never before have I seen such a scene ! In an
instant, the populace were over every spot, as if a cork
had been drawn out of a bottle, of which the contents
overflowed the whole square and up the steps to the
doors of the Cathedral, howling, baying, like mad dogs !
And yet the constables assured us " this was nothing !
This was a crowd in high good humour ! Had it been
otherwise, they could never have been held so long ! "
Meanwhile, as soon as the exuberance had somewhat
abated, we were driven home in the carriage of a foreign
Ambassador, which the police discovered in a by-street,
quite astray ; and the populace, baulked of a close view
of all the preceding grand equipages, hailed our appearance with rounds of cheering all along the route !

For the Diamond Jubilee in 1897, Her Majesty sent
me tickets for the Household stand in the forecourt of
Buckingham Palace, where we saw the Procession both
starting and returning, and the Queen's appearance
afterwards on the famous balcony over the entrance—
this time, alas ! without the well-known form of her
eldest and best-loved son-in-law ! *

One little incident in connection with the 1887
Jubilee I may mention. We noticed, while the Royal
Procession was still being marshalled at the West door,
a sudden commotion in the North Transept, and a
group of personages, clad in robes of black and purple,
surrounding a tall figure, scarlet from head to foot,
swept hurriedly, conducted by an official bearing a wand

* Seats in this same position were given also to my mother, by the King's
desire, for the Coronation of King Edward VII.

of office, inside the gates of the sanctuary, evidently belated guests of importance. One of my daughters, who was not with me at the Abbey, but to whom Mr. John Bright had given his own ticket at the Reform Club, told us afterwards, how that when the salute of guns announced that the Sovereign had reached Westminster, suddenly, to everyone's amazement, a magnificent equipage, recognised as the Duke of Norfolk's, came tearing down Piccadilly at full gallop, along the route kept open for the return procession. It was at once surmised that some essential for the Earl Marshal's department had been forgotten, and must *coûte que coûte* arrive before the function was over.

On relating this next day to a Roman Catholic lady, she exclaimed : " That explains what the Papal Envoy was after ! We were all intensely annoyed, because the Cardinal-Archbishop of Westminster, fixed the same hour for the Te Deum and Pontifical Mass, at the Pro-Cathderal, as the actual ceremony at the Abbey, and thus prevented us from being in our allotted seats as Peers and Peeresses, as we had intended. I heard the Papal Envoy was furious, as the Holy Father " (His Holiness Leo XIII.) " has a special veneration for Her Majesty, and had ordered him to attend the service in the Abbey, as a State ceremony. He seemed in a tremendous fluster and hurry, all the time, for of course he had to be at a mass of the kind at the Oratory,* but he actually left the church with his whole train, the moment mass was over, and before the benediction was given ! I am glad to hear that he succeeded in carrying out the Pope's instructions. Had the Archbishop had his way, it would have seemed like a slight to our Sovereign."

* The Cathedral at Westminster was not in being at that date.

It was in the years between the two Jubilee celebrations, that I was able to attempt a last act of service
to my dear mistress, and though my efforts were not
suffered to avert in time the mischief I foresaw, owing
to the self-importance, and want of perception, of some
who then surrounded her, I had the satisfaction of
proving that my warnings only erred in under-estimat-
ing the risk of danger to her dignity.

The story I am now about to relate, deals with an
imposture one would hardly have believed possible
in these days of enlightenment, and frequent intercourse
between outlying portions of the globe. It sounds more
like the fables of the charlatan Cagliostro, of the
eighteenth century, or a page out of Gulliver's travels,
so wild, and so easily detected (one would think), were
the fabrications with which the leaders of society, in
two capitals, were gulled !

I was then, and for several years after, a Vice-President
of the Kent Nursing Institution, whose headquarters
are at West Malling, and took a very close interest in
all that concerned the welfare of nurses. It was in
1888 or 1889 that a friend returned from a stay in New
Zealand, who had herself previously had training at
the London Hospital, and was afterwards a ward-sister
there for sixteen years. She told me about a most
extraordinary woman, who was causing an immense
amount of talk, in both Wellington and Nelson, and who
posed as having been a nurse in the Russo-Turkish war,
though from her own testimony she could not well have
been more than fifteen at the time. My young friend—
" Miss H." I will call her—the daughter of an old friend,
who had held one of the very highest Civil appointments
in India, was on a visit to relatives, and much in the
intimate circle of the Governor of the Dominion and his

family, and in constant association with the colonial dignitaries of the church.   All were greatly scandalised by the vagaries of this Miss K. M——, who had been given the appointment of Matron of the Government Hospital at Wellington, on the strength of her own assurances as to her qualifications (certificated nurses were then almost unknown there), but had had to resign on account of health, and had come to recuperate in the lovely climate of Nelson.   She seemed to be entirely without means, but was most kindly, and generously received, in the houses of several residents in succession, treated as one of the family, and even supplied with pocket money and clothes.   One or two of these were the households of clergymen, for Miss M—— made a point of standing well with the clergy, and opened her heart to many, in confidence, concerning her spiritual difficulties and troubles.   In these matters she was ready to accept the most varied teaching, all denominations had a turn in the forming of her opinions, and though many had had doubts of her straightforwardness in small matters, and—like Miss H.—questioned her capabilities and knowledge as a nurse, it was only after she had left for England, that it transpired that, within a few days of being confirmed privately, by her own wish, by the Bishop of Nelson, she had been received into the Church of Rome, and had been for some time back, endeavouring to proselytise for that communion, various ladies of her acquaintance ! Her fascination and powers of persuasion were so great that, in spite of many stories against her, there were still those that believed in her, and gave her introductions to friends and relatives in the mother-country, asking them to befriend her in the same way as they had done.

Soon, strange tales began to arrive at the Antipodes,

and newspaper articles full of marvellous accounts of a
sort of crusade against leprosy that Miss M—— had
inaugurated in New Zealand—Father Damien, and the
Hawaiian leper settlement, were then much in the
public mind—and thrilling descriptions of the addresses
she was giving, all over England, especially in fashionable
drawing-rooms in London, graphically describing the
work to which she had devoted herself for some considerable time, in alleviating the terrible ravages of this dire
disease, amongst the Maoris on the western coast of the
South Island! and telling of the large sums of money
contributed by the charitable for the fund she had
started to carry on this work!

My friend Miss H. was then still with her uncle, the
Bishop of Nelson, when this bomb-shell burst on the good
folk of that distant city. Their indignation was almost
ludicrous—for they were as wroth at the crass ignorance
of the (supposed) educated classes in England, in swal-
lowing such a farrago of nonsense, as with Miss M—— for
having fabricated it!

So far as was known, Miss M—— had only, on one
occasion, paid a flying visit, of a couple of weeks, to the
district which she pretended to describe, throughout the
length and breadth of which there are *no Maoris*, and
no cases of leprosy, to the knowledge of the Archdeacon, who had laboured there for over twenty years.
This he himself assured my friend Miss H.

Anyhow, whatever became of the money Miss M——
collected for the Maoris, certainly none of it reached
New Zealand, and her former acquaintances learned
that she had now turned her attention to India, and was
trying to get sent out there by the Zenana Missionary
Branch of the C. M. S., in order to bring help (quite
oblivious of the fact that the Indian Government

already took charge of them !) to the suffering thousands of India's lepers. But Indian Missionary Societies have an awkward habit of asking too searching questions about their would-be assistants, and their funds they keep under their own supervision.

Miss M—— had by now sponged to such an extent upon her friends, that she began to look round for "pastures new," and more secluded, on the surface of the globe, on which the fierce light of publicity, and geographical knowledge, might not be directed so unflinchingly. She pitched upon the wilds and forests of North-eastern Siberia, as being sufficiently off the beaten track for her purpose, and apparently this was so at that date (1890), so she suddenly announced that she had received intelligence of a marvellous herb, for the cure of leprosy, somewhere in Siberia, and also that there were lepers in large numbers, utterly neglected, in another part of that vast territory. She resolved to employ the highest influences she could, to get the Empress of Russia interested in her project, and give her authority to carry out her search.

It was when I heard that she had succeeded in ingratiating herself with several ladies of good position, known to me by name, had actually been granted interviews by two or three of our Royal Family, and had had her name put down on the Lord Chamberlain's list, for presentation at Court, that I felt it my duty to take some steps to warn those in authority to make inquiries about her antecedents. I was the more moved to do this on hearing a story of her unscrupulousness and mendacity, which, in spite of its heartlessness, is not without a certain element of humour !

It seems that amongst those to whom she was consigned as a martyr suffering from unjust accusations,

were two maiden ladies whose sister had implored them
to receive her, and show her all kindness in their power.
Though by no means in affluence, they took her into
their house, and in spite of her being a most exacting
guest, put up with all her whims, supplied her with
money and clothes, until, at last, she became tired of
living in such a simple and quiet way, and left them for
more wealthy acquaintances, not without hints at their
" penurious ways." Not a word did they hear from
her till they received an imploring letter, begging for
immediate assistance, as she was in dire straits, ill and
friendless, and no money for fire or clothes ! Putting
their slender resources together, they spared her some
garments, and a five-pound note, and despatched this
by return of post, only to read, on opening the daily
paper next morning, her name amongst the presen-
tations at Court the day before !

Meanwhile, Miss M—— in 1890, did go to St. Petersburg, armed with introductions from royalties here,
was received by the Empress Marie, who gave her a
letter commending her to all Russian local authorities.
By her own account* she returned thence to London,
and was presented to Miss Nightingale, started once
more viâ Paris (where she interviewed M. Pasteur and
went over the S. Louis Hospital), Egypt (audience of
H.H. the Khedive), Jaffa, Jerusalem (introductions to
Bishop Blyth, who took her over the Leper Hospital of
the Moravian Brothers), Constantinople, Scutari, Tiflis,
and so to Moscow, where she arrived in November,
doing the whole distance from London, with stoppages,
in two months ! From that point, according to her
story, she departed on her mission to the wilds of
Eastern Siberia ; but in the book which she published

* " Life of K—— M——" published in London, 1895.

on her return to civilised regions,* and which professes
to give details of this journey, there is a beautiful
vagueness as to dates, distances and localities, which
makes it quite impossible to determine where she
really got to, though evidence afterwards proved that
Viliusk, a town of 600 inhabitants, between 250 and
300 miles from Yakutsk, the capital of the Province,
was the utmost limit of her wanderings; but I believe
she made it out to be an expedition of 3,000 versts
(2,000 miles), and that it required a cavalcade of thirty
horses, and food for three months!

Certain nebulous, and laudatory reports of her
"mission," began to appear in English and Russian
newspapers, and I had given hints, and warnings for
caution, in many directions, hoping that they would
reach influential quarters; but when, in the October
of 1892, the lady in question—after being fêted,
acclaimed, and almost *canonised* in Russia—returned
to England, started on another tour of lectures and
collections, was given audiences by six of our royalties,
inscribed on the roll of the British Nurses Association
(even, so she averred, made a Fellow of the Royal
Geographical Society!), and sent for to Balmoral, my
conscience would allow me to keep silence no longer,
and on the 30th October, I wrote to the President of
my Nursing Association, who I knew was on a visit at
White Lodge, Richmond, telling her what I had heard
about Miss M—— from those who had known her in
New Zealand (her "crusade" in that direction was
now never alluded to), and begged her to plead for an
inquiry into her antecedents before proceeding further!
I was indignant that the carelessness, and want of
discretion, of those about her, should allow my beloved

* "On sleigh and horseback to Outcast Siberia."

Sovereign to lend her countenance to one already proved an imposter in another field.

Unfortunately, the lady I had made my representations through, and who placed my notes in the quarter I requested, did so without mentioning my name, believing that to be the wisest course, and unaware that an intimation of the kind would carry more weight, if known to emanate from one, in whom, I think I may say without undue assertion, Her Majesty had already reposed much confidence, believed to be cautious in her statements, and inspired solely by her loyalty and sense of justice. I only wish that my representations had been acted on at once, before further evidences of K—— M——'s unworthiness reached me during the following year, from all directions. I could not feel as comfortable and satisfied as the lady who had acted as my intermediary did, for she said, " that it was no use troubling further. If it is a failure *we* can have no blame ; we have done all that is necessary."

Therefore, further unimpeachable testimony having come to me, I dared to stir her once more, and induced her to forward documents and letters in support of what I had already said, and she herself warned ladies of position in philanthropic circles. " I am rather alarmed at all I have done," she wrote, " but I feel I did my duty, and that thanks are all due to *you*, not to me. . . . I will see Lady L——, and will write to you the moment I hear from H.R.H. If *I ever do !* . . . . As you know, all your letters to me are in the possession of H.R.H. Princess ——, and as she thinks Miss M—— is persecuted, I dare not ask for them back ! I told Lady L—— . . . she is very cautious and diplomatic, and far from satisfied with the letters she has received . . . Please tell her details. . . . I feel pretty sure that slowly and carefully Miss M—— is being watched, and her overthrow not far off. . . . I believe the extraordinary exaggerations of numbers in her books has awakened suspicion in *print*, which seems not to have been noticed in talking." It would really appear that this was the case, for a letter was sent to me from the Treasurer of K—— M——'s Leper Fund in England, in which he mentioned that, in response to questions, Miss M—— still maintained that the distances given in her book were correct, and were supplied to her by " the Bishop Maletie of Yakutsk "—also " that the ride certainly took her two months ! " For a lady who only took the same length of time to perambulate Europe and the Mediterranean coasts, this was remarkable ; but this London Committee of hers were out to swallow *anything*, for this same gentleman announced that the charges against Miss M——'s character in New Zealand, received from many quarters, were proved untrue, and he had most satisfactory reports from St. Petersburg about her, and was expecting fuller details when the lady who accompanied her to Siberia returned to London, the following week, Miss M—— herself having sailed for America !

Almost immediately upon this, I was startled by a visit from a complete stranger, from St. Petersburg, who came armed with the *very highest* credentials, and injunctions to ascertain the truth. He had been one of her warmest supporters, and had acted as Secretary of the very influential Committee formed there to further her work, and gather in the enormous funds being collected in Russia for the purpose. The whole movement was under the protection, and direction, of the renowned Minister, M. Pobedonotseff, Procurator of the Holy Synod, and the Committee consisted of some of the foremost names in the Russian Empire.

To them also had come reports and rumours against the lady's character, which filled them with indignation, but which, to clear her, they proceeded to investigate, and drew up a report, completely exculpating her, and asseverating their confidence in her blameless integrity. Of this report, not yet signed, a copy fell into her hands, and she lost no time in getting signatures from persons of distinction, only three of whom, however, were members of the said Committee. Then she left Russia for Berlin. Hardly had she done so when most damning proofs, substantiating charges against her character far worse than had gone before, fell into the hands of the Committee. So bad were they, that her friends warned her not to return to Russia !

She came to England, found some hint of this had preceded her, and started for America on April 1st, 1893, believing that at the World's Fair, at Chicago, she would find the very environment suitable for her propaganda—Russia not having proved satisfactory, from a pecuniary point of view, all charitable collections being paid into a Treasury controlled by M. Pobedonotseff !

But it was here actually that Nemesis overtook her ! Instead of proving more gullible than European society, American philanthropists had made investigations into her antecedents, on their own account, and had no hesitation, moreover, in making them public ! So outspoken was the Press in remarking on her effrontery and shamelessness, that wherever her steps may have wandered since, she certainly has not ventured again into the States. The result does infinite credit to the perspicacity of the American people.

Of course, I once more sent warning, the moment all this became known to me. My intermediary sent copies of the information I had got to the necessary persons, and measures were at length taken to modify the scandal of such a *dénouement*.

My correspondence with St. Petersburg continued fast and furious throughout 1895, and, apart from its subject, was exceedingly lively and entertaining, for my new acquaintance was an accomplished letter writer, most original, and full of epigram and wit. He paid several flying visits to this country, when I met him in London, and it gave one a curious insight into the conditions of life, at that time, in St. Petersburg that, even in his case, precautions had to be taken to insure our letters passing direct into one another's hands !

Amongst other little items of information he communicated to me, in conversation, was, that letters had come into his possession, written by Miss M—— to a confidante or accomplice, in which she retailed, with glee, the amounts pouring into her coffers, for her supposed " charity," and sketched the delightful trip, and " spree on the Rhine " they were going to have on the proceeds ! The Russian contributions, alas ! she had no chance of pocketing ! He told also, how she had managed to hoodwink her Russian Committee, and the Vice-President of the Imperial Geographical Society of Russia, by her descriptions of her journeys in N.E. Siberia. A lady was sent with her to Siberia, as a companion, by her London Committee. She succeeded, however, in giving her the slip, and left her stranded without money at Tomsk, half-way to her destination ! There was thus no one to contradict her assertions. She then secured a Russian courier, to accompany her, whom she bribed to corroborate all her story—in fact, it was concocted

between them ! They disappeared into the forests for
a few days, and on returning to civilised parts, had it
all ready !

Miss M—— tried in every way to contradict the
accusations brought against her, defying them to produce their proofs ; and when, on August 16th, 1894, the
Rev. Alexander Francis, Pastor of the British-American
Church at St. Petersburg, and Secretary of the Committee of Investigation, was obliged to make public,
by a letter to the *Times*, that the Committee required
her, according to her own engagement if the decision
went against her, to surrender all decorations, and letters
of commendation, bestowed on her under false pretences
by Imperial and Royal personages, she retorted by
publishing the unsigned report before referred to, and
instituted a lawsuit for defamation of character against
both Mr. Francis, and the Editor of the *Times !*

On one plea, and another, she kept this lingering on,
without bringing it into court ; and finally said she was
without money to pay a lawyer to defend her, when it
was merely a matter of replying " Yes," or " No,"
to half a dozen questions, which anyone could have done
on a half-sheet of notepaper—questions affecting her
own character, which no one, with a spark of shame in
their composition, would have left for half an hour
without an indignant denial. This fact was brought out
in an article in *Truth* on January 9th, 1896—yet it was
only in June of that same year that the case was finally
dismissed, and expenses awarded Mr. Francis—" Don't
you wish that I may get them ? " was his comment !—
and *Truth* gave her a final article, entitled " Exit
Miss M—— ! "

Thus for a space of seven years, this ingenious and
unscrupulous adventuress, with no special advantages

of face or form, only an ingratiating personality, managed to mystify, perturb, and turn to her own advantage, the best society in four quarters of the globe ! Not only so, but actually she was the cause of estrangement between ladies of exalted rank, who reproached each other for having sent her with letters of high commendation. As one of them exclaimed indignantly : " She begged me to treat Miss M—— as a *sister*, and I *did !* "

I had the satisfaction of knowing that I had done my part in the unmasking of her ; but as my St. Petersburg friend wrote : " there does not seem to be much courtesy extended to those who are trying to shield their Queen from an impostor ; but that is a detail which concerns only those who are discourteous. I am sure that your services will be very fully acknowledged before long, but that is not what you care about. *Fais ce que tu dois, advienne que pourra.*"

Thus ended the last service I was privileged to attempt for the Sovereign I had been closely associated with for over forty years ! One year only her junior in age, it has pleased God that I should survive her passing from amongst us. But although I have lived to see him, whom I first knew as a slender, fair-haired boy of thirteen, hailed, a grandfather of sixty, as King, and Padishah, over the world-wide Empire that she ruled so well, hailed moreover as the wisest monarch of his generation, and one of the greatest that have filled the English throne ; yet something has gone from my life that can never be replaced ! I cannot face a future that has been shorn of that central figure in the picture. From the moment that I knew my Mistress gone hence, I felt the time would not be long before there came " the one clear call " for me !

POSTSCRIPT.

On the 22nd of January, 1901, Queen Victoria passed away at Osborne. A letter from her Private Secretary, Sir Fleetwood Edwards, written from that residence at the commencement of her fatal illness, was the last communication that passed between her and her faithful subject.

Three years later, in the early morning of April 17th, 1904, my mother died at Cedars, Aylesford, Kent, in her eighty-fourth year, and was laid in Felixstowe churchyard, beside the husband she had been parted from forty years before. Three of her children had gone before her, and three survived her, whereof two are now also gone.

To the end she retained her clear intellect, and her faculties undiminished, save for a slight deafness; and without undue presumption, her daughter may perhaps claim that her memory remains green in the hearts of those who knew and loved her?

FINIS.

INDEX

" A " " for the 'osses ! " 121, 122
Abbot, General Sir F., 46, 165
Adams, Colonel Robert, 80
Albert, H.R.H. Prince (Prince Consort), 116—119, 122, 123, 125, 164, 218, 253, 267
Alexander III., 297
Alexander, General Sir James (K.C.B.), 97, 226
Alexander, Mrs. (*see* Mrs. Drummond)
Alexandra, H.M. Queen, 121, 297, 325
Alfred, H.R.H. Prince, of Saxe-Coburg-Gotha, 116, 119
Ali Bux and the " Fair Fatimah," 49—51
Anson, H.M.S., visits of Kaiser Wilhelm to, 164—167
Ash-Wednesday ceremonies at the Sixtine Chapel, 201
Asquith, Mrs., 279

Baird, Vice-Admiral, 298, 300
Bantry, Earl and Countess of, 277
Bartlett, Mr. and Mrs., 284, 285
Beatrice, H.R.H. Princess, 287
Beebeepore Palace, 38
Beecher-Stowe, Mrs., 199—200
Benson, Dr. Edward (Archbishop of Canterbury), 273, 274
Bentinck, Lady William " to Joseph Wolff," 83
Bernard, Dr., 70—71
Bernard, Mrs., 69—71
Bhajun Lal, 95, 136
" Bhuggut Ram " (Major D'Arcy Todd), 50
Bhugwan Doss (*major domo*), 55
Biddulph, Sir Thomas, 289, 295, 296
Blackamoor, the, 197
Blake, Canon J. S., 293
Bismarck, Prince (and Delagoa Railway), 127

Blyth, Bishop, of Jerusalem, 332
Boileau, Colonel Frank, 265
Breadalbane, 1st Marquess and Marchioness, 26—30, 128
Brewster, Sir David, 196
Bright, Mr. John, 137, 138, 195, 198, 205, 235, 236, 266, 306, 325, 327
Bruce, General, 169
Bruce, Mr. 113
Bugnano, Marchese di, 204
Burdett-Coutts, Baroness, 27, 28
Burne, Colonel Sir Owen, 248, 257

Campbell, Annie (daughter of General Charles), 196
Campbell, Charles (laird of Kinloch, 1760), married niece of Bishop of Oporto, 4
Campbell, Maj.-General Charles, 31, 38, 48, 146, 281, 319
Campbell, Maj.-General Charles William (Borland), 281
Campbell, Major Colin, 12, 13, 14, 283
Campbell, Lt.-Colonel C. G. L. (Borland), 318, 319
Campbell, Euphrosia Maria Ferreira (Mrs. White), 8, 10, 246, 247
Campbell, Gregorio, 16, 283
Campbell, Captain J. (7th Madras Cav.), 94
Campbell, John (or Juan), laird of Kinloch, 5—17
Campbell, Colonel John, 190, 279—282
Campbell, José (laird of Kinloch, 1784), 320
Campbell, Margaret (Mrs. Meiklejohn), 9, 18, 25, 31, 33, 34, 36
Campbell, Miss Neilena, 15
Campbell, Patricia, 37
Campbell, Maj.-General R. B. P. P. (C.B.), 281 *note*

Campbell, Victoria Gouramma (Mrs. Yardley), 285—288
Cambridge, H R.H. the Duchess of, 121, 130, 131
Cambridge, H.R.H. the Duke of, 311
Canning, Lord, 143, 144, 186, 188
Cape Town, 33—35
Cardinal Archbishop of Westminster and Pope Leo XIII., 327
Cardwell, Lord, 306
Cartridges, greased, 141, 142
Castor and Pollux, two Heràti ponies, 52
Cautley, Sir Proby, 65
Chantreuse, 11, 12
Charikar with Eldred Pottinger, 52
Christian, H.R.H. Princess, 243
Christian IX. and Queen Louise, of Denmark, 297
Christian X. and Prince Axel, 298
Christina of Spain, Queen, 201, 202; British Legion for, 12—14
"Christmas Day," 17
Clarence, H.R.H. Duke of, 298
Clarendon, Lord, 128
Clark, Admiral Sir Bouverie F. (K.C.B.), 296
Cobbold, Mr. John Chevalier, 312, 313
Colvin, Mr , 65
Conolly, Lieut., 66
Coorg, Rajah of, 98, 99 note, 109, 148 —150, 158, 160, 186, 187
Coorg, Rajah of, family of, 187—189
Coorg, Princess Victoria Gouramma of, 148, 151—163, 168—173, 176—194, 217, 279, 283, 295
Couper, Sir George, 110, 131
Cross, Viscount, 248, 269
Cullum, Lady, 317
Currie, Sir Frederick (Bart.), 85, 226, 263
Cusins, Mr. W. G., 117

Dalhousie, Marquess of, 73, 75, 79— 82, 87, 94—100, 103, 105, 108—113, 250, 257, 263, 268
Dasent, Mr. G. W. (Editor of Times), 128, 139
Davidson, Colonel, 46
Dawkins, Mr. Clinton, 248
Delane, Mr. (Editor of Times), 128, 139
Derby, Earl of, 143

Dick, Mrs. Hope, 31, 36, 38
Dips, tallow, 20, 21
Drummond, Mrs. (afterwards Mrs. Alexander), 150—153, 161
Dufferin, Lady, and her son, 198
Duleep Singh, H.H. the Maharajah, 73, 74, 84—86, 88—91, 94—105, 108—119, 122—133, 145—148, 168 —183, 190, 195—199, 201—205, 207—209, 214—224, 226, 229— 234, 237—272
Duleep Singh's coat of arms, 118; dress, 113
Duleep Singh, Prince Edward, 270
Duleep Singh, Prince Frederick, 260, 270
Duleep Singh, Prince Victor, 260, 261, 269
Duleep Singh, Princesses, 259

Edward VII., H.M. King, 116—119, 145, 169, 297, 319, 325, 326 note
Edwardes, Sir Herbert, 71, 74, 263
Edwards, Sir Fleetwood, 340
Elephant, the must, 53, 54
Elephants, 59, 60
Ellenborough, Lord, 143
Elliot, Sir Henry, 81, 82
Elliott, Rev. Vaughan, 156
Ely, Marquis and Marchioness of, 126, 197, 198
"Ely Cathedral," 301
Esher Church, Royal closet in, 130

Fakir Azizudeen, 77
Felixstowe, 223, 226, 230, 231, 309— 319
Felixstowe, Vicar of, 302—309
Ferrier, General, 46
Fife, H.R.H. the Duchess of, 298
"Fifteen above proof," 321
Fitzgerald, Mr. Edward, 315
Francis, Rev. A., 338
Fraser, Colonel James, 150
Frederick III. of Germany, 323, 324, 326
Frederick VII. of Denmark, 297
Frederick William IV. of Prussia, 177, 178, 203, 204
Frere, Sir Bartle, 188, 222
Funerals and honeymoons, 237
Futtehghur, fate of establishment at, 135, 136

ANGES water, 97
augers, dodging the, 24
orge V., H.M. King, 298
arīb-Khana (hospital) at Lucknow, 49, 57
bbs, Mr., the Princes' tutor, 117, 119
mm, Field-Marshal and Lady, 133, 134
rdon, Duchess of, 196
rdon-Duff, Mrs , 279
reh, Father Nehemiah (see Pundit Nilakanth Goreh)
uise, Mr. Walter, 97, 136

AAKON, H.M. King, and Queen Maud of Norway, 298
alifax, Lord (Sir Charles Wood), 129, 186, 188, 221
arland, Sir R. and Lady, 317
arcourt, Colonel and Lady Catherine, 183, 184, 190
ardinge, Lord and Lady, 128, 129, 157
artington, Marquess of, 259
atherton, Lord and Lady, 112, 129, 130, 132, 133
avelock, Sir Henry, 66
Henri Cinq," Comte de Chambord, 202
enry, Mr. Mitchell, M.P., 254
eràt, 46, 49, 51
ewett, Captain Sir William, R.N., 290
ighland dress, 16
ighland farmer, 321
ighland superstitions, 25, 26
inghan Khan, the Heràti, 51—55
ogg, Colonel (Lord Magheramorne), 240
ogg, Sir James Weir (see Weir-Hogg)
ohlub, Herr Emil, 316
ooker, Sir Joseph, 316
ooker, Sir William, 316
orses, stories of, 52, 60—62

BRAHIM PASHA, Viceroy of Egypt, 113
ndian Army, scheme for re-organization of, 140, 141
ndian Mutiny, 145
nglis, Sir Robert, 114, 115
' Is he keeping quate ? " 146

JACKSON, Mr., the sculptor, 231
Jarvis, Mrs. (marriage of), 3, 4
Jay, Rev. W. J., 96, 226
" Jerusalem, my happy home ! " 35, 36
John of Glücksburg, Prince, 298
José and Joséphine, 15, 16
Jung Bahadour, 87, 88, 99 note, 109, 188, 206

KAMRAN, Shah, 53 note
K—— M——, Miss, 328—339
Kaye, Sir John, 64, 69, 70, 206
Kent, H R.H. the Duchess, 110, 122, 131
Kent, Jàts and Juts, 128
Kew, Royal pew, 130
Kew Church House, 131
Khedive of Egypt, 332
Kimberley, Earl of, 248
Kinnaird, Baron, 307, 320
Kinnaird, Hon. Arthur, 320
Knatchbull, Lady, 198
Knesebeck, Baron, 131
Koh-i-noor, 73, 75—83, 123—126
Koh-i-noor, receipt for, 81, 82
Kügel, Baron, 168

"LADY LOGIN! I am a grandmother!" 163
Lassalle, Madame, 275, 276
Lawrence, Alec, 65, 67, 70, 71, 132, 133
Lawrence, Lord, 62, 66—71, 73, 221, 226, 227, 263, 266, 273
Lawrence, Lady, 69, 70, 227
Lawrence, Lady (Honoria), 63—66
Lawrence, Colonel George, 66, 73, 74
Lawrence, Sir Henry, 46, 63—66, 69, 72—74, 111, 136, 251, 263
Lawrence, Mr. P. H., 252
Lawrence, Captain Richard, 69
Leven and Melville, Countess of, 112, 238—240, 243
Leven and Melville, 11th Earl of (Ron. R. Leslie-Melville), 195, 204, 205, 237, 239, 269
Liliuo-Kalani of Hawaii, Queen, 324
Lorne, Marquis of, 289
Login, Edward William Spencer, 119, 120, 169, 170, 239, 290—292, 325
Login, Sir John, death of, 225

Login, Dr. James Dryburgh, 64, 87, 88, 206 *note*

Login, Lena, 64 *note*, 169, 227, 228, 278

Login, Louise Marion D'Arcy, 46 *note*

Login, Mabel, 278

Login, Rear-Admiral S. H. M. (C.V.O.), 64, 104, 111, 119, 120, 164, 166, 167, 211, 292—300

Longley, Dr. (Archbishop of Canterbury), 114, 115, 157

Louise, H.R.H. Princess (Duchess of Argyll), 287, 289

Low, Colonel, 45

Low, Mr., dancing-master, 12 *note*

Ludwig I. of Bavaria, King, 201, 202

MACAULAY, Lord, 200, 201

Macgregor, Sir Charles, 80, 148

Mackenzie, Colin, 66

Macnaghton, Sir William, 66

Maharanee Bamba, 237—243, 258, 276; her dress, 243

Maharanee Mai Chunda (Jinda Koür), 85, 86, 206—215, 223, 230, 237

Mahommed Ali Shah, King of Oude, 38, 44

Mahommed, Prophet, relics of, 80

Malleson, Colonel, 127, 265

Manning, Cardinal, 198

Mansel, C. G., 81, 82, 85

Maori lepers, 330

Marie Feodorovna (Dagmar), Empress, 297, 298, 331, 332

Marlborough, Duke of, 217

Marshman, Mr. John, 226

Martin, Mr. Montgomery, 187

Martyn's testament, Henry, 83

Mary, H.R.H. Princess (Duchess of Teck), 120, 122, 311

Maximilian, Emperor, 204

Mecklenburg-Strelitz, Grand Duke of, 121, 324

Melvill, Sir James, 143, 216

Menzies, Castle, 127, 128, 132—134

Misr Beelee Ram (keeper of Koh-i-noor) murdered, 79

Misr Makraj (keeper of Koh-i-noor), 75—80

Mitford, General, 46

Moolraj and other rebel chiefs, 80

Morton, Earl and Countess of, 129

Mutton Club, the, 47, 48

NADIR SHAH (exchange of turbans), 76

Nana Sahib (envoy's insult to D. S.), 108—110, 136, 138

Napier, Sir Charles (commander-in-chief), 65

Nawab Ameenoodowlah, Wuzeer of Oude, 41, 43, 44

Nelson, Bishop of, 329

Nightingale, Miss, 332

Norton, Hon. Mrs. R., 199

Nott, General Sir W., 46

OGILVY, Colonel Sir Reginald, 320

Oliphant, Mr. A., 258, 259

Oliphant, Colonel, 219, 238, 249

Orlich, Baron von, 204

Ormerod, Dr. E., 155

Oscar of Sweden, King, 300

Oude, Princesses of, 39—41

Outram, Sir James, 47, 66

PAGET, Lord Alfred and Lady Alfred, 318, 319

Paget, General Sir Arthur, 318, 319

Palmer, Mr., 311, 312

Papal Legate, 327

Partridge, Mr. and Mrs., 133, 259

Pasteur, Monsieur, 332

Pelham, Dr. (Bishop of Norwich), 307

Phipps, Colonel the Hon. Sir C., 126, 135, 139—144, 151, 157, 158, 161—163, 168, 176—186, 215, 217, 218, 221, 227—229, 233, 234, 238, 246, 253, 266, 267, 279

Phipps, Hon. Mrs. E., 199

Pobedonotseff, Monsieur, 335, 336

Pollock, Field-Marshal Sir George, 46, 66

Ponsonby, Sir Henry, 246—248, 259—269, 289

Pookraj (topaz) substituted for Koh-i-noor, 77

Pottinger, Colonel Eldred, 46, 51, 52, 66

Precedence, a question of, 114, 115

Probyn, Sir Dighton, 121

Pundit Nilakanth Goreh (Father N. Goreh of Cowley), 106—108, 207

Purdah patients, 40, 41

"QUEEN of England, Queen of Portugal!" 17

RAMSAY, Lady Edith Christian, 112
Ramsey, Colonel, 206
Ranee Duknoo, the, 89, 91—93, 101
—105, 110
Richmond, Colonel, 46
Rimbault, Dr. Edward, 117
Rio de Janeiro, 32
Rochussen, Monsieur, 100
Rudolph of Austria, Crown Prince, 324
Russia, late Dowager Empress of, 197
Rustum, sword of, 80
Ryle, Dr. (Bishop of Liverpool), 307

ST. ALBANS, Duchess of, 27, 28
Seigneurial dues, 21, 22
Servants' food, 19, 20
Seymour, Capt. (afterwards Admiral of the Fleet), Sir M. Culme-, 290
Shaftesbury, Earl of, 128, 139
Shah Soojah of Afghanistan, 76, 77, 80
Shantrews (see Chantreuse)
Sheo Deo Singh, Shahzadah, 85, 89, 91—93, 101—105, 108
Shere Singh, Maharajah, 78, 85, 91
Sleeman, Colonel Sir William, 105, 106; (Kent Juts and Jâts), 128
Soortoo, 214
Spinning-women, 22—24
Stanley, Lord, 69, 100
Stewart, Major W. M., 148
Stratford de Redcliffe, Viscount, 128
Sultans of Johore and Zanzibar, 324

TAIT, Dr. (Archbishop of Canterbury), 128
Tallow " dips," manufacture of, 20, 21
Tennant, Sir Charles and Lady, 279
Thieves and dacoits, 58, 59
Thomason, Mr. (Lieut.-Governor), 46
" Thuggee," 106
Times, editors of, 128, 139, 338

Tocqueville, M. de, 65
Todd, Major D'Arcy, 46, 66
Tomline, Colonel George, 310—315
Toshkhana, 58, 73, 75—80
Tracey, Admiral Sir R., 166
Trevelyan, Sir Charles, 68, 69, 139
Troup, 66
Truth, article in, 338

VAMBÉRY, Professor, 46
Vans Agnew, Patrick, 46, 47
Vernon, Admiral, picture of, 317
Victoria, H.M. Queen, 75, 83 (portraits of), 116—118, 122—125, 143—145, 150—164, 170—194, 217, 218, 228, 229, 231, 233, 234; autograph letter, 185; Lady Login's private correspondence with, 171—176; letter of condolence, 228
Victoria, H.R.H. Princess (Princess Royal and afterwards Empress Frederick), 145, 165, 243, 323, 324

WAJID ALI, King of Oude, 40, 44, 45
Waldemar of Denmark, Princess, 298
Waldemar, Prince, of Prussia, 65
Warren, Samuel, 315
Weir-Hogg, Sir James, 157, 190, 284, 285
Wellington, Duke of, funeral of, 324
Wemyss, Earl of (Lord Elcho), 292
Wheeler, Brigadier, 62
White, Mrs., 8, 10, 246, 247
Wilhelm II., Kaiser, 162—167, 299—301
Wilson, Dr. (Bishop of Calcutta), 96
Winchester, Bishop of, 128, 156, 158
Winterhalter, Mr., 122, 123
Wolf-children, 57, 58
Wolves, 56, 57
Wood, Sir Charles (see Lord Halifax)
Wuzeeroolniza, the little Begum, 41—43

THE WHITEFRIARS PRESS, LTD., LONDON AND TONBRIDGE

Lightning Source UK Ltd.
Milton Keynes UK
UKHW020630030621
384863UK00005B/592